THE

Expositor's Bible Commentary

with The New International Version

HEBREWS • JAMES

THE
Expositor's Bible Commentary

with *The New International Version*

HEBREWS • JAMES

Leon Morris &
Donald W. Burdick

Zondervan Publishing House
Grand Rapids, Michigan

A Division of HarperCollinsPublishers

General Editor:

FRANK E. GAEBELEIN
Former Headmaster, Stony Brook School
Former Coeditor, *Christianity Today*

Associate Editors:

J. D. DOUGLAS
Editor, *The New International
Dictionary of the Christian Church*

RICHARD P. POLCYN

Hebrews, James
Copyright © 1996 by Leon Morris, Donald W. Burdick

Requests for information should be addressed to:
   Zondervan Publishing House
   Grand Rapids, Michigan 49530

Library of Congress Cataloging-in-Publication Data

The expositor's Bible commentary : with the New International Version of the Holy Bible /
   Frank E. Gaebelein, general editor of series.
      p.   cm.
   Includes bibliographical references and index.
   Contents: v. 1–2. Matthew / D. A. Carson — Mark / Walter W. Wessel — Luke / Walter
L. Liefeld — John / Merrill C. Tenney — Acts / Richard N. Longenecker — Romans /
Everett F. Harrison — 1 and 2 Corinthians / W. Harold Mare and Murray J. Harris —
Galatians and Ephesians / James Montgomery Boice and A. Skevington Wood—Philippians,
Colossians, Philemon / Homer A. Kent Jr., Gurtis Vaughan, and Arthur A. Rupprecht—
1, 2 Thessalonians; 1, 2 Timothy; Titus / Robert L. Thomas, Ralph Earle, and D. Edmond
Hiebert—Hebrews, James / Leon Morris and Donald W. Burdick—1, 2 Peter;
1, 2, 3 John; Jude / Edwin A. Blum and Glenn W. Barker—Revelation / Alan F. Johnson
   ISBN: 0-310-20387-2 (softcover)
   1. Bible N.T.—Commentaries. I. Gaebelein, Frank Ely, 1899–1983.
BS2341.2.E96 1995
220.7-dc 00   94-47450
                                                                              CIP

Printed in the United States of America

   97 98 99 00 01 / ❖ DH / 10 9 8 7 6 5 4 3 2

CONTENTS

PREFACE

The title of this work defines its purpose. Written primarily by expositors for expositors, it aims to provide preachers, teachers, and students of the Bible with a new and comprehensive commentary on the books of the Old and New Testaments. Its stance is that of a scholarly evangelicalism committed to the divine inspiration, complete trustworthiness, and full authority of the Bible. Its seventy-eight contributors come from the United States, Canada, England, Scotland, Australia, New Zealand, and Switzerland, and from various religious groups, including Anglican, Baptist, Brethren, Free, Independent, Methodist, Nazarene, Presbyterian, and Reformed churches. Most of them teach at colleges, universities, or theological seminaries.

No book has been more closely studied over a longer period of time than the Bible. From the Midrashic commentaries going back to the period of Ezra, through parts of the Dead Sea Scrolls and the Patristic literature, and on to the present, the Scriptures have been expounded. Indeed, there have been times when, as in the Reformation and on occasions since then, exposition has been at the cutting edge of Christian advance. Luther was a powerful exegete, and Calvin is still called "the prince of expositors."

Their successors have been many. And now, when the outburst of new translations and their unparalleled circulation have expanded the readership of the Bible, the need for exposition takes on fresh urgency.

Not that God's Word can ever become captive to its expositors. Among all other books, it stands first in its combination of perspicuity and profundity. Though a child can be made "wise for salvation" by believing its witness to Christ, the greatest mind cannot plumb the depths of its truth (2 Tim. 3:15; Rom. 11:33). As Gregory the Great said, "Holy Scripture is a stream of running water, where alike the elephant may swim, and the lamb walk." So, because of the inexhaustible nature of Scripture, the task of opening up its meaning is still a perennial obligation of biblical scholarship.

How that task is done inevitably reflects the outlook of those engaged in it. Every biblical scholar has presuppositions. To this neither the editors of these volumes nor the contributors to them are exceptions. They share a common commitment to the supernatural Christianity set forth in the inspired Word. Their purpose is not to supplant the many valuable commentaries that have preceded this work and from which both the editors and contributors have learned. It is rather to draw on the resources of contemporary evangelical scholarship in producing a new reference work for understanding the Scriptures.

A commentary that will continue to be useful through the years should handle contemporary trends in biblical studies in such a way as to avoid becoming outdated when critical fashions change. Biblical criticism is not in itself inadmissible, as some have mistakenly thought. When scholars investigate the authorship, date, literary characteristics, and purpose of a biblical document, they are practicing biblical criticism. So also when, in order to ascertain as nearly as possible the original form of the text, they deal with variant readings, scribal errors, emendations, and other phenomena in the manuscripts. To do these things is essential to responsible exegesis and exposition. And always there is the need to distinguish hypothesis from fact, conjecture from truth.

The chief principle of interpretation followed in this commentary is the grammatico-historical one—namely, that the primary aim of the exegete is to make clear the meaning of the text at the time and in the circumstances of its writing. This endeavor to understand what in the first instance the inspired writers actually said must not be confused with an inflexible literalism. Scripture makes lavish use of symbols and figures of speech; great portions of it are poetical. Yet when it speaks in this way, it speaks no less truly than it does in its historical and doctrinal portions. To understand its message requires attention to matters of grammar and syntax, word meanings, idioms, and literary forms—all in relation to the historical and cultural setting of the text.

The contributors to this work necessarily reflect varying convictions. In certain controversial matters the policy is that of clear statement of the contributors' own views followed by fair presentation of other ones. The treatment of eschatology, though it reflects differences of interpretation, is consistent with a general premillennial position. (Not all contributors, however, are premillennial.) But prophecy is more than prediction, and so this commentary gives due recognition to the major lode of godly social concern in the prophetic writings.

THE EXPOSITOR'S BIBLE COMMENTARY is presented as a scholarly work, though not primarily one of technical criticism. In its main portion, the Exposition, and in Volume 1 (General and Special Articles), all Semitic and Greek words are transliterated and the English equivalents given. As for the Notes, here Semitic and Greek characters are used but always with transliterations and English meanings, so that this portion of the commentary will be as accessible as possible to readers unacquainted with the original languages.

It is the conviction of the general editor, shared by his colleagues in the Zondervan editorial department, that in writing about the Bible, lucidity is not incompatible with scholarship. They are therefore endeavoring to make this a clear and understandable work.

The translation used in it is the New International Version (North American Edition). To the International Bible Society thanks are due for permission to use this most recent of the major Bible translations. The editors and publisher have chosen it because of the clarity and beauty of its style and its faithfulness to the original texts.

To the associate editor, Dr. J. D. Douglas, and to the contributing editors—Dr. Walter C. Kaiser, Jr. and Dr. Bruce K. Waltke for the Old Testament, and Dr. James Montgomery Boice and Dr. Merrill C. Tenney for the New Testament—the general editor expresses his gratitude for their unfailing cooperation and their generosity in advising him out of their expert scholarship. And to the many other contributors he is indebted for their invaluable part in this work. Finally, he owes a special debt of gratitude to Dr. Robert K. DeVries, executive vice-president of the Zondervan Publishing House; Rev. Gerard Terpstra, manuscript editor; and Miss Elizabeth Brown, secretary to Dr. DeVries, for their continual assistance and encouragement.

Whatever else it is—the greatest and most beautiful of books, the primary source of law and morality, the fountain of wisdom, and the infallible guide to life—the Bible is above all the inspired witness to Jesus Christ. May this work fulfill its function of expounding the Scriptures with grace and clarity, so that its users may find that both Old and New Testaments do indeed lead to our Lord Jesus Christ, who alone could say, "I have come that they may have life, and have it to the full" (John 10:10).

FRANK E. GAEBELEIN

ABBREVIATIONS

A. General Abbreviations

A	Codex Alexandrinus	MT	Masoretic text
Akkad.	Akkadian	n.	note
ℵ	Codex Sinaiticus	n.d.	no date
Ap. Lit.	Apocalyptic Literature	Nestle	Nestle (ed.) *Novum*
Apoc.	Apocrypha		*Testamentum Graece*
Aq.	Aquila's Greek Translation	no.	number
	of the Old Testament	NT	New Testament
Arab.	Arabic	obs.	obsolete
Aram.	Aramaic	OL	Old Latin
b	Babylonian Gemara	OS	Old Syriac
B	Codex Vaticanus	OT	Old Testament
C	Codex Ephraemi Syri	p., pp.	page, pages
c.	*circa*, about	par.	paragraph
cf.	*confer*, compare	Pers.	Persian
ch., chs.	chapter, chapters	Pesh.	Peshitta
cod., codd.	codex, codices	Phoen.	Phoenician
contra	in contrast to	pl.	plural
D	Codex Bezae	Pseudep.	Pseudepigrapha
DSS	Dead Sea Scrolls (see E.)	Q	Quelle ("Sayings" source
ed., edd.	edited, edition, editor; editions		in the Gospels)
e.g.	*exempli gratia*, for example	qt.	quoted by
Egyp.	Egyptian	q.v.	*quod vide*, which see
et. al.	*et alii*, and others	R	Rabbah
EV	English Versions of the Bible	rev.	revised, reviser, revision
fem.	feminine	Rom.	Roman
ff.	following (verses, pages, etc.)	RVm	Revised Version margin
fl.	flourished	Samar.	Samaritan recension
ft.	foot, feet	SCM	Student Christian Movement Press
gen.	genitive	Sem.	Semitic
Gr.	Greek	sing.	singular
Heb.	Hebrew	SPCK	Society for the Promotion
Hitt.	Hittite		of Christian Knowledge
ibid.	*ibidem*, in the same place	Sumer.	Sumerian
id.	*idem*, the same	s.v.	*sub verbo*, under the word
i.e.	*id est*, that is	Syr.	Syriac
impf.	imperfect	Symm.	Symmachus
infra.	below	T	Talmud
in loc.	*in loco*, in the place cited	Targ.	Targum
j	Jerusalem or	Theod.	Theodotion
	Palestinian Gemara	TR	Textus Receptus
Lat.	Latin	tr.	translation, translator,
LL.	Late Latin		translated
LXX	Septuagint	UBS	The United Bible Societies'
M	Mishnah		Greek Text
masc.	masculine	Ugar.	Ugaritic
mg.	margin	u.s.	*ut supra*, as above
Mid	Midrash	viz.	*videlicet*, namely
MS(S)	Manuscript(s)		

vol.	volume	Vul.	Vulgate
v., vv.	verse, verses	WH	Westcott and Hort, *The*
vs.	versus		*New Testament in Greek*

B. Abbreviations for Modern Translations and Paraphrases

AmT	Smith and Goodspeed, *The Complete Bible, An American Translation*	LB	The Living Bible
		Mof	J. Moffatt, *A New Translation of the Bible*
ASV	American Standard Version, American Revised Version (1901)	NAB	The New American Bible
		NASB	New American Standard Bible
		NEB	The New English Bible
Beck	Beck, *The New Testament in the Language of Today*	NIV	The New International Version
		Ph	J. B. Phillips *The New Testament in Modern English*
BV	Berkeley Version (The Modern Language Bible)	RSV	Revised Standard Version
JB	The Jerusalem Bible	RV	Revised Version — 1881–1885
JPS	*Jewish Publication Society Version of the Old Testament*	TCNT	Twentieth Century New Testament
KJV	King James Version	TEV	Today's English Version
Knox	R.G. Knox, *The Holy Bible: A Translation from the Latin Vulgate in the Light of the Hebrew and Greek Original*	Wey	*Weymouth's New Testament in Modern Speech*
		Wms	C. B. Williams, *The New Testament: A Translation in the Language of the People*

C. Abbreviations for Periodicals and Reference Works

AASOR	*Annual of the American Schools of Oriental Research*	BAG	Bauer, Arndt, and Gingrich: *Greek-English Lexicon of the New Testament*
AB	*Anchor Bible*	BC	Foakes-Jackson and Lake: *The Beginnings of Christianity*
AIs	de Vaux: *Ancient Israel*		
AJA	*American Journal of Archaeology*		
AJSL	*American Journal of Semitic Languages and Literatures*	BDB	Brown, Driver, and Briggs: *Hebrew-English Lexicon of the Old Testament*
AJT	*American Journal of Theology*	BDF	Blass, Debrunner, and Funk: *A Greek Grammar of the New Testament and Other Early Christian Literature*
Alf	Alford: *Greek Testament Commentary*		
ANEA	*Ancient Near Eastern Archaeology*	BDT	Harrison: *Baker's Dictionary of Theology*
ANET	Pritchard: *Ancient Near Eastern Texts*	Beng.	*Bengel's Gnomon*
		BETS	*Bulletin of the Evangelical Theological Society*
ANF	Roberts and Donaldson: *The Ante-Nicene Fathers*	BJRL	*Bulletin of the John Rylands Library*
ANT	M. R. James: *The Apocryphal New Testament*	BS	*Bibliotheca Sacra*
A-S	Abbot-Smith: *Manual Greek Lexicon of the New Testament*	BT	*Babylonian Talmud*
		BTh	*Biblical Theology*
AThR	*Anglican Theological Review*	BW	*Biblical World*
BA	*Biblical Archaeologist*	CAH	*Cambridge Ancient History*
BASOR	*Bulletin of the American Schools of Oriental Research*	CanJTh	*Canadian Journal of Theology*
		CBQ	*Catholic Biblical Quarterly*

CBSC	Cambridge Bible for Schools and Colleges	HUCA	Hebrew Union College Annual
CE	Catholic Encyclopedia	IB	The Interpreter's Bible
CGT	Cambridge Greek Testament	ICC	International Critical Commentary
CHS	Lange: Commentary on the Holy Scriptures	IDB	The Interpreter's Dictionary of the Bible
ChT	Christianity Today	IEJ	Israel Exploration Journal
Crem	Cremer: Biblico-Theological Lexicon of the New Testament Greek	Int	Interpretation
		INT	E. Harrison: Introduction to the New Testament
DDB	Davis' Dictionary of the Bible	IOT	R. K. Harrison: Introduction to the Old Testament
Deiss BS	Deissmann: Bible Studies		
Deiss LAE	Deissmann: Light From the Ancient East	ISBE	The International Standard Bible Encyclopedia
DNTT	Dictionary of New Testament Theology	ITQ	Irish Theological Quarterly
EBC	The Expositor's Bible Commentary	JAAR	Journal of American Academy of Religion
EBi	Encyclopaedia Biblica	JAOS	Journal of American Oriental Society
EBr	Encyclopaedia Britannica		
EDB	Encyclopedic Dictionary of the Bible	JBL	Journal of Biblical Literature
EGT	Nicoll: Expositor's Greek Testament	JE	Jewish Encyclopedia
		JETS	Journal of Evangelical Theological Society
EQ	Evangelical Quarterly	JFB	Jamieson, Fausset, and Brown: Commentary on the Old and New Testament
ET	Evangelische Theologie		
ExB	The Expositor's Bible		
Exp	The Expositor		
ExpT	The Expository Times	JNES	Journal of Near Eastern Studies
FLAP	Finegan: Light From the Ancient Past	Jos. Antiq.	Josephus: The Antiquities of the Jews
GR	Gordon Review	Jos. War	Josephus: The Jewish War
HBD	Harper's Bible Dictionary	JQR	Jewish Quarterly Review
HDAC	Hastings: Dictionary of the Apostolic Church	JR	Journal of Religion
		JSJ	Journal for the Study of Judaism in the Persian, Hellenistic and Roman Periods
HDB	Hastings: Dictionary of the Bible		
HDBrev.	Hastings: Dictionary of the Bible, one-vol. rev. by Grant and Rowley	JSOR	Journal of the Society of Oriental Research
		JSS	Journal of Semitic Studies
HDCG	Hastings: Dictionary of Christ and the Gospels	JT	Jerusalem Talmud
		JTS	Journal of Theological Studies
HERE	Hastings: Encyclopedia of Religion and Ethics	KAHL	Kenyon: Archaeology in the Holy Land
HGEOTP	Heidel: The Gilgamesh Epic and Old Testament Parallels	KB	Koehler-Baumgartner: Lexicon in Veteris Testament Libros
HJP	Schurer: A History of the Jewish People in the Time of Christ	KD	Keil and Delitzsch: Commentary on the Old Testament
HR	Hatch and Redpath: Concordance to the Septuagint	LSJ	Liddell, Scott, Jones: Greek-English Lexicon
HTR	Harvard Theological Review	LTJM	Edersheim: The Life and Times of Jesus the Messiah

MM	Moulton and Milligan: *The Vocabulary of the Greek Testament*		*Testament aus Talmud und Midrash*
MNT	Moffatt: *New Testament Commentary*	SHERK	*The New Schaff-Herzog Encyclopedia of Religious Knowledge*
MST	McClintock and Strong: *Cyclopedia of Biblical, Theological, and Ecclesiastical Literature*	SJT	*Scottish Journal of Theology*
		SOT	Girdlestone: *Synonyms of Old Testament*
NBC	Davidson, Kevan, and Stibbs: *The New Bible Commentary*, 1st ed.	SOTI	Archer: *A Survey of Old Testament Introduction*
NBCrev.	Guthrie and Motyer: *The New Bible Commentary*, rev. ed.	ST	*Studia Theologica*
		TCERK	Loetscher: *The Twentieth Century Encyclopedia of Religious Knowledge*
NBD	J. D. Douglas: *The New Bible Dictionary*	TDNT	Kittel: *Theological Dictionary of the New Testament*
NCB	*New Century Bible*	TDOT	*Theological Dictionary of the Old Testament*
NCE	*New Catholic Encyclopedia*		
NIC	*New International Commentary*	Theol	*Theology*
NIDCC	Douglas: *The New International Dictionary of the Christian Church*	ThT	*Theology Today*
		TNTC	*Tyndale New Testament Commentaries*
NovTest	*Novum Testamentum*		
NSI	Cooke: *Handbook of North Semitic Inscriptions*	Trench	Trench: *Synonyms of the New Testament*
NTS	*New Testament Studies*	UBD	*Unger's Bible Dictionary*
ODCC	*The Oxford Dictionary of the Christian Church*, rev. ed.	UT	Gordon: *Ugaritic Textbook*
		VB	Allmen: *Vocabulary of the Bible*
Peake	Black and Rowley: *Peake's Commentary on the Bible*	VetTest	*Vetus Testamentum*
PEQ	*Palestine Exploration Quarterly*	Vincent	Vincent: *Word-Pictures in the New Testament*
PNFl	P. Schaff: *The Nicene and Post-Nicene Fathers* (1st series)	WBC	*Wycliffe Bible Commentary*
		WBE	*Wycliffe Bible Encyclopedia*
PNF2	P. Schaff and H. Wace: *The Nicene and Post-Nicene Fathers* (2nd series)	WC	*Westminster Commentaries*
		WesBC	*Wesleyan Bible Commentaries*
		WTJ	*Westminster Theological Journal*
PTR	*Princeton Theological Review*	ZAW	*Zeitschrift für die alttestamentliche Wissenschaft*
RB	*Revue Biblique*		
RHG	Robertson's *Grammar of the Greek New Testament in the Light of Historical Research*	ZNW	*Zeitschrift für die neutestamentliche Wissenschaft*
		ZPBD	*The Zondervan Pictorial Bible Dictionary*
RTWB	Richardson: *A Theological Wordbook of the Bible*	ZPEB	*The Zondervan Pictorial Encyclopedia of the Bible*
SBK	Strack and Billerbeck: *Kommentar zum Neuen*	ZWT	*Zeitschrift für wissenschaftliche Theologie*

D. Abbreviations for Books of the Bible, the Apocrypha, and the Pseudepigrapha

OLD TESTAMENT

Gen	2 Chron	Dan
Exod	Ezra	Hos
Lev	Neh	Joel
Num	Esth	Amos
Deut	Job	Obad
Josh	Ps(Pss)	Jonah
Judg	Prov	Mic
Ruth	Eccl	Nah
1 Sam	S of Songs	Hab
2 Sam	Isa	Zeph
1 Kings	Jer	Hag
2 Kings	Lam	Zech
1 Chron	Ezek	Mal

NEW TESTAMENT

Matt	1 Tim
Mark	2 Tim
Luke	Titus
John	Philem
Acts	Heb
Rom	James
1 Cor	1 Peter
2 Cor	2 Peter
Gal	1 John
Eph	2 John
Phil	3 John
Col	Jude
1 Thess	Rev
2 Thess	

APOCRYPHA

1 Esd	1 Esdras	Ep Jer	Epistle of Jeremy
2 Esd	2 Esdras	S Th Ch	Song of the Three Children
Tobit	Tobit		(or Young Men)
Jud	Judith	Sus	Susanna
Add Esth	Additions to Esther	Bel	Bel and the Dragon
Wisd Sol	Wisdom of Solomon	Pr Man	Prayer of Manasseh
Ecclus	Ecclesiasticus (Wisdom of	1 Macc	1 Maccabees
	Jesus the Son of Sirach)	2 Macc	2 Maccabees
Baruch	Baruch		

PSEUDEPIGRAPHA

As Moses	Assumption of Moses	Pirke Aboth	Pirke Aboth
2 Baruch	Syriac Apocalypse of Baruch	Ps 151	Psalm 151
3 Baruch	Greek Apocalypse of Baruch	Pss Sol	Psalms of Solomon
1 Enoch	Ethiopic Book of Enoch	Sib Oracles	Sibylline Oracles
2 Enoch	Slavonic Book of Enoch	Story Ah	Story of Ahikar
3 Enoch	Hebrew Book of Enoch	T Abram	Testament of Abraham
4 Ezra	4 Ezra	T Adam	Testament of Adam
JA	Joseph and Asenath	T Benjamin	Testament of Benjamin
Jub	Book of Jubilees	T Dan	Testament of Dan
L Aristeas	Letter of Aristeas	T Gad	Testament of Gad
Life AE	Life of Adam and Eve	T Job	Testament of Job
Liv Proph	Lives of the Prophets	T Jos	Testament of Joseph
MA Isa	Martyrdom and Ascension	T Levi	Testament of Levi
	of Isaiah	T Naph	Testament of Naphtali
3 Macc	3 Maccabees	T 12 Pat	Testaments of the Twelve
4 Macc	4 Maccabees		Patriarchs
Odes Sol	Odes of Solomon	Zad Frag	Zadokite Fragments
P Jer	Paralipomena of Jeremiah		

E. Abbreviations of Names of Dead Sea Scrolls and Related Texts

CD — Cairo (Genizah text of the) Damascus (Document)

DSS — Dead Sea Scrolls

Hev — Nahal Hever texts

Mas — Masada Texts

Mird — Khirbet mird texts

Mur — Wadi Murabba'at texts

P — Pesher (commentary)

Q — Qumran

1Q, 2Q, etc. — Numbered caves of Qumran, yielding written material; followed by abbreviation of biblical or apocryphal book.

QL — Qumran Literature

1QapGen — Genesis Apocryphon of Qumran Cave 1

1QH — *Hodayot* (Thanksgiving Hymns) from Qumran Cave 1

1QIsa a, b — First or second copy of Isaiah from Qumran Cave 1

1QpHab — Pesher on Habakkuk from Qumran Cave 1

1QM — *Milhamah* (War Scroll)

1QpMic — Pesher on portions of Micah from Qumran Cave 1

1QS — *Serek Hayyahad* (Rule of the Community, Manual of Discipline)

1QSa — Appendix A (Rule of the Congregation) to 1Qs

1QSb — Appendix B (Blessings) to 1QS

3Q15 — Copper Scroll from Qumran Cave 3

4QExod a — Exodus Scroll, exemplar "a" from Qumran Cave 4

4QFlor — Florilegium (or Eschatological Midrashim) from Qumran Cave 4

4Qmess ar — Aramaic "Messianic" text from Qumran Cave 4

4QpNah — Pesher on portions of Nahum from Qumran Cave 4

4QPrNab — Prayer of Nabonidus from Qumran Cave 4

4QpPs37 — Pesher on portions of Psalm 37 from Qumran Cave 4

4QTest — Testimonia text from Qumran Cave 4

4QTLevi — Testament of Levi from Qumran Cave 4

4QPhyl — Phylacteries from Qumran Cave 4

11QMelch — Melchizedek text from Qumran Cave 11

11QtgJob — Targum of Job from Qumran Cave 11

TRANSLITERATIONS

Hebrew

א = ʾ		ד = $\underline{d}$		י = y		ס = s		ר = r
בּ = b		ה = h		כ = k		ע = ʿ		שׂ = ś
ב = $\underline{b}$		ו = w		כ = $\underline{k}$		פּ = p		שׁ = š
גּ = g		ז = z		ל = l		פ = $\underline{p}$		תּ = t
ג = $\underline{g}$		ח = ḥ		מ ם = m		צ ץ = ṣ		ת = $\underline{t}$
ד = d		ט = ṭ		נ = n		ק = q		

(ה)ָ = â (h)	ָ = å	ַ = a	ֲ = a
ֵה = ê	ֶה = ė	ֵ = e	ֱ = e
ִי = î		ִ = i	ְ = e (if vocal)
וֹ = ô	ֹ = ô	ָ = o	ֳ = o
וּ = û		ֻ = u	

Aramaic

ʾ b g d h w z ḥ ṭ y k l m n s ʿ p ṣ q r š š t

Arabic

ʾ b t ṯ ǧ ḥ ḫ d ḏ r z s š ṣ ḍ ṭ ẓ ʿ ǵ f q k l m n h w y

Ugaritic

ʾ b g d ḏ h w z ḥ ḫ ṭ ẓ y k l m n s ṣ ʿ ǵ ṗ ṣ q r š t ṯ

xv

Greek

α	—	a	π	—	p	αι	—	ai
β	—	b	ρ	—	r	αυ	—	au
γ	—	g	σ,ς	—	s	ει	—	ei
δ	—	d	τ	—	t	ευ	—	eu
ε	—	e	υ	—	y	ηυ	—	ēu
ζ	—	z	φ	—	ph	οι	—	oi
η	—	ē	χ	—	ch	ου	—	ou
θ	—	th	ψ	—	ps	υι	—	hui
ι	—	i	ω	—	ō			
κ	—	k				ῥ	—	rh
λ	—	l	γγ	—	ng	‘	—	h
μ	—	m	γκ	—	nk			
ν	—	n	γξ	—	nx	ᾳ	—	ā
ξ	—	x	γχ	—	nch	ῃ	—	ē
ο	—	o				ῳ	—	ō

HEBREWS

Leon Morris

HEBREWS

Introduction

1. Literary Form
2. Destination
3. Authorship
4. Use of the Old Testament
5. Date
6. Bibliography
7. Outline

This book is unlike any other in the NT, though not without resemblance to 1 John. In subject matter it is distinctive, and its picture of Jesus as our great High Priest is its own. It is not easy to see who wrote it, to whom it was written, or why. It lacks an epistolary opening but has an epistolary conclusion. Difficulties abound, but the profundity of its thought gives it a significant place in the NT.

1. Literary Form

Though we usually call Hebrews an epistle, important features of a letter are lacking for this book. But if we cannot straightforwardly label it a letter, there are at least indications that it was meant for a restricted circle of readers, not the general public or even the general Christian public. The recipients are a group who ought to be teachers (5:12). The writer knows them and looks forward to visiting them (13:19, 23). He has a good opinion of them (6:9). He can ask for their prayers (13:18) and give them news of their mutual friend Timothy (13:23). The writer recalls "earlier days" (10:32) and remembers persecutions his friends had endured (10:32; 12:4), their generosity to other believers (6:10), and their cheerful attitude when their property had been confiscated. He knows their present attitude toward their leaders (13:17). In the light of such statements, it is plain that the writer is addressing a definite, known group, and a small one at that (not many Christians would qualify for the position of teacher).

Moreover, the intended recipients were a group whose needs the writer knew. He wanted them to advance to the level of being teachers (5:12) and to avoid apostasy (6:4ff.). There is a homiletic air about much that he writes; so it is not surprising that many have considered the book a sermon—one the author had preached earlier or one he was now composing for the benefit of his friends. He himself calls his work "my word of exhortation" (13:22; cf. Acts 13:15, where a sermon is similarly styled; NIV has "a short letter" at the end of 13:22, but the Gr. means simply "briefly," *dia bracheōn*). There are oratorical touches, and E.F. Scott calls it "one of the noblest examples of Christian eloquence" (p. 2). The style makes it not unlikely that there is a sermon behind it. But as it stands, the book is addressed to a specific group. So it may be called a letter, though the lack of the usual epistolary framework shows that the writer is paying no attention to conventional niceties. He is concerned for his friends and writes to correct some specific erroneous tendencies he sees in them.

2. Recipients

The title "To the Hebrews" is attested by Pantaenus (Eusebius *Ecclesiastical History* 6.14.4) and in the West by Tertullian (*De Pudicitia* 20). It is in the oldest MSS. It is often said that the title was not original, and this may be the case, though it should be added that we have no knowledge of any other title or any time when it lacked this one. If the title is accurate, then it follows that the letter was written to a group of Jews. However, it would still remain to be determined whether they were Jewish Christians or non-Christians. The traditional view is that the recipients were Christian Jews, but some recent scholars doubt whether there is enough evidence to sustain this position. Some think it better to see the original recipients as Gentiles.

The most persuasive argument for Jewish recipients is the way the book moves so consistently within the orbit of the OT Scriptures and Jewish liturgy. The writer has much to say about the worship of the tabernacle, the priests and the kind of sacrifice they offered, the covenant that meant so much to the Jews, and Jewish worthies like Abraham, Moses, Joshua, and a host of others mentioned in chapter 11. Topics like the sufferings of the Messiah and the replacement of the Levitical priesthood by a priesthood after the order of Melchizedek would interest Jews. Incidental references such as "surely it is not angels he helps, but Abraham's descendants" (2:16) are more likely to appeal to Jews than Gentiles. The argument that Jesus is superior to Moses (3:1ff.) would have more weight with Jews than with anyone else. (What would it matter to Gentiles who was superior to Moses?)

Some have thought that the recipients were a group of Jewish priests—perhaps specifically Essene priests—or members of the Qumran community.[1] Such positions, however, are scarcely tenable. The readers were certainly members of the Christian community (e.g., 3:1; 6:9; 10:23). Jewish Christians they may have been, but we cannot place them as non-Christian Jews.

On the other hand, some argue that the elegant Greek of the epistle indicates that neither the writer nor the recipients were Jews. But this argument is not relevant. The Jews of the Diaspora were familiar with Greek; after all, the LXX had been written for them. So there would be no problem for Jews either to write or to read "elegant" Greek. Furthermore, it is not necessary that the author himself be a Jew. A Gentile could certainly write to Jews. Nor is the argument from the book's use of the LXX decisive, for many Jews used this version instead of the Hebrew OT.

More significant is the appeal to fundamentals in chapter 6. The "elementary teachings" are listed as "repentance from acts that lead to death, . . . faith in God, instruction about baptisms, the laying on of hands, the resurrection of the dead, and eternal judgment" (vv.1–2). It is urged that this is the basis of the Gentile mission, but it would have been necessary in the first stages to teach Jews that Jesus is the

---

[1]W.G. Kümmel, *Introduction to the New Testament* (London: SCM, 1966), p. 279.

Christ and perhaps that God is present in the Holy Spirit. Again, people who turned back to Judaism would not be turning away "from the living God" (3:12), though those who returned to Gentile ways would. Jewish regulations about foods are said to be "strange teachings" (13:9). The epistle never contrasts Jew and Gentile and indeed never mentions either in set terms.

Many do not regard the constant reference to the OT as significant, for from the first the OT was the Bible of Gentile Christians as well as Jewish Christians. The church saw itself as the true Israel, as the heir of the promises of the OT. And while the author makes a good deal of the Jewish priesthood and Jewish practices, it must be borne in mind that he does not take his information and symbolism from the temple that existed in the first century. Rather, he referred to the much earlier tabernacle, about which all the available information is in the OT.

Not all this evidence is equally convincing. The appeal to the OT would be valid for Gentiles only if they were Christians. But if they were falling away from the faith, the OT would hold no authority for them. However, it was authoritative for Jewish readers, whether they were Christians or not. Also, one could fairly argue that 3:12 does not tell against Jewish recipients of the letter because the author sees all apostasy as falling away from the "living God." Indeed, he illustrates this by referring to the Israelites in the wilderness who rejected Moses' leadership and rebelled against God (3:16ff.). The "elementary teachings" of chapter 6 might be taken as being just as applicable to Jews as to Gentiles. So we might go on. And when we are through, we may conclude that it cannot be proved beyond any doubt that Hebrews was written for either Jews or Gentiles.

On the whole, it seems that more is to be said for Hebrews having been written for Jewish rather than Gentile readers. I find it hard to think that a writing that moves so much in the area of Jewish ritual was in the first instance intended for non-Jews, however readily they may have embraced the OT. And it is conjecture that the title "To the Hebrews" was not original. The evidence favors it. While absolute certainty is impossible, it is best, therefore, to see the epistle as written for a group of able Jewish Christians. They seem to have been hesitant about cutting themselves off decisively from the Jewish religion (which was tolerated by the Romans) in favor of the Christian way (which was not).

Many consider the recipients to have been Palestinian Jews. Specifically, some suggest that these Jews had a connection with the Qumran community. But the evidence for this is slight. These people had helped others (6:10), whereas Palestinian Christians were poor (Acts 11:27–30; Rom 15:26; 2 Cor 8–9). They had not seen Jesus (2:3), but many Palestinian Christians must have done so. There is more to be said for indications that point to recipients in Rome. For example, the epistle is first attested in Clement of Rome's letter. The greeting "Those from Italy send you their greetings" (13:24) is perhaps most naturally understood of a group of Italian origin, now living elsewhere, sending greetings back home. The word hēgoumenos ("leader") applied to church leaders (13:7, 17, 24) occurs in a similar way in 1 Clement and Hermas, both connected with Rome. Also, there was more hesitation at Rome to regard Hebrews as canonical than there was elsewhere, and a big factor in this hesitation was doubt that Paul wrote the epistle. The argument is that the Romans knew who wrote it and that the author was not Paul. Obviously all this falls far short of proof. Yet there do seem to be more reasons for connecting the letter with Rome than with any other place.

3. Authorship

The epistle was used by Clement of Rome (e.g., 1 Clement 17; 36) probably also by Polycarp (*To the Philippians* 6; 12) and Hermas (*Visions* 2.3.2; 3.7.2; *Similitudes* 9.13.7). Therefore the author was an early Christian. The earliest reference to authorship is a statement of Clement of Alexandria that Paul wrote it in Hebrew and that Luke translated the work into Greek (quoted in Eusebius *Ecclesiastical History* 6.14.2). When it was accepted as part of the NT, this was partly at least because contemporaries held Paul to be the author. This view, however, appears to rest on no reliable evidence but rather to be a deduction from the facts that Paul was a prolific writer of epistles and that Hebrews is a noble writing that must have had a distinguished author. But both the language and thought forms are unlike those of Paul. The Greek is polished; Paul's is rugged, though vigorous. This book moves in the context of Levitical symbolism, about which Paul elsewhere says nothing. The same argument also tells against Clement of Alexandria's view that Luke translated it. While there are some interesting coincidences of language between Hebrews and Luke-Acts, there are also some differences. And it is incredible that if Luke knew Hebrews, he should have made no reference whatever to its teaching either in his Gospel or in the Acts.

None of the early writers who cites the epistle mentions its author. Nor does internal evidence help us much. The author was plainly a teacher, a second generation Christian (2:3). The style is unlike that of any other NT document; consequently, we have nothing more to go on to determine authorship than conjecture. Though many suggestions have been made, it will suffice to mention only a few of them. The allegation that Barnabas was the author is as old as Tertullian (*De Pudicitia* 20), but little can be said in its support. Barnabas was a Levite (Acts 4:36), and there is much about Levitical ritual in the epistle. Again, in Acts 4:36 Barnabas was called *huios parakleseos* ("Son of Encouragement"); and in Hebrews 13:22 the epistle refers to itself as *tou logou tes parakleseos* ("my word of exhortation," NIV). But it is hard to see 2:3 as applying to Barnabas.

Luther suggested that Apollos was the author. A number of modern scholars support this view. Apollos was an eloquent man (Acts 18:24), and there is indeed eloquence in this epistle. Apollos came from Alexandria, a center where allegorical interpretation, which might be said to be akin to the method used in Hebrews, flourished (cf. Philo). Apollos had "a thorough knowledge of the Scriptures" (Acts 18:24), a description particularly appropriate for the author, who did not simply use the "proof-text" method but applied a thorough knowledge of Scripture in an original manner. Apollos must remain a possible author, but the evidence is far from conclusive.

Harnack thought that Priscilla probably wrote the epistle.[2] His strong point is that this would account for the suppression of the author's name. It was a man's world, and there would be every reason for keeping it quiet that a woman had written an epistle intended to be authoritative and to have wide circulation. Priscilla and her husband were cultured Hellenistic Jews, and the woman who could instruct Apollos

---

[2]Adolph von Harnack, "Probabilia über die Adresse und den Verfasser des Hebräerbriefes," ZNW, i (1900), 16ff.

in the faith (Acts 18:26) was no mean teacher. The interest in the tabernacle would be natural in a family whose living came from tentmaking (Acts 18:3), and the outlook of a pilgrim would be natural to one who did so much traveling. All this is interesting, but plainly it falls far short of proof. And against it stands the masculine participle *diēgoumenon* ("to tell") used of the author in 11:32.

In the end we must agree that we have no certain evidence about the authorship of Hebrews. Who wrote it remains unknown to us. We can scarcely improve on the words of Origen's conclusion, that "who wrote the Epistle, God only knows the truth" (Eusebius *Ecclesiastical History* 6.25.14).

4. The Use of the Old Testament in Hebrews

There are some interesting features of the author's use of the OT. To begin with, he uses the LXX almost exclusively. Now and then he bases his argument on the LXX where that differs from the Hebrew (e.g., 10:5–7). G. Howard argues that the author seems to have used a variety of Greek texts, some agreeing with our LXX and some differing from it (NovTest 10 [1968], pp. 208–16).

The author's favorite sources are the Pentateuch and the Psalms. Westcott finds him quoting from the Pentateuch twelve times and alluding to it without direct quotation thirty-nine times. The figures for the other parts of the OT are Historical books, one quotation, no allusions; the Prophets, four quotations, eleven allusions; Psalms, eleven quotations, two allusions; Proverbs, one quotation, one allusion. This means twenty-three out of twenty-nine quotations come from the Pentateuch and the Psalms. It is curious that there is so little from the Prophets, especially in view of the author's attitude toward the sacrifices. One would think he would have found much in the Prophets that was applicable to his purpose. There are no quotations from the Apocrypha, though there appears to be an allusion to an event narrated in 2 Maccabees 6–7 (11:35).

The author has an unusual method of citation; he almost always neglects the human author of his OT quotations (exceptions are 4:7; 9:19–20), though throughout the rest of the NT the human author is often noted. Instead, without actually saying "God says," he normally ascribes the passage he quotes to God, except, of course, where God is addressed, as in 2:6. Twice he attributes words in the OT to Christ (2:11–12; 10:5ff.) and twice to the Holy Spirit (3:7; 10:15). No other NT writer shares this way of quoting the OT. Elsewhere in the NT words are normally ascribed to God only when God is the actual speaker in the OT. This is not invariable, but the habit in Hebrews is only the occasional use in the other books. The effect is to emphasize the divine authorship of the whole OT. For the author, what Scripture says, God says.

A further point is that the author sees Scripture as pointing to Jesus. What the ancient writings say is fulfilled in him. This means more than that specific prophecies are fulfilled in Jesus. Rather the thrust of the whole OT is such that it leads inescapably to him. The author writes of Christianity as the final religion, not because he regards the faith of the OT as mistaken, but because he sees it as God's way of pointing men to Jesus. Judaism is not so much abrogated by Christianity as brought to its climax. The fuller meaning of the OT is to be seen in the person and work of Jesus. The OT and the new way are rightly seen only when they are recognized as parts of one whole. And it is Jesus who enables us to discern that whole and its meaning.

5. Date

The mention of Timothy (13:23) shows that the writing must be early, unless the reference is to a Timothy other than Paul's companion. But this is highly improbable. However, as we know nothing about the dates of Timothy's birth and death, this reference to him does little to narrow down our search. The words "you have not yet resisted to the point of shedding your blood" (12:4) points to a date before the persecutions, or at least before the lives of any of the community the letter was written to had been lost in the persecutions. Once again we have an indication of an early date, but one we cannot narrowly tie down.

The principal indication of the date is that the epistle says nothing about the destruction of the temple but leaves the impression that the Jewish sacrificial system, with its ministry of priests and all that that involved, was a continuing reality (cf. 9:6–9). But the author is arguing that Judaism is superseded by Christianity and specifically that the sacrifices of the old system are of no avail now that the sacrifice of Jesus has been offered. It would have been a convincing climax had the author been able to point out that the temple and all that went with it had ceased to exist. "The best argument for the supersession of the old covenant would have been the destruction of the Temple" (Montefiore, p. 3). The author's failure to mention this surely means that it had not yet occurred.

This seems about as far as we can go. A date before A.D. 70 is indicated, but how much before that we cannot say. Some passages in the epistle gain in force if we think of a time not long before, when there was a compelling call to loyal Jews to cast in their lot with those fighting against Rome. So perhaps we should think of a date near or even during the war of A.D. 66–70.

6. Bibliography

Barclay, William. *The Letter to the Hebrews*. Edinburgh: Saint Andrew, 1955.

Bowman, J.W. *Hebrews, James, I and II Peter*. London: SCM, 1962.

Brown, J. *An Exposition of Hebrews*. 1862. Reprint. London: Banner of Truth, 1961.

Bruce, F.F. *The Epistle to the Hebrews*. Grand Rapids: Eerdmans, 1964.

Buchanan, G.W. *To the Hebrews*. New York: Doubleday, 1972.

Calvin, J. *The Epistle of Paul the Apostle to the Hebrews and the First and Second Epistles of St. Peter*. Edinburgh: Oliver and Boyd, 1963.

DuBose, W.P. *High Priesthood and Sacrifice*. London: Longmans, 1908.

Héring, J. *The Epistle to the Hebrews*. London: Epworth, 1970.

Hewitt, T. *The Epistle to the Hebrews*. London: Tyndale, 1960.

Kent, H.A. *The Epistle to the Hebrews*. Grand Rapids: Baker, 1972.

Manson, W. *The Epistle to the Hebrews*. London: Hodder and Stoughton, 1951.

Moffatt, J. *A Critical and Exegetical Commentary on the Epistle to the Hebrews*. ICC. Edinburgh: T. & T. Clark, 1924.

Montefiore, H.W. *A Commentary on the Epistle to the Hebrews*. London: Black, 1964.

Nairne, A. *The Epistle of Priesthood*. Edinburgh: T. & T. Clark, 1913.

Purdy, A.C. *The Epistle to the Hebrews*. New York: Abingdon, 1955.

Robinson, T.H. *The Epistle to the Hebrews*. London: Hodder and Stoughton, 1933.

Scott, E.F. *The Epistle to the Hebrews*. Edinburgh: T. & T. Clark, 1922.

Snell, A. *New and Living Way*. London: Faith, 1959.

Spicq, C. *L'Épître aux Hébreux*. Paris: Gabalda, 1952.

Tasker, R. V. G. *The Gospel in the Epistle to the Hebrews*. London: Tyndale, 1950.
Westcott, B. F. *The Epistle to the Hebrews*. London: MacMillan, 1892.
Williamson, R. *Philo and the Epistle to the Hebrews*. Leiden: Brill, 1970.

7. Outline

Text and Exposition

I. Introduction

1:1–4

> [1]In the past God spoke to our forefathers through the prophets at many times and in various ways, [2]but in these last days he has spoken to us by his Son, whom he appointed heir of all things, and through whom he made the universe. [3]The Son is the radiance of God's glory and the exact representation of his being, sustaining all things by his powerful word. After he had provided purification for sins, he sat down at the right hand of the Majesty in heaven. [4]So he became as much superior to the angels as the name he has inherited is superior to theirs.

The author begins with a magnificent introduction in which he brings out something of the greatness of Jesus and his saving work. He goes on to point out that Jesus is superior to the angels and thus leads into the first main section of the epistle. In the Greek this is a single, powerful sentence that shows the difference between the old revelation, which is fragmentary and spoken through prophets, and the new, which is complete and comes from one who has all the dignity of being Son of God (cf. v.2 for comment on "being Son").

1 It is significant that the subject of the first verb is "God," for God is constantly before the author; he uses the word sixty-eight times, an average of about once every seventy-three words all through his epistle. Few NT books speak of God so often. Right at the beginning, then, we are confronted with the reality of God and the fact that he has been active. The first divine activity commented on is that God has spoken in a variety of ways. He spoke to Moses in the burning bush (Exod 3:2ff.), to Elijah in a still, small voice (1 Kings 19:12ff.), to Isaiah in a vision in the temple (Isa 6:1ff.), to Hosea in his family circumstances (Hos 1:2), and to Amos in a basket of summer fruit (Amos 8:1). God might convey his message through visions and dreams, through angels, through Urim and Thummim, through symbols, natural events, ecstasy, a pillar of fire, smoke, or other means. He could appear in Ur of the Chaldees, in Haran, in Canaan, in Egypt, in Babylon. There is no lack of variety, for revelation is not a monotonous activity that must always take place in the same way. God used variety.

"In the past" (*palai*) means "of old," rather than simply "formerly." The revelation the writer is speaking of is no novelty but has its roots deep in the past. He is not referring here to what God does continually but to what he did in days of old, in the time of "our forefathers." The expression is usually translated "fathers" and is normally used in the NT of the patriarchs (cf. KJV, John 7:22; Rom 9:5, et al.), but here the contrast to "us" in v.2 shows that the term "forefathers" is a shorthand way of referring to OT believers in general. There is a problem concerning the phrase "through the prophets," for scholars are not agreed on how we should take *en* (translated "through"). Moffatt takes the word as equivalent to "through," though noting that in antiquity Philo saw the prophets as God's interpreters in a way that requires us to see God as really "in" them (in loc.). This latter view is held by a number of exegetes. Westcott, for example, explicitly rejects the rendering "through" in favor of "*in them* . . . as the quickening power of their life . . . they were His messengers, inspired by His Spirit, not in their words only but as men" (in loc.). Kent reminds us that the construction is parallel to that in v.2: God was in Christ and before that he was in the prophets (in loc.). It seems best to see the meaning in some such way as this. God not only used the prophets as his voice but was "in" them. The "prophets" here may mean more than the canonical prophets and may include the men of God, like Abraham, who preceded them.

2 "In these last days" is more literally "on the last of these days." The expression is found in the LXX, where it not infrequently refers in some way to the days of the Messiah (e.g., Num 24:14). Here, in Hebrews, it means that in Jesus the new age, the Messianic Age, has appeared. Jesus is more than simply the last in a long line of prophets. He has inaugurated a new age altogether. In Jesus there is continuity and there is discontinuity. The continuity comes out when we are told that God "has spoken to us by his Son." The verb "spoken" is the same one used in v.1 of the prophets, and there is a grammatical connection: "God, having spoken in the prophets . . . has spoken in the Son" (personal translation). The earlier revelation is not irrelevant to the later one but is continuous with it. The same God has spoken in both. The old prepares the way for the new, a truth that will be brought out again and again in this epistle as the author backs up his arguments with quotations from Scripture. The discontinuity is seen when we come to the reference to the Son. It is noteworthy that in the Greek there is no article or possessive; there is nothing corresponding to NIV's "his." In essence the writer is saying God spoke "in one who has the quality of being Son." It is the Son's essential nature that is stressed. This stands in contrast to "the prophets" in the preceding verse. The consummation of the revelatory process, the definitive revelation, took place when he who was not one of "the goodly fellowship of the prophets" but the very Son of God came. Throughout the epistle we shall often meet such thoughts. The writer is concerned to show that in Jesus Christ we have such a divine person and such divine activity that there can be no going back from him.

This emphasis on the Son leads to a series of seven propositions about him (eight if we include v.4). In the first we find that God "appointed" him "heir of all things." The verb "appointed" is somewhat unexpected. We should have anticipated that the Son would simply *be* heir. Perhaps there is a stress on the divine will as active. In the term "heir" there is no thought of entering into possession through the death of a testator. In the NT the word and its cognates are often used in a sense much like "get possession of" without reference to any specific way of acquiring the property in question. In other words, the term points to lawful possession but without indicating in what way that possession is secured. "Heir of all things," then, is a title of dignity and shows that Christ has the supreme place in all the mighty universe. His exaltation to the highest place in heaven after his work on earth was done did not mark some new dignity but his reentry to his rightful place (cf. Phil 2:6–11).

The second truth about the Son is that it is "through" him that God "made the universe." The "through" (*di'*) preserves the important truth that God is the Creator. But as elsewhere in the NT the thought is that he performed the work of creation through the Son (cf. John 1:3; 1 Cor 8:6; Col 1:16). The term rendered "the universe" is literally "the ages" (*tous aiōnas*) and has a temporal sense. While the universe may well be in mind (it is the natural object of the verb "made"), it will be the universe as "the sum of the periods of time, including all that is manifested in them" (A-S, s.v.). Buchanan thinks that the word here (and in 11:3) means "ages," arguing that it was a Jewish idea that God created the ages (in loc.). This may be so. Yet it seems that in this context "the universe" makes better sense, though the word may be meant to hint at the temporal nature of all things material.

3 The one long sentence (Gr.) continues, but there is a change of subject. NIV has supplied "The Son," which gives the sense of it; but the Greek has simply the relative *hos* ("who"). The Son is described first as "the radiance of God's glory." There is ambiguity in the Greek term *apaugasma,* which may mean "radiance," a shining forth because of brightness within, or "reflection," a shining forth because of brightness from without. Jesus is thus spoken of as the outshining of the brightness of God's glory, or as the reflection of that glory. In either case we see the glory of God in Jesus, and we see it as it really is. "Glory" can be used of literal brightness (Acts 22:11). However, it is more commonly used in the NT of the radiance associated with God and with heavenly beings in general. "Glory" sometimes indicates the presence of God (e.g., Ezek 1:28; 11:23), and, to the extent that man is able to apprehend it, the revelation of God's majesty.

"The exact representation of his being" is the fourth of the statements about the Son. "Exact representation" translates *charaktēr,* a very unusual word (here only in the NT). Originally it denoted an instrument for engraving and then a mark stamped on that instrument. Hence it came to be used generally of a mark stamped on a thing, the impress of a die. It might be used figuratively, for example, of God as making man in his own image (1 Clement 33:4). In its literal sense it was used of the impression on coins; RSV's "bears the very stamp of his nature" brings out something of this meaning. Here the writer is saying that the Son is an exact representation of God. The word *hypostaseōs,* rendered "being," is difficult. Its etymological equivalent in English is "substance," viz., that which stands under a thing, that which makes it what it is. The Son is such a revelation of the Father that when we see Jesus, we see what God's real being is.

"Sustaining" translates *pherōn,* which has a meaning like "carrying along." The author does not see Christ's work in sustaining creation as holding up the universe like a dead weight (as Atlas was supposed to do!). Rather his thought is that of carrying it along, of bearing it toward a goal. The concept is dynamic, not static. "All things" is *ta panta,* the totality, the universe considered as one whole. Nothing is excluded from the scope of the Son's sustaining activity. The author pictures the Son as in the first instance active in creation and then as continuing his interest in the world he loves and bearing it onward towards the fulfillment of the divine plan. And all this he does "by his powerful word," or, as Knox renders it, by "his enabling word." The "word" (*rhēma* here, "command," "order," according to BAG) is thought of as active and powerful. The universe (*aiōnas,* "ages") was created by this "word" (11:3). The "word" is not empty. It has force. It does things. The word for "powerful" (lit., "by the word of his power") is *dynamis,* which may be used of literal physical power or in more metaphorical usages like "capability," "wealth," or the like. Here it has something like the literal meaning.

With the statement about the Son's having effected purification of sins, the author comes to what is for him the heart of the matter. His whole epistle shows that the thing that had gripped him was that the very Son of God had come to deal with the problem of man's sin. He sees him as a priest and the essence of his priestly work as the offering of the sacrifice that really put sin away. The author has an unusual number of ways of referring to what Christ has done for man: The Savior made a propitiation for sins (2:17). He put sins away so that God remembers them no more (8:12; 10:17). He bore sin (9:28), he offered a sacrifice (*thysia*) for sins (10:12), he made an offering (*prosphora*) for sin (10:18), and brought about remission of sin (10:18). He annulled sin by his sacrifice (9:26). He brought about redemption from transgressions (9:15). In other passages the author speaks of a variety of things the former covenant could not do with respect to sin, the implication in each case being that Christ has now done it (e.g., 10:2, 4, 6, 11). It is clear from all this that the author sees Jesus as having accomplished a many-sided salvation. Whatever had to be done about sin he has done.

The word "purification" (*katharismos*) is most often used in the NT of ritual cleansing (e.g., Mark 1:44), but here (and in 2 Peter 1:9) it refers to the removal of sin. It also points to the defiling aspect of sin. Sin stains. But Christ has effected a complete cleansing. The verb "provided" is in the aorist tense; the cleansing in question, being based on a past action, is complete. The purification was accomplished at Calvary. The genitive "of sins" probably means that Christ took the sins away rather than that the person was cleansed "from sins." The word for sin (*hamartia*) occurs in this epistle twenty-five times, a total exceeded only by Romans with forty-eight. The author sees *hamartia* ("sin") as a great problem; and in this epistle "sin appears as the power that deceives men and leads them to destruction, whose influence and activity can be ended only by sacrifices" (BAG, s.v.). But the usual sacrifices could not remove sin, and it is the author's conviction that Jesus Christ was needed to remove it. In him and him alone are sins really dealt with.

The seventh in the series of statements about the Son is that when his work of purification was ended, "he sat down at the right hand of the Majesty in heaven." Sitting is the posture of rest, and the right-hand position is the place of honor. Sitting at God's right hand, then, is a way of saying that Christ's saving work is done and that he is now in the place of highest honor. By contrast, the posture for a priest is standing (10:11). The word translated "Majesty" (*megalōsynē*) appears again in the NT only in 8:1; Jude 25. It means "greatness" and thus came to signify "majesty." Here it is obviously a periphrasis for God himself. "In heaven" is more literally "in the heights," but clearly this means "heaven" (for the thought cf. Eph 4:10; Phil 2:9). Some take the expression with "sat down"; i.e., "sat down in heaven at the right hand." This makes it refer to the exaltation, but this scarcely seems warranted. The Greek word order as well as the general sense make it better to link "in heaven" with "the Majesty."

4 "He became" is again somewhat unexpected (cf. "appointed," v.2). The writer has made some strong statements about the excellence of Christ's person, and so we should expect him to describe Christ as eternally superior to the angels rather than as "becoming" superior to them. But the writer says it this way because he was thinking of what the Son did in becoming man and putting away the sins of men. Of course, the Son was also eternally superior to the angels. That, however, is not what is in mind here. It was because he had put away sins that he sat down on the throne in the place of highest honor, and it is in this aspect that he is seen as greater than any angel.

"Superior" is the translation of *kreittōn*, which is more usually rendered "better." This is one of the author's favorite words. He uses it thirteen out of the nineteen times it appears in the NT (1 Cor, with three occurrences, is the only other book that has the word more than once). So we read in Hebrews that there are better things (6:9) and that the less is blessed of the better (7:7); there is a better hope (7:19) and a better covenant (7:22; 8:6); there are better promises (8:6) and better sacrifices (9:23); there are a better possession (10:34), a better country (11:16), a better resurrection (11:35), something better (11:40), and blood that speaks better (12:24). This strong emphasis on what is "better" arises from the author's deep conviction that Jesus Christ is "better" and that he has accomplished something "better" than anyone else.

Another word that appears frequently in this epistle is "angel." The author uses it thirteen times. The only NT books that use it more often are Matthew, Luke, Acts, and Revelation. While the term can be used of a human messenger (Luke 9:52), sometimes sent by God (Mark 1:2), in the overwhelming number of cases it means a spirit being from the other world. In many cases the idea of a messenger remains. Sometimes, however, the thought is simply that of beings intermediate between God and man. It also may be used of evil beings, but references to good angels are much more common.

In antiquity "the name" meant much more than it does today. We use a name as little more than a distinguishing mark or label to differentiate one person from other people. But in the world of the NT the name concisely sums up all that a person is. One's whole character was somehow implied in the name. Opinions differ as to what is meant here by "the name." Some take this to mean that in his whole character and personality Christ was superior to any angel. Others think the reference is simply to the name "Son," which is a better name than "angel" because it denotes superiority in character and personality. Either interpretation is possible.

The word "superior" as applied to "the name" is *diaphorōteron* (not *kreitton*, which is translated the same way earlier in the verse). *Diaphorōteron* is the comparative of the adjective meaning "different" and, in a derived sense, "excellent." The name of the Son is "more excellent" than that of any angel. "Inherited" (*keklēronomēken*) is not quite the verb we expect, for there is no question of entering into possession as the result of the death of someone. On the contrary the word as used in the NT denotes entering into possession without regard to the means. So here we should think of Christ as obtaining the more excellent name as the result of his atoning work. The main idea is that of an abiding possession in Christ's capacity as heir (see comments on v.2).

Notes

2 Bruce sees ἐπ' ἐσχάτου τῶν ἡμερῶν (*ep eschatou tōn hēmerōn*, "from the last days") as a Septuagintalism that reflects a Hebrew expression meaning literally "in the latter end of the days" and that "according to the context may mean 'hereafter,' 'ultimately' or 'in the end-time.'" Here it "implies an inaugurated eschatology" (p. 3).

3 According to Westcott (in loc.), the Greek fathers unanimously take the sense of ἀπαύγασμα (*apaugasma*) as "effulgence" ("radiance"). This he sees as the preferable sense here, for the truth involved in "reflection" is conveyed also in χαρακτήρ (*charaktēr*), whereas "effulgence" adds another thought.

4 The perfect κεκληρονόμηκεν (*keklēronomēken*, "inherited") puts some stress on the continuing possession of the more excellent name. The writer is referring to a present fact, not simply to past history.

II. The Excellence of the Christ 1:5—3:6

In the introduction the author has drawn attention to the excellence of the Christ; now he dwells on the point. He brings out the fact that Christ is possessed of a greater dignity than any other being, so great indeed that he must be classed with God rather than with men. This does not mean any weakening of the doctrine of the Incarnation. On the contrary, in this epistle as high a Christology as is conceivable is combined with an emphasis on the real humanity of Jesus. Nobody insists on the limitations of Jesus' human frame as does the writer of Hebrews. But he unites with this the thought that Jesus is exalted far above all creation.

A. *Superior to Angels*

1:5–14

⁵For to which of the angels did God ever say,

"You are my Son;
today I have become your Father"?

Or again,

"I will be his Father,
and he will be my Son"?

⁶And again, when God brings his firstborn into the world, he says,

"Let all God's angels worship him."

⁷In speaking of the angels he says,

"He makes his angels winds,
his servants flames of fire."

⁸But about the Son he says,

"Your throne, O God, will last for ever and ever,
and righteousness will be the scepter of your kingdom.
⁹You have loved righteousness and hated wickedness;
therefore God, your God, has set you above
your companions
by anointing you with the oil of joy."

¹⁰He also says,

"In the beginning, O Lord, you laid the foundations
of the earth,
and the heavens are the work of your hands.
¹¹They will perish, but you remain;
they will all wear out like a garment.
¹²You will roll them up like a robe;
like a garment they will be changed.
But you remain the same,
and your years will never end."

¹³To which of the angels did God ever say,

"Sit at my right hand
until I make your enemies
a footstool for your feet"?

¹⁴Are not all angels ministering spirits sent to serve those who will inherit salvation?

17

The discussion of the excellence of the Son begins with a series of seven quotations from the OT, five being from the Psalms. They all stress the superiority of Christ to the angels.

5 The opening question, "For to which of the angels did God ever say . . . ," implies that Christ is to be seen in all the Scriptures because there is no explicit reference to him in the passage cited. In the OT angels are sometimes called "sons of God" (cf. mg., Job 1:6; 2:1); and the term was applied to Israel (Exod 4:22; Hos 11:1) and Solomon (2 Sam 7:14; 1 Chron 28:6). But none of the angels nor anyone else was ever singled out and given the kind of status this passage gives to Christ. The first quotation comes from Psalm 2:7. Among the rabbis, the "Son" is variously identified as Aaron, David, the people of Israel in the messianic period, or the Messiah himself (SBK, pp. 673–77). But clearly our writer is taking the psalm as messianic and sees it as conferring great dignity on Jesus. We should not concern ourselves overmuch with trying to identify the day meant in "today." Since the writer seems to be quoting the text to bring out the greatness of the Son, he could scarcely pass over the word rendered "today." But his interest was not here, and he makes no special reference to the day.

The second quotation comes from 2 Samuel 7:14 (= 1 Chron 17:13). Though the words were originally used of Solomon, the writer of Hebrews is applying them to the Messiah, a usage which does not seem to occur among the rabbis (SBK, p. 677). There was, however, a widespread expectation that the Messiah would be a descendant of David (de Jonge, TDNT, 9:511ff.). The quotation points to the father-son relationship as the fundamental relationship between God and Christ. No angel can claim such a relationship. This and 12:9 are the only passages in Hebrews in which the term "Father" is applied to God.

6 This verse is the only place in the NT where "firstborn" (*prōtotokos*) is used absolutely of Christ. Elsewhere it is used with reference to Jesus' birth (Luke 2:7) and it is linked with many brothers (Rom 8:29), all creation (Col 1:15), or the church (Col 1:18; Rev 1:5). It represents Christ in his relationship to others and gives the word a social significance. Here, however, it signifies that he has the status with God that a firstborn son on earth has with his father (cf. reference to "heir" in v.2). Some hold that the bringing of the firstborn into the world should be closely linked with "again" (*palin*). If this is done, there is a reference to the Second Coming. The arguments in support of this are not convincing, however, nor are those that see a reference to the Incarnation. It is probably better to think of Christ's "exaltation and enthronement as sovereign over the inhabited universe, the *oikoumenē*, including the realm of angels" (Bruce, in loc.), without emphasis on when this takes place.

The quotation is from Deuteronomy 32:43 in the LXX; it is absent from our Hebrew text, though attested in the Qumran material. The LXX reads "sons of God" where our quotation has "God's angels," but "angels" occurs later in the verse and again in a similar context in Psalm 97:7. Justin quotes it in the same form as here (*Dialogue* 130), which may indicate that the early Christians had it in their text. "All" shows that this is no small, hole-in-the-corner affair but one in which the worship of all heaven is offered the Son. The one the angels worship is clearly superior by far to them.

7 The Hebrew of Psalm 104:4 can mean either that God makes the winds his messengers and the flames his servants or that he makes his messengers (angels) into winds and his servants into flames. The LXX, which the author quotes, takes the latter view. This means no downgrading of the angels as the Targum quoted by Buchanan (in loc.) shows: "Who makes his messengers swift as the wind, his ministers mighty as flaming fire." But if the angels are immeasurably superior to men, the Son is immeasurably superior to the angels. Whereas he has sonship, they are reducible to nothing more than the elemental forces of wind and fire. Also, the implication is probably that the angels are temporary in contrast to the Son, who is eternal.

8–9 Some translations render the opening words of v.8 as "God is your throne" or the like (cf. RSV, NEB mg.). But it is better to take the Greek as a vocative as NIV: "Your throne, O God." The quotation from Psalm 45:6–7 is referred to the Son who is then addressed as "God." His royal state is brought out by the references to the "throne," "scepter," and "kingdom" and by his moral concern for the "righteousness" that is supreme where he reigns. This concern continues with loving righteousness and hating wickedness (better: lawlessness), which lead to the divine anointing. We should perhaps take the first occurrence of the word "God" as another vocative: "Therefore, O God, your God has set you." Anointing was usually a rite of consecration to some sacred function (e.g., Exod 28:41; 1 Sam 10:1; 1 Kings 19:16). This is in view here as the Son is set above his companions, who are probably the "brothers" of 2:11.

10–12 The author next quotes from Psalm 102:25–27 to bring out the Son's eternality and his supremacy over creation. In the OT these words are applied to God. Here, however, they apply to Christ without qualification or any need for justification. Christ was God's agent in creation, the one who laid the earth's foundations and constructed heaven. All these will in due course perish, but not their maker.

The metaphor of clothing has a twofold reference: the created things will wear out (the process is slow but certain); and the Son deals with them as with clothing, rolling them up and changing them. He began the universe and he will finish it. Clearly the final transformation of all things is in mind (cf. Isa 66:22; Rev 6:14; 21:1). This universe that seems so solid and permanent will be rolled up, changed, and replaced by a totally new heaven and earth. But through it all the Son remains unchanged. Our years come to an end, but his will never do so.

13 The quotation from Psalm 110:1 is introduced with a formula that stresses its inapplicability to angels (see comment on 1:4). This psalm is accepted by the NT writers as messianic. It is repeatedly applied to Christ; and apparently even Jesus' opponents accepted it as messianic (Mark 12:35–37), though, of course, they would not apply it to Jesus. Since the angels stand before God (Luke 1:19; Rev 8:2; cf. Dan 7:10), it is a mark of superior dignity that the Son sits. And the statement that God discharges the task of a servant in preparing a footstool for the Son is a striking piece of imagery. The angels are God's servants. How great then is he whom God deigns to serve! To make the enemies a footstool means to subject them utterly. Consequently, God will render all Christ's enemies utterly powerless.

14 We now consider the angels who are contrasted with the Son. He sits in royal state; they, however, are no more than servants. "All" applies without distinction. Not only are they servants, but they are servants of saved men. "Spirits" preserves their place of dignity, but their function is service (*eis diakonian*, "to serve"). *Diakonia* is the usual NT term for the service Christians render God and man, but nowhere else is it used of the service angels render. "Inherit" is often used in the NT in senses other than the strict one of obtaining something by a will. It can mean "obtain possession of" without regard to the means. It is used of possessing the earth (Matt 5:5), the kingdom of God (1 Cor 6:9–10), eternal life (Mark 10:17), the promises (Heb 6:12), incorruption (1 Cor 15:50), blessing (Heb 12:17), a more excellent name (v.4, where see comments).

"Salvation" is a general word, but among first-century Christians it was used of salvation in Christ, either in its present or, as here, future aspect. The word "salvation" (*sōtēria*) is used in Hebrews seven times, the most of any NT book; so the concept clearly matters to the author. His use of it here without explanation or qualification shows that it was already accepted by the readers as well as the author as a technical term for the salvation Christ brought. And the angels are the servants of those saved in this way.

Notes

6 Δέ (*de*, "and," NIV) has here no strong adversative force, for this quotation reinforces the preceding rather than contrasts with it. The point of the δέ is possibly the fact that now the relation of the angels to the Son is dealt with, whereas in the previous quotations it was that of the Son to the Father, a different relation.

8 Δέ (*de*, "but," NIV) certainly has adversative force here: the Son is set in strong contrast with the angels (cf. the μέν [*men*, an untranslatable emphatic particle] in v.7).

12 The words ὡς ἱμάτιον (*hōs himation*, "like a garment") are not found in the LXX but are well attested here and are certainly part of the true text.

14 The adjective λειτουργικά (*leitourgika*, "ministering") is especially appropriate to the service of God and may be used, for example, of ritual (cf. our word "liturgical"). These "ministering spirits" are "spirits in holy service" (BAG, p. 472).

B. *Author of "Such a Great Salvation"*

2:1–9

¹We must pay more careful attention, therefore, to what we have heard, so that we do not drift away. ²For if the message spoken by angels was binding, and every violation and disobedience received its just punishment, ³how shall we escape if we ignore such a great salvation? This salvation, which was first announced by the Lord, was confirmed to us by those who heard him. ⁴God also testified to it by signs, wonders and various miracles, and gifts of the Holy Spirit distributed according to his will.

⁵It is not to angels that he has subjected the world to come, about which we are speaking. ⁶But there is a place where someone has testified:

"What is man that you are mindful of him,
    the son of man that you care for him?
⁷You made him a little lower than the angels;
    you crowned him with glory and honor
⁸ and put everything under his feet."

In putting everything under him, God left nothing that is not subject to him. Yet at present we do not see everything subject to him. [9]But we see Jesus, who was made a little lower than the angels, now crowned with glory and honor because he suffered death, so that by the grace of God he might taste death for everyone.

The second step in the argument for Jesus' superiority shows him to be infinitely great because of the nature of the salvation he won. He who brought about a salvation that involved tasting death "for everyone" (v.9) cannot but be greater by far than any angel. The author precedes the development of this thought with a brief section in which he exhorts his readers to attend to what has been said, a feature we shall notice elsewhere (e.g., 3:7-11; 5:11-14).

1 "Therefore" might refer to what immediately precedes. Because angels are sent to minister to the saved, certain consequences follow. It is more likely that the term refers to the argument as a whole. Since the Son is so far superior to the angels, we should give heed to what he says. His message is superior to theirs. So we must "pay more careful attention" to it. The verb *prosechein* means not only to turn the mind to a thing but also to act upon what one perceives (see its use in Acts 8:6; 16:14). Inaction in spiritual things is fatal. The author does not explain what he means by "what we have heard," but we need not doubt that the whole Christian gospel is in mind. (Notice that his "we" puts him in the same class as his readers, i.e., dependent on others for the message. He was not one of the original disciples. Of course, a writer will sometimes class himself with his readers without actually meaning that he is in quite the same position. But it is difficult to think of Paul or one of those who followed Jesus in the days of his flesh writing exactly these words.) The danger is that we might "drift away" (*pararyōmen*). While this verb may mean "lest we let them slip," the more likely meaning is as in NIV. It is used of such things as a ring slipping off a finger, a vivid figure for the man who lets himself drift away from the haven of the gospel. One need not be violently opposed to the message to suffer loss; one need only drift away from it.

2 "Message" translates *logos*, more commonly rendered "word." It means in the first place a word spoken (as opposed to a deed) and then a series of words, a statement. What the statement is varies with the context. It can mean a message from God, a revelation, and so the Christian gospel (Acts 4:4; 8:4). The final revelation is, of course, Christ. He himself is "the Word" (John 1:1). In Hebrews the "word" is usually God's word (e.g., 2:2; 4:2, 12), though it can also be the writer's own word (5:11, "to say," NIV) or the word the Israelites did not wish to hear (12:19). Or it may be used in the sense of giving account (13:17). Here in v.2 it is the divinely given law. "By angels" is literally "through (*di'*) angels," which stresses the important truth that the law came from God. The OT does not speak of angels in connection with the giving of the law; but their presence is mentioned in other NT passages (Acts 7:53; Gal 3:19), in the LXX of Deuteronomy 33:2, and in Josephus (Antiq. XV, 136). The rabbis also thought of angels as there on that great occasion (SBK, 3:554–56). Thus the author is appealing to this well-attested view for his "how shall we?" argument (v.3). If the law came through angels, how much more should respect be given the message that came, not through angels, but through the Son? The law was "binding," i.e., fully valid. And it had provision for the proper punishment of wrongdoers so that every transgression was dealt with in the proper way.

3 The just penalties meted out under the law show that where God is concerned strict standards apply. This makes it imperative that those to whom a great salvation is offered do something about the offer. The emphatic pronoun "we" (*hēmeis*) is found only five times in Hebrews. Therefore its occurrence here is significant. It probably means "we, in contrast to those who had only the law," though it may be taken to mean "we, with our privileged position." Notice that the disaster that threatens is brought on by nothing more than neglect. It is not necessary to disobey any specific injunction. For had we done nothing when we were offered salvation, we would not have received it. This is the first of a number of warnings to the readers not to surrender their Christian profession. Clearly the writer is determined to guard against that possibility. He distinguishes the salvation he writes about from the many other kinds of salvation offered in the ancient world by calling it "such a great salvation" and then by telling us three things about it. In the first place, it was "announced by the Lord." Once more "by" is literally "through" (*dia*), with the implication that the salvation originates with the Father. The verb rendered "announced" is *laleisthai*, which is unusual in such a connection. But the meaning is plain enough. This is one of the places where this epistle has a point of contact with the Gospel of Luke, for there only does Jesus announce salvation (Luke 19:9, though cf. John 4:22). Luke also calls Jesus "Savior" (Luke 2:11) and tells us that he brings salvation (Luke 1:69, 71, 77). We have already seen that the writer has much to say about salvation (see comments on 1:14). Anything Jesus said is of interest and importance to his followers, but his proclamation of salvation must be regarded as especially important.

The second point about this salvation is that it "was confirmed to us by those who heard him." The author is appealing to the first hearers as those to whom the authentic gospel was entrusted (cf. Luke 1:2). Any later preaching must agree with theirs. If it does not, then it will stand convicted of being an innovation instead of the genuine article. Once more we see an indication that the author of Hebrews was not one of the original disciples. For him as for his readers the message was "confirmed" by the original disciples. The verb "confirm" (*bebaioō*) is used as a legal technical term "to designate properly guaranteed security" and in this context means "the saving message was guaranteed to us" (BAG, p. 138). Its frequent use in a legal sense gives it great force here; i.e., there cannot be the slightest doubt about the salvation offered. It came through Christ and that this is the salvation Christ offered is guaranteed by its apostolic attestation.

4 The third and clinching point is that God himself has also "testified" to our great salvation. The compound "with" (*syn*) shows that the preachers were not left to bear their witness alone. No less a one than God has shared in this. In John's Gospel we have the bold thought that God has borne witness to Christ (John 5:37). Since anyone who bears witness commits himself by that very act, God has gone on record, so to speak, that he too is a witness to the great salvation of his Son.

Here, however, we have an even bolder thought: God has been pleased to commit himself through the original disciples. He gave the signs that attested their preaching. The gospel is not a human creation, and the early hearers were not left in doubt as to its origin. They actually saw the way God attested it. So the author stresses the miraculous accompaniments of the preaching. "Signs" (*sēmeia*), a word used often in John to designate miracles, puts emphasis on the meaning of the miracles. They were not pointless displays of power but, in the literal sense of the word, they were *sig*nificant. They pointed beyond themselves. The miracles were full of spiritual meaning and led those who heeded them to see that they were signs from God and conveyed his message. "Wonders" emphasizes the marvelous aspect of the signs. They were such that no man could produce them and they were not explicable on merely human premises. It is this wonder-producing aspect that comes spontaneously to mind when we think of miracles. Yet to NT people this was far from being the most important aspect, for they never use this term by itself when they speak of Christ's miracles. They always link it with some other word or words, usually with "sign" and commonly in the expression "signs and wonders." "Miracles" is properly "mighty works" and is the term usually employed in the synoptic Gospels. It brings out the truth that in Christ's miracles there is superhuman power. The mighty works prove something about the gospel because they are not of human origin and thus show that the gospel they attest is not human either. "Various" (*poikilais*) means "many-colored" and is a vivid word. There was no flat uniformity about the accompaniments of the preaching of the gospel but a many-hued attestation.

There is a problem about the "gifts of the Holy Spirit" in that it is not clear whether we should take this in the sense of "gifts the Holy Spirit gives" (as in 1 Cor 12:11) or "gifts of the Holy Spirit himself" (as in Gal 3:5). Either way, there were manifestations of the Holy Spirit in believers, and the author sees these as confirming the gospel. But on the whole it seems more likely that he is speaking about God as giving men the gift (and the gifts) of the Holy Spirit. God does this as he wills, the reference to "his will" reminding us of the divine overruling. It is God who is supreme, not man nor angel. When God gives his attestation, it must accordingly be taken with full seriousness.

5 Having looked at "such a great salvation" that Christ won for his own, the author goes on to the further point that the subjection of the world to man spoken of in Psalm 8 is to be seen in Christ, not in mankind at large. "Not to angels" implies that the subjection was made to someone other than the angels, not that it has not been made at all. The world in question was subjected, but not to angels. "The world" (*tēn oikoumenēn*) is a term that normally denotes the inhabited earth. The Greeks often used it of countries occupied by men of their own race as opposed to barbarians. Later it came to be used for the Roman Empire. It is unusual to have it employed of the Messianic Age (BAG, p. 564, notes this usage only here), "age" (*aiōn*) being much more common in this sense (e.g., Matt 12:32).

6 A quotation from Psalm 8:4–6 is introduced by the unusual verb *diamartyromai* ("testify"). Only here in the NT does it introduce a quotation from Scripture. More often it is used in a sense like "adjure" or "testify solemnly." It shows that the words following it are to be taken with full seriousness. The author tells us neither the place where the words are found nor who said them. Consistently he regards all that is in his Bible as coming from God and puts no emphasis on the human author. It is impossible to hold that his general manner of citation here shows that he did not know where the words come from; for he quotes the passage exactly and his whole epistle shows that he was very familiar with the Psalms. His quotation is exact (except that he has omitted one line: "You made him ruler over the works of your hands" [Ps 8:6]).

The psalmist is concerned with both the insignificance and the greatness of man. There is, of course, no difference in meaning between "man" and "son of man" in this verse. The parallelism of Hebrew poetry requires that the two be taken in much the same sense; and in any case it is quite common in Hebrew idiom for "the son of" to denote quality, as, for example, "the son of strength" means "the strong man." So "son of man" means one who has the quality of being man. (We should not be led astray by recollecting that in the Gospels Jesus often calls himself "Son of man"; that usage is quite different.) God is said to be "mindful of" (*mimnēskē*) and to "care for" (*episkeptē*) man. The former thought has the sense of remembering with a view to helping. O. Michel warns against misinterpreting the word as used in the Bible "along historicising or intellectualistic lines. It includes total dedication to God, concern for the brethren, and true self-judgment (Hb. 13:3). It carries with it the thinking in terms of salvation history and the community which the whole of Scripture demands" (TDNT, 4:678). As used with God as subject much of this must be modified, but the word *mimnēskē* is clearly one with far-reaching implications.

Episkeptē may mean "visit in order to punish for wrongdoing," or, as here, "visit in order to 'care for.'" The psalmist asks what there is about man that the great God should stoop to help him. The rabbis endorsed the sentiment, and there is a saying attributed to R. Joshua b. Levi that when Moses came to receive the law the angels objected: "That secret treasure," they said, "which has been hidden by Thee for nine hundred and seventy-four generations before the world was created, Thou desirest to give to flesh and blood! *What is man, that thou art mindful of him?*" (*Shabbath* 88b).

7 Having asked the rhetorical questions that pinpoint man's insignificance, the psalmist goes on to his greatness. God has given man an outstanding position, one but a little lower than that of the angels. In the psalm the meaning may be as in RSV: "Yet thou hast made him little less than God," where the final word translates *'elōhîm*. Some prefer to understand this as "gods," but LXX renders it "angels" (as does the Targum, according to Buchanan). As he usually does, the author follows the LXX. Man's dignity, then, is such that he is placed in God's order of creation only a short way below the angels, and this seems to set him above all else in creation, an impression that the rest of the passage confirms. God "crowned him with glory and honor." "Glory" denotes brightness or splendor and is used of the splendor of God as well as of the glory of earthly potentates. "Honor" is frequently linked with "glory" and the combination stresses the supreme place of man in creation.

8 The dignity of man is further brought out by the fact that God has "put everything under his feet." Man is supreme among the beings of this created world. "Under his feet" shows that he has complete supremacy. Having completed the quotation, the writer goes on to draw out an important implication. In that God put all things in subjection to man, he left nothing unsubjected. It is a picture of a divinely instituted order in which man is sovereign over all creation. A few commentators see "him" as referring in this place to Christ, to whom alone all things are rightly subjected. But grammatically there is no reason for this. The passage is describing the place of mankind in God's order, and we do not come to Christ's place until v. 9. While there is a sense in which it is only Christ everything is subject to, there is another sense in which man has his rightful place of supremacy over the other created things. It is this latter sense that is in view here.

From this ideal picture the writer turns his attention to current reality. As things are now, we do not see the subjection of all things to man. The writer's use of *oupō* ("not yet") shows his optimistic outlook. One day this subjection will be fully realized. But for the present there is a difference between what the psalm promises and what we see around us. While man has his powers and dignity, there are many limitations. The full promise of the psalm awaits realization. It is part of the frustration of life that in every part of it there are the equivalents of the "thorns and thistles" (Gen 3:18) that make life so hard for the tiller of the soil. Everyone knows what it is to chafe under the limitations under which he must do his work while he glimpses the vision of what would be possible were it not for those cramping limitations.

9 But if we do not see the fulfillment of this passage from Scripture in the way we might have expected, we do see a fulfillment in another way. We see it fulfilled in Jesus. He has gone through the experience of living out this earthly life, and he is now "crowned . . . with glory and honor" (the very words of the psalm) because of his saving work for man. The writer calls the Savior by his human name, Jesus, a usage we find nine times in this epistle (here, 3:1; 4:14; 6:20; 7:22; 10:19; 12:2, 24; 13:12); and on each occasion he seems to place emphasis on the humanity of our Lord. He was Jesus, the man. In this book the writer uses "Jesus Christ" three times and "our Lord Jesus" once, as well as "Christ" nine times (see comments on 3:6). Clearly, in this epistle there is a high proportion of passages with the name "Jesus." That Jesus was true man meant a good deal to the writer of Hebrews. Here he is saying that we do not see the psalm fulfilled in mankind at large but we do see it fulfilled in the man Jesus. He had a genuine incarnation because he "was made a little lower than the angels." But we do not now see him in this lowly place. Now we see him crowned with glory and honor. He is in the place of supremacy that the psalmist envisaged. And he is there because of his saving work, "because he suffered death."

"So that" looks back to the reference to suffering rather than to "crowned" (which immediately precedes it in the Gr.); and the clause it introduces gathers up "the full object and purpose of the experience that has just been predicated of Jesus" (Moffatt, in loc.). This is one of several places in the NT where someone is said to taste death (Matt 16:28; Mark 9:1; Luke 9:27; John 8:52). The verb means to taste with the mouth, from which the metaphorical sense "come to know" develops. It means here that Jesus died, with all that that entails. There is a problem as to whether we should read "by the grace [chariti] of God" or "apart from [chōris] God." The latter is read by a few MSS only, but it has strong patristic support. The author has a variety of ways of viewing the atoning work of Christ; and it would not be surprising if at this point he made a passing reference to our Lord's death as one in which the Sin-Bearer was forsaken by God (cf. Matt 27:46; Mark 15:34). Others see "apart from God" to mean that his divine nature was not involved in his death or that he died for all, God excepted. But it seems better to accept the reading of most of the MSS. It was by God's grace that Christ's saving work was accomplished. Grace is one of the great Christian words, and it is not surprising to find it connected with the Atonement here.

Notes

1 Μήποτε παραρυῶμεν (mēpote pararyōmen, "lest we should drift") is literary rather than vernacular. Μή (mē, "not") is used in the negative of apprehension followed by the subjunctive when the meaning is to ward off something that depends on the will (the indicative would be used if the thing had happened or if it was independent of the will; see BDF, par. 370).
4 Θέλησις (thelēsis, "will") is found only here in the NT, whereas θέλημα (thelēma, "will,"

"desire") occurs sixty-two times. It is spoken of as a "vulgar word" and it means "the act of willing," whereas θέλημα (*thelēma*) is "what is willed" (BAG, p. 355).

9 Διὰ τὸ πάθημα τοῦ θανάτου (*dia to pathēma tou thanatou*) is more literally "on account of the suffering of death"; and some take it with "made a little lower than the angels," i.e., "Jesus was made man in order to suffer death." It is doubtful whether the Gr. will stand this meaning (διὰ, *dia*, means "on account of" something that is, not "with a view to" something being realized). And in any case this interpretation ignores both the thrust of the present passage and the consistent view throughout Heb that the glory follows the passion.

C. *True Man*

2:10–18

10In bringing many sons to glory, it was fitting that God, for whom and through whom everything exists, should make the author of their salvation perfect through suffering. 11Both the one who makes men holy and those who are made holy are of the same family. So Jesus is not ashamed to call them brothers. 12He says,

> "I will declare your name to my brothers;
> in the presence of the congregation I will sing
> your praises."

13And again,

> "I will put my trust in him."

And again he says,

> "Here am I, and the children God has given me."

14Since the children have flesh and blood, he too shared in their humanity so that by his death he might destroy him who holds the power of death—that is, the devil—15and free those who all their lives were held in slavery by their fear of death. 16For surely it is not angels he helps, but Abraham's descendants. 17For this reason he had to be made like his brothers in every way, in order that he might become a merciful and faithful high priest in service to God, and that he might make atonement for the sins of the people. 18Because he himself suffered when he was tempted, he is able to help those who are being tempted.

It has been argued that Jesus was greater than the angels and that his greatness is to be seen in the salvation he obtained for us. But he had lived on earth as an ordinary man. There was nothing about the Teacher from Nazareth to show that he was greater than the angels. Indeed, the reverse was true, for he had undergone humiliating sufferings culminating in a felon's death. The author proceeds to show, however, that, far from this being an objection to his greatness, this was part of it. This was the way he would save men. He would be made like those he saves.

10 Usually we do not speak of things as being "fitting" for God, but here the word is appropriate. The way of salvation is not arbitrary but befitting the character of the God we know, the God "for whom and through whom everything exists" (i.e., he is the goal and the author of all that is). The words show that the sufferings of Jesus did not take place by chance. They have their place in God's great eternal purpose. "Many sons" is an unusual expression for the total number of the saved. But sonship is important and so is the fact that the number of the saved will not be few. "Glory" points to what Montefiore calls "the splendour of ultimate salvation" (in loc.). It is no mean state into which we are saved but one actually to be thought of in terms of splendor.

Christ is "the author of their salvation." The word *archēgos*, "author," may be used in more senses than one (just as there are differing meanings for *archē*, "beginning," "first," etc.). It can denote a leader, a ruler, or one who begins something as the first in a series; RSV renders the word "pioneer." Or it might mean the originator or founder. Bowman thinks that "the picture is of one who, as a member of the fellowship, moves ahead, leading the way to ever higher ground of experience" (in loc.). The word contains the thoughts of supremacy, personal participation, and originating something. Any one of these may be prominent. Here it is surely the thought of origination that is stressed, but the choice of word enables the author to see Jesus as one who trod this earthly way before us as he established the way of salvation.

The idea of being made perfect is at first sight a startling one to apply to Jesus, but it is one the author repeats. He is fond of the word *teleioō* ("make perfect") and uses it nine times altogether (five times in John is the next most frequent use of it in the NT). BAG (pp. 817–18) sees the present passage as usually understood in the sense of "the *completion* and *perfection* of Jesus by the overcoming of earthly limitations" and notes the use of the verb in the mystery religions in senses like "consecrate" and in the passive "be consecrated," "become a *teleios*." Neither, however, seems probable. There is nothing to indicate an allusion to the mystery religions. A reference to transcending earthly limitations is more possible. Yet it may be fairly objected that suffering is the means of perfecting, not resurrection, ascension, or the like. What the author is saying is that there is a perfection that results from actually having suffered and that this is different from the perfection of being ready to suffer. The bud may be perfect, but there is a difference between its perfection and that of the flower. There is, of course, no thought of perfecting what was morally imperfect. No imperfection is implied (cf. 4:15).

11 Here the writer has emphasized the link between Jesus and those he saves. He "who makes men holy" is, of course, Jesus. He makes them into God's people by his offering of himself (10:10). The passive, "those who are made holy," coming, as it does, from the same verb, puts some emphasis on the unity of Christ and his own. But the writer does not say they are one; he says they are "of one" (NIV, "of the same family," though the Gr. has nothing corresponding to "family"). If the reference to spiritual unity is pressed, then this "one" will be God. All are "from" him. It is, however, more in keeping with the thrust of the passage to see a reference to earthly descent. In that case the "one" is Adam (as in Acts 17:26). The thought, then, is that Jesus is qualified to be our Priest and Savior because he shares our nature, because he is not some remote being but truly "one of us." Since the entire universe and angels as well as men have their origin in God, it is merely a truism to say that it is he from whom we all come. That gives no reason for Christ's being qualified to save. But that he shares with us a descent from Adam does. This enables him to call us "brothers."

Those who follow Christ are often called "brothers"; rarely, however, are they called his brothers in the NT. Indeed, sometimes the two are differentiated, as when Jesus says, "You have only one Master and you are all brothers" (Matt 23:8). Mostly Jesus' "brothers" refers to those in his immediate family (e.g., Matt 12:46–48; Luke 8:19–20; John 2:12). Sometimes, however, the word is used in a spiritual sense while linking people to Christ (Matt 12:49–50; Mark 3:33–35; Luke 8:21; Rom 8:29). So this passage in Hebrews, while somewhat unusual, is not unparalleled. There is a sense in which Jesus is brother to all who call God "Father." That is why it is important to identify the "them" in "Jesus is not ashamed to call them brothers." It is not people as such he calls brothers but only those who are sanctified.

12 The writer clarifies the point of spiritual brotherhood with an appeal to Scripture. Psalm 22 was regarded as messianic in the early church. As he hung on the cross, Jesus quoted its opening words: "My God, my God, why have you forsaken me?" (Mark 15:34). And the words about dividing garments (Ps 22:18) are seen as fulfilled in what the soldiers did as they crucified Jesus (John 19:24). It was thus the most natural thing in the world for the writer of Hebrews to see Jesus as the speaker in this psalm. He will declare his name to his brothers. In antiquity "name" generally signified more than an identifying label. It stood for the whole character, the whole person. So in this psalm the writer sees Jesus as saying that he will proclaim God's character as he has revealed himself, not simply that he will declare the name of God. The important thing in this quotation is that Jesus will do this "to [his] brothers." Jesus recognizes them as kin. The parallel statement in the next line reinforces the idea.

The word "congregation" (*ekklēsia*) can mean a properly summoned political group (Acts 19:39) or an assembly of almost any kind, including the rioting Ephesians (Acts 19:32, 41). But it is also used of the congregation of ancient Israel (Acts 7:38). In the NT *ekklēsia* ("assembly") became the characteristic word for the gatherings of Christians. Now he who sings God's praises in the midst of God's people is by that very fact showing that he is one of them, their spokesman. The "brothers" are the church.

13 Two further citations from Scripture underline the point. The second of these is from Isaiah 8:18, and this makes it almost certain that the first is from Isaiah 8:17, not Isaiah 12:2 or 2 Samuel 22:3 (all three are identical in LXX). The reason the author cites this first passage is not obvious. The context in Isaiah, however, speaks of difficulties, and the thought may be that just as Isaiah had to trust God to see him through, so was it with Jesus. In this he was brother to all God's troubled saints. The second quotation continues the first, but it is introduced here with "and again he says" because it makes a new point. The author now sees believers as "the children God has given" Christ. The word *paidion*, normally used of literal children, is not infrequent in the NT. This is, however, the one place where it is used of "children" of Christ (though in John 21:5 the risen Christ greets the disciples as "children," *paidia* [NIV, "friends"]). These children are "given" by God as the disciples were given to Jesus (John 17:6).

All three quotations from the OT, then, place the speaker in the same group as God's children. The actual word "brothers" occurs only in the first, but they all locate Christ firmly among people. He had a real community of nature with those he came to save.

14–15 The author now develops the thought of community of nature. Jesus shared "blood and flesh" with the children. (This order is found only in Eph 6:12; NIV for some reason reverses the order of the Gr.) He really came where they are. The word "humanity" is not in the Greek; it is "blood and flesh" that Christ shared with "the children." He did this for the purpose of nullifying the power of the devil, who is described as the one "who holds the power of death." This raises a problem because it is God alone who controls the issues of life and death (Job 2:6; Luke 12:5). But it was through Adam's sin, brought about by the temptation of the devil, that death entered the world (Gen 2:17; 3:19; Rom 5:12). From this it is logical to assume that the devil exercises his power in the realm of death. But the death of Christ is the means of destroying the power of the devil.

The author does not explain how Christ's death does this but contents himself with the fact that it does. In doing so he stresses the note of victory that we find throughout the NT (e.g., 1 Cor 15:54–57). The defeat of the devil means the setting free of those he had held sway over, those who had been gripped by fear of death. Fear is an inhibiting and enslaving thing; and when people are gripped by the ultimate fear—the fear of death—they are in cruel bondage. In the first century this was very real. The philosophers urged people to be calm in the face of death, and some of them managed to do so. But to most people this brought no relief. Fear was widespread, as the hopeless tone of the inscriptions on tombs clearly illustrates. But one of the many wonderful things about the Christian gospel is that it delivers men and women from this fear (cf. Rev 1:18). They are saved with a sure hope of life eternal, a life whose best lies beyond the grave.

16 "Surely" translates *dēpou*, a word used only here in the NT. It makes a strong affirmation and appeals to information shared by the reader. There is a problem about the verb rendered "helps" (*epilambanetai*). It means "to take hold of," "take by the hand," from which sense "helps" is derived. But the statement may also be understood in the following sense: "For it was not the angels that he took to himself" (JB); i.e., he became man. The fact that the Incarnation is in view in v.17 supports the rendering "helps." Furthermore, the verb is thought to mean "take hold with a purpose," i.e., to help. The author has in mind that Jesus came to rescue people. This is not in dispute; yet it is another question whether this is all contained in the verb. On the whole it seems better to see the statement as pointing to the fact of the Incarnation rather than to its purpose. "Abraham's descendants" particularizes the manner of the Incarnation and makes it harder to see the meaning of the verb as "helps," for Jesus helps many more than Jews. But he became incarnate as a Jew. He did not descend to the level of the angels and become one of them. He descended to the level of mankind and became a Jew.

17 The purpose of salvation involved a genuine incarnation. "He had to" means "he owed it" (the verb can be used of financial debts), "he ought." There is the sense of moral obligation. The nature of the work Jesus came to accomplish demanded the Incarnation. In view of this work, he ought to become like the "brothers." "In order that" renders the conjunction *hina*, which expresses purpose. The Incarnation was not aimless; it was for the specific purpose of Jesus' becoming a high priest, another way of saying that it was to save men. "Merciful" receives emphasis from its position (the Gr. word order is "that a merciful he might become and faithful high priest").

There is an interesting contrast in Philo, who thinks of the Jewish high priest as one who will not show his feelings: "He will have his feeling of pity under control" (*De Specialibus Legibus* 1.115). Not so our great High Priest. He is one who is first and foremost merciful. He is also "faithful." This adjective can refer to the faith that relies on someone or something or that on which one can rely, i.e., "relying" or "reliable." Jesus is, of course, both. But here the emphasis is on his relationship to God the Father, and so the first meaning is more probable (cf. Rev. 1:5; 3:14; 19:11).

Only in Hebrews is the term "high priest" applied to Jesus in the NT. This is the first example of its use, and the author does not explain it. He may want us to see

Jesus as superior to all other priests. Or he may be using the term because he sees Jesus' saving work as fulfilling all that is signified by the ceremonies of the Day of Atonement, for which the high priest's ministry was indispensable. Sometimes in this epistle the author calls Jesus simply a "priest," but there seems to be no great difference in meaning.

"In service to God" (i.e., "with respect to the things of God" [*ta pros ton theon*]) shows where Christ's high priestly work is carried out. Some of the service of the high priest was directed toward the people, but this is not in view here. The service Christ was to render was "that he might make atonement for the sins of the people." The introductory conjunction denotes purpose: he became high priest with a view to this.

"Make atonement" is a curious rendering. The word *hilaskesthai* means "to propitiate," not "to make atonement," and relates to putting away the divine wrath (NIV mg.). When people sin, they arouse the wrath of God (Rom 1:18); they become enemies of God (Rom 5:10). One aspect of salvation deals with this wrath, and it is to this the author is directing attention at this point. Christ saves us in a way that takes account of the divine wrath against every evil thing. *Hilaskesthai* ("make atonement") is followed here by the accusative case of "sins" (*tas hamartias*), an unusual construction that means "to make propitiation with respect to the sins of the people." "The people" (*tou laou*) in some contexts indicates the people in contrast to their leaders or their priests. But it is frequently used for the people of God—those Christ died for—and this is the meaning here.

18 The sufferings Jesus endured enable him to help others. "He himself" (*autos*) is emphatic. Contrary to what might have been expected, *he* suffered. The verb *peponthen* ("suffered") naturally applies to the cross, but the context shows that a wider reference is in mind. Throughout his earthly life Jesus suffered. Being what he is, temptation must have been far more distasteful for him than it is for us. The verb *peirastheis* ("tempted") sometimes means "tested," and here it might conceivably apply to the sufferings simply as trials to be endured. But the verb is more often used in the sense of "tempt." The author is saying that Jesus can help the tempted because he has perfect sympathy with them. He too has been tempted and knows what temptation is. The words "he is able" are important and mean more than "he helps." Only he who suffers *can* help in this way. Jesus went all the way for us. He was not only ready to suffer, but he actually did suffer.

Notes

10 Δι' οὗ (*di' hou*) would normally be taken of the agent "through" whom a task was accomplished. But it can also denote the originator (1 Cor 1:9; cf. Rom 11:36). The participle ἀγαγόντα (*agagonta*, "bringing") must be taken in sense with αὐτῷ (*autō*, "to him"; NIV, "God"), even though the case is different. Here the aorist is timeless, drawing attention to the act as a simple fact, not as an event in the past.

15 The articular infinitive with an attributive in the same case, διὰ παντὸς τοῦ ζῆν (*dia pantos tou zēn*, "through all of life"; NIV, "all their lives"), is without parallel in the NT (BDF, par. 398). Τὸ ζῆν (*to zēn*) was evidently regarded as equivalent to a noun, "the life" (cf. 2 Cor 1:8).

D. *Superior to Moses*

3:1–6

> [1]Therefore, holy brothers, who share in the heavenly calling, fix your thoughts on Jesus, the apostle and high priest whom we confess. [2]He was faithful to the one who appointed him, just as Moses was faithful in all God's house. [3]Jesus has been found worthy of greater honor than Moses, just as the builder of a house has greater honor than the house itself. [4]For every house is built by someone, but God is the builder of everything. [5]Moses was faithful as a servant in all God's house, testifying to what would be said in the future. [6]But Christ is faithful as a son over God's house. And we are his house, if we hold on to our courage and the hope of which we boast.

The author steadily develops his argument that Jesus is supremely great. He is greater than the angels, the author of a great salvation, and great enough to become man to accomplish it. Now the author turns his attention to Moses, regarded by the Jews as the greatest of men. They could even think of him as greater than angels (SBK, 3:683). Perhaps then he was superior to Jesus? The writer does nothing to belittle Moses. Nor does he criticize him. He accepts Moses' greatness but shows that as great as he was, Jesus was greater by far.

1 The address "holy brothers" is found only here in the NT (though cf. Col. 1:2 and some MSS of 1 Thess 5:27). It combines the notes of affection and consecration. These people are members of the brotherhood and dear to the writer. They are also people who have been set apart for the service of God. The reference to "the heavenly calling" shows that the initiative comes from God. He has called them to be his own. "Therefore" links this section to the preceding. Because Christ has taken our nature and can help us, therefore we are invited to consider him in his capacities as apostle and high priest.

"Apostle" is applied to Jesus only here in the NT, but the idea that God "sent" him is more frequent, especially in the fourth Gospel. The basic idea is that of mission. Jesus was sent by the Father to accomplish his purpose. "High priest" brings before us the sacrificial nature of that mission. In the Greek the verse ends by naming him simply "Jesus." Though he is the most glorious of beings, this name draws attention to his humanity. It is as man that his work as apostle and high priest is accomplished.

2 The point could have been made that there were times when Moses was not as faithful as he might have been. But the writer makes no criticism of the man held in such honor by the Jews. He prefers to accept Moses as "faithful." Yet he sees Jesus' faithfulness as much more comprehensive. Moses was no more than part of the "house," but Jesus made the house. Again, Jesus as Son was over the house, whereas Moses was a servant in it. The "house," of course, is the household, the people, not the building; and it is God's house, the people of God. Moses was a member of that house and proved faithful there (the words are a quotation from Num 12:7). The adjective "all" may point to a concern both Moses and Jesus had for the whole house. Others, such as prophets, kings, or priests, dealt with restricted areas.

3 The first point of comparison pronounces Jesus as "worthy of greater honor than Moses" because he was builder of the house rather than part of it, as was Moses. Incidentally, *doxa,* which is the usual word for "glory," and *timē* are both translated "honor" in this verse by NIV. Though Moses was a glorious person, his glory did not measure up to that of Christ. But the word *doxa* ("glory") is close in meaning to *timē* ("honor"), and the two often occur together (e.g., 2:7, 9). He who makes a house is worthy of more honor than the house, glorious though the house may be. Moses was at all times a member of the people of God, that and no more. He had great honor within that people, but there was no way for him to be any other than one of them. Not so Jesus! He was more. The author has just made the point that Jesus became true man and could truly call men "brothers." But that does not alter his conviction that Christ is also more than man. He is the founder of the church, and the church was continuous with the OT people of God. The author will come back to this thought in v.6.

4 Parenthetically, this verse makes the point that God is over all. The author does not want us to lose sight of this fact. So he points out that the existence of a house is an argument for a builder. Houses do not build themselves. "But" (the adversative *de*) introduces something different. There is, of course, similarity. A house argues for a builder, and all that is argues for God. There is also a difference, because God is not to be put on a level with any builder of a house.

5 Having made his point that God transcends everyone, for he made everything, the writer returns to Moses. He repeats his statement that Moses was faithful in God's house (v.2; in both places and again in v.6 the Gr. reads "his house," but NIV has correctly interpreted it as "God's house"). Now he makes a further point: Whereas Moses was no more than a servant, Jesus was greater, for he was Son over the house. The thought is still that of Moses' faithfulness. There is no criticism of him, but his faithfulness consisted in his discharge of his role as servant.

The word for "servant" (*therapōn*) is found only here in the NT. It denotes an honored servant, one who is far above a slave but still a servant. It can be used for "henchman, attendant . . . companion in arms, squire" (LSJ, p. 793). Here the emphasis is on the subordinate, if honorable, capacity: It is the "squire" rather than the "companion in arms." The writer goes on to say that Moses' faithfulness did not relate to his own day only. He was "testifying to what would be said in the future." Some hold that this means what Moses himself would say and points perhaps to Deuteronomy. But it seems more likely that the thought is that there would be revelations to others. This epistle began with a reference to such revelations and to the importance of what God said (the verb *laleō* ["speak"] is the same as that used in 1:1). And there is a reference to our Lord's speaking about salvation in 2:3 (same verb again).

6 The name "Christ" is used here for the first time in this epistle, without the article (as in 9:11, 24). It has the article six times (3:14; 5:5; 6:1; 9:14, 28; 11:26) and the expression "Jesus Christ" occurs three times (10:10; 13:8, 21). Here, where a name of dignity is called for, it is a proper name. Christ is contrasted with Moses "as a son over God's house." Moses was no more than a member—even though a very distinguished member—of the house. He was essentially one with all the others. Christ has an innate superiority. He is the Son and as such is "over" the household.

The author adds a most important explanation as to the composition of this house. One might easily suppose that he was referring to the Jews or at least to the Jews of the OT. They were, of course, in mind. But he is not thinking of the Jews as a race nor of a group of historical figures. He is thinking of the people of God. In OT days this had been the people Israel. But Israel had rejected the Son of God when he came, and now the people of God is the church. Perseverance is one of the marks of being a Christian. Without it we are not Christ's. As F.F. Bruce puts it, "The doctrine of the final perseverance of the saints has as its corollary the salutary teaching that the saints are the people who persevere to the end" (in loc.).

We are to hold on to "our courage." The word *parrēsia* has about it the feeling of being quite at home when words flow freely and so means "confidence" or "courage." "The hope of which we boast" may perhaps be not quite it. The word for "boast" is *kauchēma*, which means something one can boast about, rather than *kauchēsis*, the act of boasting. Our position as God's "house" is something of which we may be proud. We have a good gift from God. Instead of being ashamed of this gift, we should glory in it. "Boast" is connected with "hope." "Hope" is used in the NT in much the same way as we use it, now in ordinary speech. But more characteristically it is the Christian hope, the certainty that God will carry out his promises, especially those in the gospel. The Christian looks forward eagerly, expecting God's triumph. To be God's house, then, means to persevere in quiet confidence, knowing that one has matter for pride in the Christian hope.

Notes

2 Ποιήσαντι (*poiēsanti*) is correctly translated "appointed." It cannot mean "created" since the Son is not a created being (1:3). There might be a reference to the Incarnation, but it seems more probable that it is the Son's appointment as apostle and high priest that is meant. The same verb is used of the appointment of Moses and Aaron (1 Sam 12:6 LXX), the apostles (Mark 3:14), and Christ himself (Acts 2:36).

III. The Promised Rest

The comparison between Christ and Moses leads to one between their followers. The writer uses the conduct of the Israelites as a means of challenging his readers to a closer walk with God. There was a promise in the OT that God's people would enter into rest. The writer sees this promise as fulfilled—not in anything in the OT—but in Christ. In drawing attention to this, he shows from another angle that Christ is God's final word to mankind (cf. 1:2).

A. Scriptural Basis

3:7–11

⁷So, as the Holy Spirit says:

"Today, if you hear his voice,
⁸ do not harden your hearts
as you did in the rebellion,
   during the time of testing in the desert,
⁹where your fathers tested and tried me
   and for forty years saw what I did.

> ¹⁰That is why I was angry with that generation,
>   and I said, 'Their hearts are always going astray,
>   and they have not known my ways.'
> ¹¹So I declared on oath in my anger,
>   'They shall never enter my rest.' "

The writer begins this section with a quotation from Psalm 95:7–11. Israel did not walk in fellowship with God but disobeyed and provoked him. Therefore they did not enter his rest. Judaism is not the way of entry into that rest.

7 Some see the quotation as a long parenthesis, "so" being followed by v. 12: "So . . . see to it. . . ." But it seems better to take "so" with the quotation "So . . . do not harden your hearts." Do not repeat the mistake the Israelites made. The quotation is ascribed directly to the Holy Spirit (cf. 9:8; 10:15; Acts 28:25; the human author is mentioned in 4:7). The author is fond of the word "today," using it eight times (Luke and Acts are the only NT books that use it more). Here its prominent position gives it emphasis. Immediate action is imperative. The voice of God is sounding now. It must not be neglected.

8 To "harden" the heart is to disobey the voice of God and act in accordance with one's own desires. This is what Israel did in the wilderness. Here the reference is to the incident when there was no water and the Israelites "put the Lord to the test" (Exod. 17:1–7). In the LXX the place names Massah and Meribah are always translated by words such as those here rendered "rebellion" and "testing." Through lack of faith and failure to appreciate God's purposes of grace, the people of Israel put him to the test.

9 The thought of "testing" God continues. NIV may be correct in rendering "tested and tried me," but there is no "me" in the Greek. This opens up the alternative possibility that "my works" (NIV, "what I did") is the object of both the preceding verbs: "Your fathers tested and saw my works for forty years." They ought to have proceeded in faith. Since God had done so much for them, they should have trusted him when they could not see. Instead, they tested his works where they could see ("saw" puts stress on visibility). This faithlessness was no passing phase but something that went on for forty years. In the LXX the "forty years" is connected with God's anger, not with the testing. The author may have had other MSS with this way of taking the words. Or he may have put the words in a new position himself. It may well be that at the time he wrote this epistle, the author reflected on the fact that it was the fourth decade since Jesus' crucifixion. The Israelites had rejected God for forty years, and it was now nearly forty years since their descendants had rejected Jesus—a reason for serious concern.

10 We should not miss the reference to the anger of God. The Bible is clear that God is not impassive or indifferent in the face of human sin. He is a "consuming fire" (12:29), and his inevitable reaction to sin is wrath. "Generation" may mean a "clan" or "race," sometimes those living at a particular time or those who have the characteristics of a particular age. Here it is all the Israelites living at a particular time. They showed constancy in error, "always going astray." "Heart" (*kardia*) as used in the Bible does not stand for the emotions as with us but for the whole inner being—

thoughts, feelings, and will. Often the emphasis is on the mind. Here the thought is that Israel went wholly astray. Their inner state was not right with God. The last line of the verse implies that if people really knew the ways of God, they would walk in them. But these people did not know. Their ignorance was culpable, not innocent. They were not blamed simply for not knowing but for not knowing things they ought to have known and acted on. They did not take the trouble to learn. To neglect opportunity is serious.

11 The seriousness with which God viewed Israel's sin is shown by the divine oath. This points to an unshakable determination. The form of the oath in the Hebrew, reflected in the LXX, is "If they shall enter." This construction implies an ending that occurs only rarely; e.g., "If I have done evil to him who is at peace with me . . . let my enemy pursue and overtake me" (Ps 7:4–5). Here it will be something like "If they shall enter into my rest . . . then my name is not God!" (NIV, "They shall never enter"). The oath refers to the time when the spies had returned from their survey of the Promised Land (Num 14:21ff.).

The psalmist has brought together two incidents, one from the beginning and one from the end of the wilderness period, to make the impressive point that the Israelites of old consistently provoked God. God swore the oath in his "anger." Here the word *orgē* is from a different root from that rendered "angry" in v.10 (*prosōchthisa*). *Orgē* is the usual word for the "wrath" of God and points to the strong and settled opposition of God's holy nature to all that is evil. God is not passive in the face of wrongdoing; he actively opposes it. "Wrath" may not be the perfect word with which to express this (as used of men it implies lack of self-control and the like that do not apply to God). But it seems the best word we have and it does bring out God's passionate opposition to evil and his concern for the right. Those who reject its use are in danger of misrepresenting God as one who does not care. But God does care, and he did not allow the sinning Israelites to enter the rest.

The author has a fondness for the verb "enter" (*eiserchomai*) and uses it seventeen times, more than any other NT book except the Synoptics and Acts. Eleven times in chapters 3–4 he speaks of entering rest. "Rest" (*katapausis*), as used here, points to a place of blessing where there is no more striving but only relaxation in the presence of God and in the certainty that there is no cause for fear. R. Akiba understood Psalm 95 (in conjunction with Num 14:35) to mean that the wilderness generation would have no part in the world to come (Talmud *Sanhedrin* 110b; M *Sanhedrin* 10.3 bases the same thought on Num 14:35). Disobedience cut them off from the blessing. Buchanan thinks of the "rest" as "the promised heritage of the land of Canaan under the rule of the Messiah to be fulfilled for Jesus and his followers" (in loc.). This would give us an easy interpretation to the word "rest," but it is more than difficult to fit it in with what the writer says elsewhere. It is better to take "rest" in a spiritual sense.

B. *Some Did Not Enter the Rest*

3:12–19

> ¹²See to it, brothers, that none of you has a sinful, unbelieving heart that turns away from the living God. ¹³But encourage one another daily, as long as it is called Today, so that none of you may be hardened by sin's deceitfulness. ¹⁴We have come to share in Christ if we hold firmly till the end the confidence we had at first. ¹⁵As has just been said:

"Today, if you hear his voice,
do not harden your hearts
as you did in the rebellion."

¹⁶Who were they who heard and rebelled? Were they not all those Moses led out of Egypt? ¹⁷And with whom was he angry for forty years? Was it not with those who sinned, whose bodies fell in the desert? ¹⁸And to whom did God swear that they would never enter his rest if not to those who disobeyed? ¹⁹So we see that they were not able to enter, because of their unbelief.

Having shown that Scripture looks for a rest for God's people, the author proceeds to show that Israel of old did not enter that rest. The implication is that it is still available for others. And there is a warning. When God opens up an opportunity, that does not necessarily mean that those who have that opportunity will take it.

12 The writer has a tender concern for every one of his readers. He exhorts them to beware lest any one of them fall away. The "sinful, unbelieving heart" stands in marked contrast to the faithfulness ascribed to both Jesus and Moses (v.2). It is an unusual and emphatic expression. The author stresses the heinousness of this by speaking of turning away from the living God. "Turn away" is perhaps not strong enough; the meaning is rather "rebel against." The author is fond of the expression "the living God" (cf. 9:14; 10:31; 12:22). The rebellion he warns against consists of departing from a living, dynamic person, not from some dead doctrine. Jews might retort that they served the same God as the Christians so that they would not be departing from God if they went back to Judaism. But to reject God's highest revelation is to depart from God, no matter how many preliminary revelations are retained. A true faith is impossible with such a rejection.

13 Contrariwise, they must encourage one another constantly and urgently. The author sees Christian fellowship as very important. It can build people up in the faith and form a strong bulwark against sin and apostasy (cf. 10:25; Matt 18:15–17). "Daily" means that encouragement should be habitual. "As long as it is called Today" adds a touch of urgency, for "Today" does not last forever. The aim of the swift action the writer looks for is that not one of his readers be hardened. Once again we see his concern for every individual reader. The verb "hardened" does not refer only to "the heart" but is quite general. One's whole life may be hard and in that case one is no candidate for spiritual progress. What hardens is "sin's deceitfulness." The readers were tempted to go back to Judaism in the belief that by doing so they would be better off. But sin deceived those who thought like this. Temporal and physical safety would be bought only at the price of spiritual disaster.

14 The expression *metochoi tou Christou* can be understood as "participators in Christ" (NIV, Moff., RSV, etc.) or as "participators with Christ" (NEB, TEV, JB, etc.). The former is supported by the use of the same noun of sharing (*metochoi*) in the Christian calling (v.1) and in the Holy Spirit (6:4), the latter by the use of partnership with Christ in 1:9. It seems to me that there is more to be said for the former rendering. It may be supported by the context, for it is the privilege we have in being Christians that is stressed, not the kind of work Christians do alongside Christ. The two sides of a paradox appear when we have, on the one hand, "we have come" and, on the other hand, "if we hold firmly." What God has done God has done. But it is important that the believer hold firmly to what God has given him (cf. v.6). The word *hypostasis* means literally "that which stands under" and may be used of essential "being" (as in 1:3). Here it will rather be that which undergirds the Christian's profession, and "confidence" is a good translation. "The confidence we had at first" is that experienced when the readers first believed. They had no doubts then, nor should they have any now. "Till the end" may point to the end of the age or the end of the believer's life.

15 The construction is uncertain. This verse may be taken with the preceding one, as in NIV, or with what follows, as NEB, which starts a new paragraph with "When Scripture says . . . who, I ask, were those who heard?" This is attractive, but it ignores the *gar* ("for") at the beginning of v.16. Some link the words with v.13 and regard v.14 as a parenthesis: "Exhort one another while it is called today . . . while it is said. . . ." The question is not an easy one, but it seems best to take things in order, as NIV does. The words, of course, have already been quoted (vv.7-8, where see commentary).

16 The author presses home his point by three questions that emphasize that it was the people who were in a position of spiritual privilege and yet sinned grievously who were in mind in Psalm 95. Some scholars, it is true, take *tines* as the indefinite pronoun and not as an interrogative (as does KJV, "for some . . . did provoke"). But "some" is a strange designation for practically the whole nation, and in any case it is better to see the same construction in all three of these verses. The first question, then, asks, "Who were they who heard and rebelled?" The verb "rebelled" (*parepik-ranan*) is found only here in the NT (though a cognate noun occurs in v.8). It means "embitter," "make angry," and is a strong expression for the rebellious attitude that characterized the Exodus generation.

The writer answers his question with another, this one phrased so as to expect the answer yes. "All those Moses led out of Egypt" is comprehensive, but that Joshua and Caleb are not mentioned does not invalidate the argument. The nation was character- ized by unbelief, and the faithfulness of two men does not alter this. NIV says that Moses "led" the people out of Egypt; but, more literally, the author said that they "came out through [*dia*] Moses"— implying that they acted of their own volition and made a good start.

17 The second question refers to those God was angry with those forty years. (For the anger of God, see comments on vv.10-11.) In the earlier treatment of the incident (vv.7-8), the forty years referred to testing God and seeing his works. Here it refers to the continuing wrath of God (as in the Heb. and LXX). The wrath of God was not something transitory and easily avoided. It lasted throughout the wilderness period. The question "Was it not. . . ?" employs the emphatic *ouchi*, found in only one other place in this epistle (in 1:14). Its use leaves no doubt whatever that God was angry with the sinners in question. Their punishment is mentioned in words taken from or reminiscent of Numbers 14:29, 32. The author may be quoting or he may simply be using scriptural language to add solemnity to his point. He reminds his readers that in the past those who sinned against God had been destroyed, and, indeed (as the verbs in the Numbers passage are future since they were spoken before the event), that they were destroyed as it was prophesied. The word rendered "desert" refers to "deserted" land. It is wilderness country in contrast to cultivated and inhabited land.

It can be used for pasture (Luke 15:4). Here it is the uninhabited area the Israelites passed through on their wanderings.

18 The third question refers to those to whom the oath was sworn (cf. v.11). Those who would not enter God's rest were "those who disobeyed." The verb *apeitheō* means properly "disobey," but some accept the meaning "disbelieve" (as NIV mg.). This is possible since for the early Christians "the supreme disobedience was a refusal to believe their gospel" (BAG, p. 82). But here it seems that we should take the meaning "disobey." God did much for these people. Yet in the end they went their own way and refused to obey him.

19 The depressing conclusion sums up what has gone before. The author does not say that they did not enter but that they "were not able to enter." Sin is self-defeating and unbelief of itself prevents us from entering God's rest. This is not an arbitrary penalty imposed by a despotic God. It is the inevitable outcome of unbelief. In the Greek the final word in this section of the argument, thrown to the end of the sentence for greater emphasis, is *apistia* ("unbelief"). That is what robbed the wilderness generation of the rest they had every reason to expect when they came out of Egypt. The warning to the people of the writer's day is clear. To slip back from their Christian profession into unbelief would be fatal.

Notes

12 Ἐν (*en*) with the dative of the articular infinitive τῷ ἀποστῆναι (*tō apostēnai*, "turns away from") is rather more frequent in Heb than in most of the other NT writings. The tense is usually the present and the sense temporal. However, exceptions to both occur, as here where the tense is aorist and the meaning something like "in that." There is probably another nontemporal example, this time with the present, in v.15.

C. Christians Enter the Rest

4:1–10

¹Therefore, since the promise of entering his rest still stands, let us be careful that none of you be found to have fallen short of it. ²For we also have had the gospel preached to us, just as they did; but the message they heard was of no value to them, because those who heard did not combine it with faith. ³Now we who have believed enter that rest, just as God has said,

"So I declared on oath in my anger,
'They shall never enter my rest.' "

And yet his work has been finished since the creation of the world. ⁴For somewhere he has spoken about the seventh day in these words: "And on the seventh day God rested from all his work." ⁵And again in the passage above he says, "They shall never enter my rest."

⁶It still remains that some will enter that rest, and those who formerly had the gospel preached to them did not go in, because of their disobedience. ⁷Therefore God again set a certain day, calling it Today, when a long time later he spoke through David, as was said before:

"Today, if you hear his voice,
do not harden your hearts."

[8]For if Joshua had given them rest, God would not have spoken later about another day. [9]There remains, then, a Sabbath-rest for the people of God; [10]for anyone who enters God's rest also rests from his own work, just as God did from his.

The author argues that the purposes of God are not frustrated because Israel of old disobeyed him and failed to enter the rest he had promised his people. The promise remains. If the ancient Israel did not enter God's rest, then someone else will; namely, the Christians. But this should not lead to complacency. If the Israelites of an earlier day, with all their advantages, failed to enter the rest, Christians ought not to think there will be automatic acceptance for them. They must take care lest they, too, fail to enter the blessing.

1 NIV's "let us be careful" is more strictly "let us fear," and the exhortation comes first in the sentence. It is emphatic because the writer does not want his readers to be complacent. There is real danger. God's promises mean much to the writer, and indeed the word *epangelia* ("promise") occurs more often in Hebrews than in any other NT book (fourteen times; next is Gal with ten). The promise in question "still stands." That is to say, though it has not been fulfilled, it has not been revoked. In one sense, of course, there was a fulfillment, for the generation after the men who died in the wilderness entered Canaan. But throughout this section it is basic to the argument that physical entry into Canaan did not constitute the fulfillment of the promise. God had promised "rest" and that meant more than living in Canaan.

There is a problem about the word translated "be found." The verb is *dokeō*, which means "think," "suppose" if transitive, and "seem," "have the appearance of" if intransitive. Moffatt points out that a meaning like "judge," "adjudge" is also attested in some passages in Josephus, LXX, and Attic. There are two main possibilities. The one accepts "think" as the meaning and sees the writer as reassuring fearful Christians who thought they might miss the rest. (The earlier generation had missed it, and why should not they?) The other interpretation prefers "seem," "be judged," or "be found" and takes the words as a warning to the readers to take care lest they miss the promised rest. ("Seem" is a way of softening the warning so that the writer refrains from saying that any of them actually missed or will miss the promise.) A decision is not easy, but on the whole it seems that this second interpretation fits the context better. The author, then, is reminding his readers that there was a generation to whom the rest was promised and who missed it. They should beware lest they make the same mistake.

2 There is a question about following the rendering "we have had the gospel preached to us" or whether the phrase should be taken as general—i.e., "we have heard the good news as well as they." The verb *euangelizomai* is used of preaching good news in general, but in a Christian context it is much more often used of the specific good news of the gospel; indeed, it becomes the technical term for preaching the gospel. Here everything turns on whether we think that what was preached to Israel of old was what Christians call "the gospel." If it was, then NIV is correct. If we think otherwise, we will follow the rendering "heard the good news." The first half of the verse makes it clear that on the score of hearing God's Good News there was not much

to choose between the wilderness generation and the readers: "We also have had the gospel preached to us, just as they did." The stress is on the readers. They have the message. They must act on it in contrast to the men of old who did not.

"The message they heard" (i.e., "the word of hearing," an expression much like that in 1 Thess 2:13) brought them no profit. A difficult problem remains at the end of the verse, where the reason for this is given. While there are several textual variants in the MSS, they boil down to two—whether we take the participle of the verb "to combine" or "unite" as singular, in which case it agrees with "word" (in "word of hearing") or as plural, in which case it goes with "them." Only a few MSS have the singular reading, some of them very old, but many scholars favor it on grammatical grounds. If adopted, it gives this sense: "It [the word] was not mixed with faith in them that heard." On the other hand, if we take the plural, the meaning is, "They were not united by faith with them that heard" (i.e., real believers, men like Caleb and Joshua). The resolution of the question is difficult and may be impossible with the information at our disposal. The main thrust, however, is plain enough. The writer is saying that it is not enough to hear; the message must be acted on in faith.

This is the writer's first use of *pistis* ("faith"), a term he will employ 32 times (out of the 243 times it occurs in the NT), a total exceeded only in Romans (40 times). *Pistis* means "faithfulness" as well as "faith," but the latter preponderates in the NT. Sometimes faith in God is meant and sometimes faith in Christ. In this epistle it is often the former. In the NT, the term is usually used without an object, i.e., as "true piety, genuine religion" (BAG, p. 669). Here the term points to the right response to the Christian message. It is the attitude of trusting God wholeheartedly. The writer speaks of "those who heard" without specifying what it was they heard. But there can be no doubt that he is looking for a right response to what God has done and to what God has made known.

3 "We who have believed" once more stresses the necessity of faith. This is one of only two places where the verb *pisteuō* ("to believe") occurs in Hebrews (the other is in 11:6)—a contrast to the frequency of the noun. It is believers who enter God's rest, not members of physical Israel, and they do so through a right relationship to God, with an attitude of trust. The verb *eiserchomai* ("enter") is in the present tense. Montefiore, for one, regards this as important: "Contrary to some commentators, the Greek means neither that they are certain to enter, nor that they will enter, but that they are already in process of entering" (in loc.). By contrast Bruce complains of translations that "suggest that the entrance is here and now, whereas it lies ahead as something to be attained. The present tense is used in a generalizing sense" (in loc.). Either view is defensible and probably much depends on our idea of the "rest." If it lies beyond death, then obviously "rest" must be understood in terms of the future. But if it is a present reality, then believers are entering it now. Characteristically, the writer supports his position by an appeal to Scripture.

There is nothing in the Greek to correspond to NIV's "God" ("God has said"). Yet this is a correct interpretation because the writer habitually regards God as the author of Scripture. The perfect tense *eirēken* ("has said") puts some emphasis on permanence. What God has spoken stands. The quotation is from Psalm 95:11 (already cited in 3:11, where see comments). Its point appears to be that those to whom the promise was originally made could not enter the rest because of the divine oath. This does not mean any inadequacy on God's part. He had completed his works from of old, in fact from the Creation. The writer is saying that God's rest was available from the time

Creation was completed. The "rest" was thus the rest he himself enjoyed. The earthly rest in Canaan was no more than a type or symbol of this.

4 The writer does not precisely locate his quotation (Gen 2:2) but contents himself with the general "somewhere." Nor does he say who the speaker is, though once again it will be God, the author of all Scripture. Locating a passage precisely was not easy when scrolls were used; and unless it was important, there would be a tendency not to look it up. In the present case the important thing is that God said the words, not where and when they were spoken. The passage speaks of God as resting from his work on the seventh day.

It is worth noticing that in the creation story each of the first six days is marked by the refrain "And there was evening, and there was morning." However, this is lacking in the account of the seventh day. There we simply read that God rested from all his work. This does not mean that God entered a state of idleness, for there is a sense in which he is continually at work (John 5:17). But the completion of creation marks the end of a magnificent whole. There was nothing to add to what God had done, and he entered a rest from creating, a rest marked by the knowledge that everything that he had made was very good (Gen 1:31). So we should think of the rest as something like the satisfaction that comes from accomplishment, from the completion of a task, from the exercise of creativity.

5 The writer adds a second quotation (Psalm 95:11). It is one that is central to his argument at this point. As here, he often uses "again" where a further quotation is added to a preceding one (e.g., 1:5; 2:13; 10:30). In this case, however, it does more than that; it introduces a second point in the argument. The first passage said that God rested (and by implication that the rest was open to those who would enter it); the second passage said that the Israelites did not enter that rest because God's judgment fell on them. So the way is prepared for later steps in the argument.

6–7 "It still remains" misses some of the force of the original, which is rather: "Since therefore it remains. . . ." The argument moves along in logical sequence. Some will enter that rest because it is unthinkable that God's plan should fail of fulfillment. If God prepared a rest for humanity to enter into, then they will enter into it. Perhaps those originally invited would not do so, for there is often something of the conditional about God's promises. This is not to say that one is to fear that these promises will not be kept. It is precisely the force of the present argument that nothing can stop the promises from being kept. But they must always be appropriated by faith. There is no other way of laying hold on them. So if one does not approach the promises by faith, he does not obtain what God offers and the offer is made to others. Some, then, must enter God's rest; but the first recipients of the Good News (cf. comment on v.2) did not.

The writer concentrates on two generations only: the wilderness generation and his contemporaries. There had been other generations who might have appropriated the promise. But the focus is on the first generation who set the pattern of unbelief and then on the writer's generation, who alone at that time had the opportunity of responding to God's invitation. All the intervening generations had ceased to be and could be ignored for the purpose of the argument.

The reason the first group did not enter God's rest was "their disobedience." The word *apeitheia* ("disobedience") is always used in the NT of disobeying God, often with the thought of the gospel in mind; so it comes close to the meaning disbelief (cf. v.11; Rom 11:30). Because the first generation had passed the opportunity by, God set another day. The idea that the wilderness generation was finally rejected was one the rabbis found hard to accept. In their writings we find statements such as the following: "Into this resting-place they will not enter, but they will enter into another resting-place" (Mid *Qoheleth* 10.20.1). The rabbis also had a parable of a king who swore in anger that his son would not enter his palace. But when he calmed down, he pulled down his palace and built another, so fulfilling his oath and at the same time retaining his son (ibid.). Thus the rabbis expressed their conviction that somehow those Israelites would be saved. The author, however, has no such reservations about the wilderness generation. They disobeyed God and forfeited their place. Psalm 95 was written long after that generation had failed to use its opportunity and had perished. Its use of the term "Today" shows that the promise had never been claimed and was still open. The voice of God still called. The author has already used the quotation in 3:7ff. (cf. comments). But its point this time is the word "Today." There is *still* a day of opportunity, even though the fate of the wilderness generation stands as an impressive witness to the possibility of spiritual disaster.

8 The form of the Greek sentence indicates a contrary-to-fact condition: "If Joshua had given them rest [as he did not], God would not have spoken later about another day [as he did]." The name "Joshua" is the Hebrew form of the Greek name "Jesus." "Joshua" is a good way of rendering the text, as it makes clear to the English reader who is in mind. The Greek text, however, says "Jesus"; and both the writer and his original readers would have been mindful of the connection with the name of Christ, even though the emphasis in the passage lies elsewhere. There had been a "Jesus" who could not lead his people into the rest of God just as there was another "Jesus" who could.

9 The sentence begins with the inferential *ara* ("so," "as a result"). What follows is the logical consequence of what precedes. The term "Sabbath-rest" (*sabbatismos*) is not attested before this passage and looks like the author's own coinage. He did not have a word for the kind of rest he had in mind; so he made one up. There were various kinds of "rest." There was, for example, the kind Israel was to get in its own land when it had rest from wars (Deut 25:19). When the psalmist wrote Psalm 95, he knew firsthand what this kind of rest in Palestine meant, and he still looked for "rest." So this is not what the author of Hebrews had in mind.

Buchanan has a long note on rest in which he surveys a number of opinions and rejects all spiritualizing interpretations. He thinks that many scholars read their own ideas into "rest"; and he thinks it impossible for the word to be used in a nonnational, nonmaterial sense: "They were probably expecting a rest that was basically of the same nature as Israelites had anticipated all along" (in loc.). But surely this is precisely what the author is rejecting. He knew that Israel had been in its own land for centuries. There had been quite long periods of peace and independence. Yet the promise of rest still remained unfulfilled.

Jesus spoke of quite another kind of rest—rest for the souls of men (Matt 11:28–30). This is nearer to what the author means. We might also notice an idea of the rabbis. The Mishnah explains the use of Psalm 92 (a psalm headed "A Psalm: A Song for the Sabbath") in these terms: "A Psalm, a song for the time that is to come, for the day that shall be all Sabbath and rest in the life everlasting" (*Tamid* 7:4). This is the kind of rest the author refers to, though his idea is not the rabbinic one. He links rest with the original Sabbath, with what God did when he finished Creation and what Christians are called into. This, then, is a highly original view, not simply an old idea refurbished. The author sees the rest as for "the people of God"—an expression found elsewhere in the NT only in 11:25 (though 1 Peter 2:10 is similar, and expressions like "my people" occur several times). In the OT "the people of God" is the nation of Israel, but in the NT it signifies believers. The rest the author writes about is for such people. Others cannot enter into it. This is not so much on account of a law or rule denying them entrance as that they shut themselves out by disobedience and unbelief.

10 We now have a description of at least part of what the rest means. The writer reverts to the word for rest he has been using earlier instead of the "Sabbath-rest" of v.9. To enter rest means to cease from one's own work, just as God ceased from his. There are uncertainties here. Some think the reference is to Jesus, who would certainly fit the description except for the "anyone" (which is a reasonable interpretation of the Gr.). But the general reference is there, and we must take it to refer to the believer.

The question then arises whether the rest takes place here and now, or (as Kent, for example, holds) after death, as seen in Revelation 14:13: "Blessed are the dead who die in the Lord . . . they will rest from their labor, for their deeds will follow them." Bruce thinks it is "an experience which they do not enjoy in their present mortal life, although it belongs to them as a heritage, and by faith they may live in the good of it here and now" (in loc.). I should reverse his order and say that they live in it here and now by faith, but what they know here is not the full story. That will be revealed in the hereafter. There is a sense in which to enter Christian salvation means to cease from one's works and rest securely on what Christ has done. And there is a sense in which the works of the believer, works done in Christ, have about them that completeness and sense of fulfillment that may fitly be classed with the rest in question.

Notes

1 There is a variety of constructions with ἐπαγγελία (epangelia, "promise"). The genitive may denote the one who makes the promise (Rom 4:20), the one to whom the promise is given (Rom 15:8), or the thing promised (Heb 9:15). Or the genitive "of promise" may be added to a noun, as in "land of promise" = "promised land" (11:9). This seems to be the only place where a following infinitive gives the content of the promise. The tense of ὑστερηκέναι (hysterēkenai, "fallen short") is perfect, which points to a permanent condition. It is not a past defeat or a present momentary failure but a continuing failure.

3 Καίτοι (kaitoi) is rare in the NT (John 4:2; Acts 14:17). The use here with a following genitive absolute is not classical. The meaning is "and yet."
The writer does not use κτίσις (ktisis), the usual word for "creation," but καταβολή (katabolē), which means a "throwing down." Among other things it is used of laying foundations; and in the NT it is generally used, as here, of the foundation of the world and thus the Creation.

7 Ἐν Δαυίδ (en Dauid, "in David") is an example of the instrumental ἐν (en). God used David as his means or instrument. David is not mentioned as the author of this psalm in the Hebrew, but he is in the LXX.

9 Ἄρα (*ara*) is found in Hebrews only again at 12:8. It does not begin a clause in the classics as it does quite often in the NT. It is an inferential particle meaning "so, as a result."

D. *Exhortation to Enter the Rest*

4:11-13

> ¹¹Let us, therefore, make every effort to enter that rest, so that no one will fall by following their example of disobedience.
> ¹²For the word of God is living and active. Sharper than any double-edged sword, it penetrates even to dividing soul and spirit, joints and marrow; it judges the thoughts and attitudes of the heart. ¹³Nothing in all creation is hidden from God's sight. Everything is uncovered and laid bare before the eyes of him to whom we must give account.

The idea of the rest of God is not simply a piece of curious information not readily accessible to the rank and file of Christians. It is a spur to action. So the writer proceeds to exhort his readers to make that rest their own.

11 It is possible that this verse should be attached to the preceding paragraph but it seems meant to introduce an exhortation based on the penetrating power of the Word of God. Notice that the writer includes himself with his readers in urging a quick and serious effort to enter the rest "so that no one will fall by following their example of disobedience." Paul refers to the same generation to hammer home a similar lesson, and he regards the wilderness happenings as types (1 Cor 10:1–12; cf. *typikōs*, "examples," v.11). These earlier people had perished. Let the readers beware!

12 "The word of God" means anything that God utters and particularly the word that came through Jesus Christ. He is called "the Word" in John 1:1, but that is not the thought here (though there have been exegetes who have taken this line). The comparison with a sharp sword and its penetration into human personality shows that it is not the incarnate Word that is in mind. "Living and active" shows that there is a dynamic quality about God's revelation. It does things. Specifically it penetrates and, in this capacity, is likened to a "double-edged sword" (for the sword, cf. Isa 49:2; Eph 6:17; Rev 19:15; and for the double-edged idea, cf. Rev 1:16; 2:12).

The Word of God is unique. No sword can penetrate as it can. We should not take the reference to "soul" and "spirit" as indicating a "dichotomist" over against a "trichotomist" view of man, nor the reference to "dividing" to indicate that the writer envisaged a sword as slipping between them. Nor should we think of the sword as splitting off "joints" and "marrow." What the author is saying is that God's Word can reach to the innermost recesses of our being. We must not think that we can bluff our way out of anything, for there are no secrets hidden from God. We cannot keep our thoughts to ourselves. There may also be the thought that the whole of man's nature, however we divide it, physical as well as nonmaterial, is open to God. With "judges" we move to legal terminology. The Word of God passes judgment on men's feelings (*enthymēseōn*) and on their thoughts (*ennoiōn*). Nothing evades the scope of this Word. What man holds as most secret he finds subject to its scrutiny and judgment.

13 Here the same truth is expressed in different imagery. This time the impossibility of hiding anything from God is illustrated by the thought of nakedness. "Nothing in all creation," or "no created being" (*ktisis* means "the act of creating" and then "a created being," "a creature"), remains invisible to God. "Uncovered" renders *gymna*, a word used of the soul being without the body (2 Cor 5:3), of a bare kernel of grain (1 Cor 15:37), or of a body without clothing (Acts 19:16). Here it means that all things are truly uncovered before God. The word rendered "laid bare" (*trachēlizō*) is an unusual one, found here only in the NT and not very common outside it. It is obviously connected with the neck (*trachēlos*), but just how is not clear. It was used of wrestlers who had a hold that involved gripping the neck and was such a powerful hold that it brought victory. So the term can mean "to prostrate" or "overthrow." Those who accept this meaning render this verse in this way: "All things are naked and prostrate before his eyes."

Most scholars, however, think a meaning like "exposed" is required. Yet it is not easy to see how it is to be obtained. It has been suggested that the wrestler exposed the face or neck of his foe by his grip. While this may be so, it entails reading something into the situation. Another suggestion is the bending back of the head of a sacrificial victim to expose the throat. Unfortunately, no example of the word used in this way is attested. In the end we must probably remain unsatisfied. Clearly the author is saying that no one can keep anything hidden from God, but the metaphor by which he brings out this truth is not clear.

The verse contains yet another difficulty, namely, the precise meaning of its closing words. KJV renders them "him with whom we have to do," and this may be right. But the expression is used of accounting, and it seems more likely that NIV's "him to whom we must give account" is correct. Nothing is hidden from God, and in the end we must give account of ourselves to him. The combination makes a powerful reason for heeding the exhortation and entering into the rest by our obedience.

Notes

13 The problem is that there is no verb in the expression πρὸς ὃν ἡμῖν ὁ λόγος (*pros hon hēmin ho logos*), while both πρός (*pros*) and λόγος (*logos*) can have more than one meaning. "To whom we must give account" takes the most natural meaning of *pros* ("to") and is supported by a good deal of the exegesis of the Greek fathers and by the fact that *logos* is often used in the papyri in the sense "account," "reckoning" (see MM, s.v.). "With whom we have to do" can claim support from LXX (1 Kings 2:14; 2 Kings 9:5).

IV. A Great High Priest

One of the major insights of this epistle is that Jesus is our great High Priest. The author proceeds to reinforce his exhortation to enter the rest with a reminder of the character of our High Priest. Jesus is one with his people and for them he offers the perfect sacrifice. This is seen largely in terms of the Day of Atonement ceremonies in which the role of the high priest (and not simply any priest) was central.

A. *Our Confidence*

4:14-16

14Therefore, since we have a great high priest who has gone through the heavens, Jesus the Son of God, let us hold firmly to the faith we profess. 15For we do not have a high priest who is unable to sympathize with our weaknesses, but we have one who has been tempted in every way, just as we are—yet was without sin. 16Let us then approach the throne of grace with confidence, so that we may receive mercy and find grace to help us in our time of need.

The first point is that Jesus knows our human condition. It is not something he has heard about, so to speak, but something he knows; for he, too, was man. We may approach him confidently because he knows our weakness.

14 Our confidence rests on Jesus. He is "a great high priest," a title that suggests his superiority to the Levitical priests ("high priest" in Heb. is lit. "great priest"; the author's usage is not common in the OT, though it does occur there). Jesus has "gone through the heavens." The Jews sometimes thought of a plurality of heavens, as in Paul's reference to "the third heaven" (2 Cor 12:2) or the Talmud's reference to seven heavens (*Hagigah* 12b). The thought is that Jesus has gone right through to the supreme place. His greatness is further emphasized by the title "Son of God." All this is the basis for an exhortation to hold firmly to our profession.

15 Our High Priest has entered into our weakness and so can sympathize meaningfully with us. He "has been tempted . . . just as we are" (*kath' homoiotēta*) may mean "in the same way as we are tempted" or "by reason of his likeness to us"; both are true. There is another ambiguity at the end of the verse where the Greek means "apart from sin." This may mean that Jesus was tempted just as we are except that we sin and he did not. But it may also mean that he had a knowledge of every kind of temptation except that which comes from actually having sinned. There are supporters for each interpretation. But it may be that the writer was not trying to differentiate between the two. At any rate his words can profitably be taken either way. The main point is that, though Jesus did not sin, we must not infer that life was easy for him. His sinlessness was, at least in part, an earned sinlessness as he gained victory after victory in the constant battle with temptation that life in this world entails. Many have pointed out that the Sinless One knows the force of temptation in a way that we who sin do not. We give in before the temptation has fully spent itself; only he who does not yield knows its full force.

16 Having this High Priest gives confidence. So the writer exhorts his readers to approach God boldly. The word "us" does away with the mediation of earthly priests. In view of what our great High Priest has done, there is no barrier. *We* can approach God. "The throne of grace" occurs only here in the NT. It points both to the sovereignty of God and to God's love to men. The rabbis sometimes speak of a "throne of mercy" to which God goes from "the throne of judgment" when he spares people (Lev R 29. 3, 6, 9, 10). The idea here is not dissimilar, all the more so since the writer goes on to speak of receiving mercy. We need mercy because we have failed so often, and we need grace because service awaits us in which we need God's help. And help is what the writer says we get—the help that is appropriate to the time, i.e., "timely help." The writer is urging a bold approach. Christians should not be tentative because they have the great High Priest in whom they can be confident. His successful traverse of the heavens points to his power to help, and his fellow-feeling with our weakness points to his sympathy with our needs. In the light of this, what can hold us back?

B. The Qualities Required in High Priests

5:1–4

[1]Every high priest is selected from among men and is appointed to represent them in matters related to God, to offer gifts and sacrifices for sins. [2]He is able to deal gently with those who are ignorant and are going astray, since he himself is subject to weakness. [3]This is why he has to offer sacrifices for his own sins, as well as for the sins of the people.
[4]No one takes this honor upon himself; he must be called by God, just as Aaron was.

The author now directs his readers to the qualities required in the well-known institution of high priests, though he confines his attention to the Aaronic priesthood in the LXX and does not consider contemporary Jewish priests who fell far short of the ideal. He shows that the necessary qualifications include oneness with the people, compassion, and appointment by God. Then he goes on to show that Christ had these qualifications.

1 The author proposes to explore something of the nature of high priesthood and begins by showing that it has both a manward and a Godward reference. It is of the essence of priesthood that the priest has community of nature with those he represents. But his work is "in matters related to God," specifically in offering "gifts and sacrifices for sins." These two are sometimes differentiated as cereal and animal offerings. It seems more likely, however, that the writer is summing up the priestly function of offering.

2 It is not easy to translate *metriopathein* (NIV, "to deal gently with"). It refers to taking the middle course between apathy and anger. A true high priest is not indifferent to moral lapses; neither is he harsh. He "is able" to take this position only because he himself shares in the same "weakness" as the sinners on whom he has compassion. The word may denote physical or moral frailty, and the following words show that in the case of the usual run of high priests the latter is included. The earthly high priest is at one with his people in their need for atonement and forgiveness.

3 The high priest is required to make offerings for himself just as for his people. For the Day of Atonement it was prescribed that the high priest present a bull "for his own sin offering" (Lev 16:11). And in the first century, as he laid his hands on the head of the animal, he would say, "O God, I have committed iniquity and transgressed and sinned before thee, I and my house and the children of Aaron, thy holy people. O God, forgive, I pray, the iniquities and transgressions and sins which I have committed and transgressed and sinned before thee, I and my house" (M *Yoma* 4:2). Only then was he able to minister on behalf of the people. In the matter of sins and of sacrifices the priest must regard himself in exactly the same way he regards the people. His case is identical with theirs.

4 The negative statement immediately refutes any thought that a man can take the initiative in being made high priest. It is an honor to be a high priest (cf. Jos. Antiq. III, 188 [viii. 1]). The only way to be made high priest is by divine appointment, and the appointment of Aaron sets the pattern (Exod 28:1–3). In point of fact, no other call to be high priest is recorded in Scripture, though we might reason that the call to Aaron was not simply personal but also included his family and descendants. At any rate, the Bible records disasters that befell those who took it upon themselves to perform high priestly duties, as in the cases of Korah (Num 16), Saul (1 Sam 13:8ff.), and Uzziah (2 Chron 26:16ff.).

Notes

3 Περί (peri) sometimes comes very close in meaning to ὑπέρ (hyper), as in the first two instances here. The meaning must be "on behalf of" or "in the place of."

C. Christ's Qualifications as High Priest

5:5–11

⁵So Christ also did not take upon himself the glory of becoming a high priest. But God said to him,

"You are my Son;
today I have become your Father."

⁶And he says in another place,

"You are a priest forever,
in the order of Melchizedek."

⁷During the days of Jesus' life on earth, he offered up prayers and petitions with loud cries and tears to the one who could save him from death, and he was heard because of his reverent submission. ⁸Although he was a son, he learned obedience from what he suffered ⁹and, once made perfect, he became the source of eternal salvation for all who obey him ¹⁰and was designated by God to be high priest in the order of Melchizedek.
¹¹We have much to say about this, but it is hard to explain because you are slow to learn.

Having made clear what is required in high priests, the author shows that Christ has these qualifications. Moreover, he shows that Christ is both Priest and King, which goes beyond the view expressed in some Jewish writings that there will be two messiahs, one of Aaron and another of David. No other NT writer speaks of Jesus as a high priest. It is a highly original way of looking at him.

5–6 Christ has the qualification of being called by God. There is perhaps a hint at his obedience in the use of the term "the Christ" (ho Christos) rather than the human name "Jesus." He who was God's own Christ did not take the glory on himself (cf.

John 8:54). The writer cites two passages, the first being Psalm 2:7 (cf. 1:5). He will later argue that Jesus ministers in the heavenly sanctuary. Accordingly, it is important that Jesus be seen to be the Son, one who has rights in heaven.

The second citation is from Psalm 110:4. The first verse of this psalm is often applied to Jesus (e.g., 1:13), but this appears to be the first time the Melchizedek passage is used in this way. The psalm says, "You are a priest forever," which is the first use of the term "priest" in this epistle (a term the author will use fourteen times, out of thirty-one in NT; next most frequent use is in Luke—five times). The author of Hebrews uses it of priests generally (7:14; 8:4), of the Levitical priests (7:20, etc.), of Melchizedek (7:1, 3), and of Christ (5:6; 7:11, 15, 17, 21; 10:21). When it is used of Christ, it seems to differ but little from "high priest." It is a powerful way of bringing out certain aspects of Christ's saving work for men. All that a priest does in offering sacrifice for men Christ does. But whereas they do it only symbolically, he really effects atonement.

"Forever" is another contrast. Other priests have their day and pass away. Not Christ! His priesthood abides. He has no successor (a fact that will be brought out later). He is a priest "of the same kind as Melchizedek" (J. C. Ward). Most translations render this "of the order of Melchizedek," but this is incorrect. There was no succession of priests from Melchizedek and thus no "order." Jesus, however, was a priest of this kind—not like Aaron and his successors.

7 The author turns to the second qualification—Jesus' oneness with mankind. In realistic language he brings out the genuineness of Jesus' humanity. Commentators agree that the writer is referring to the agony in Gethsemane, but his language does not fit into any of our accounts. It seems that he may have had access to some unrecorded facts. It is also possible that he wants us to see that there were other incidents in Jesus' life that fit into this general pattern. He speaks of "the days of his flesh," which NIV renders "Jesus' life on earth." But the use of the word "flesh" (*sarx*) is probably meant to draw attention to the weakness that characterizes this life.

"Prayers and petitions" (the latter word [*hiketērias*] appears only here in the NT) point to dependence on God, who alone can save from death. The "loud cries and tears" are not mentioned in the Gethsemane accounts, though there is no reason for thinking that they had no part in the incident. Westcott quotes a rabbinic saying: "There are three kinds of prayers, each loftier than the preceding: prayer, crying, and tears. Prayer is made in silence: crying with raised voice; but tears overcome all things ('there is no door through which tears do not pass')" (in loc.).

There are difficulties at the end of v.7. The word "heard" (*eisakoustheis*) is usually taken to mean that the prayer was answered, not simply noted. Most interpreters agree. But they also contend that the prayer must have been answered in the terms in which it was asked. The problem, then, is that Jesus prayed, "Take this cup from me" (Mark 14:36); but he still died. Some see the solution in holding that "from death" (*ek thanatou*) means "out of the state of death," whereas *apo thanatou* would be needed for "deliverance away from dying." This is ingenious; but the usage of the prepositions does not support it. Others draw attention to the word rendered "reverent submission" (*eulabeia*, used again in the NT only at 12:28). As it can mean "fear" as well as "reverence," or "godly fear," it has been suggested that we might understand the verse thus: "He was heard and delivered from the fear of death." This, however, does seem to be reading something into the text. Another solution is that the prayer was not that Jesus should not die but that he should not die in Gethsemane ("If Christ had died in the Garden, no greater calamity could possibly have fallen on mankind," Hewitt, in loc.). This, however, seems artificial and has not gained much support.

All in all, it seems much better to remember that Jesus' prayer was not simply a petition that he should not die, because he immediately said, "Yet not what I will, but what you will" (Mark 14:36). The important thing about answered prayer is that God does what brings about the end aimed at, not what corresponds exactly to the words of the petitioner. In this case the prayer was that the will of God be done, and this has precedence over the passing of the cup from Jesus. Since the cup had to be drunk, it was drunk! But the significant point is that the Son *was* strengthened to do the will of the Father. Yet another solution is to take some of the words over into the next verse. This involves inserting a full stop after "death" and then combining the rest as follows: "Having been heard because of his reverent submission, although he was a son, he learned obedience from what he suffered." This, however, seems unnatural and puts too much weight on v.8.

8 We should take these words in the sense of "son though he was" rather than "although he was *a* son." It is the quality of sonship that is emphasized. Again, it is the fate of sons to suffer (12:7), but the writer does not say "because he was a son" but "although . . . ." Jesus' stature was such that one would not have expected him to suffer. But he did suffer and in the process learned obedience. This, startling though it is, does not mean that Jesus passed from disobedience to obedience. Rather, he learned obedience by actually obeying. There is a certain quality involved when one has performed a required action—a quality that is lacking when there is only a readiness to act. Innocence differs from virtue.

9 Here we must make a similar comment about Jesus' being "made perfect." This does not mean that he was imperfect and that out of his imperfection he became perfect. There is a perfection that results from having actually suffered; it is different from the perfection that is ready to suffer. "He became" indicates a change of relationship that follows the perfecting. The suffering that led to the perfecting did something. It meant that Jesus became "the source of eternal salvation." This expression can be paralleled in Greek literature, though there, of course, "salvation" is understood in very different ways. "Eternal salvation" is not a very common expression (found only here in the NT; cf. Isa 45:17). "Eternal" (*aiōnios*) means "pertaining to an age (*aiōn*)." Normally the word refers to the age to come and so means "without end," though it can also be used of what is without beginning or end (9:14) or simply of what is without beginning (Rom 16:25). It is used of what does not end in connection with redemption (9:12), covenant (13:20), judgment (6:2), and inheritance (9:15). Jesus will bring people a salvation that is eternal in its scope and efficacy, a salvation that brings them into the life of the world to come. It is a nice touch that he who learned to obey brought salvation to those who obey.

10 The writer has forcefully made his point that Jesus shared our human life. He was qualified to be high priest because of his common nature with us and his compassion. Now the writer returns to the thought that Jesus was made high priest by God. What is to become his characteristic designation throughout this epistle is a title not given by men, nor assumed by himself, but conferred on him by God the Father.

11 NIV takes this verse as the opening sentence in a new paragraph, as do some commentators. This is not impossible, but on the whole it seems better to take it as completing the preceding paragraph. The writer points out that there is a good deal that could be said about his subject. It is "hard to explain," not because of some defect in the writer or the intrinsic difficulty of the subject, but because of the slowness of the learners. This leads to a new train of thought that is pursued throughout chapter 6 (we come back to Melchizedek in ch. 7). While "this" is quite general, it might be masculine and so could refer to Melchizedek or Christ. On the whole, it seems best to see a reference here to the way Melchizedek prefigures Christ. "Are" should really be "have become." It is an acquired state, not a natural one. "Slow" renders *nōthros*, which means "sluggish," "slothful." They ought to have been in a different condition. The readers of the epistle were not naturally slow learners but had allowed themselves to get lazy.

V. The Danger of Apostasy

Obviously the author was much concerned lest his readers slip back from their present state into something that amounts to a denial of Christianity. So he utters a strong warning about the dangers of apostasy. He wants his friends to be in no doubt about the seriousness of falling into it.

A. *Failure to Progress in the Faith*

5:12–14

> [12]In fact, though by this time you ought to be teachers, you need someone to teach you the elementary truths of God's word all over again. You need milk, not solid food! [13]Anyone who lives on milk, being still an infant, is not acquainted with the teaching about righteousness. [14]But solid food is for the mature, who by constant use have trained themselves to distinguish good from evil.

This little section is of special interest because it shows that the recipients of the letter were people of whom better things might have been expected. They should have been mature Christians. Since they had evidently been converted for quite some time, they ought to have made much more progress in the faith than they in fact had. The author is troubled by their immaturity.

12 The readers had been Christians for long enough to qualify as teachers. This does not necessarily mean that the letter was written to a group of teachers, for the emphasis is on progress in the faith. Those addressed had failed to go on though they had been believers long enough to know more. Christians who have really progressed in the faith ought to be able to instruct others (as 1 Peter 3:15 shows; cf. Rom 2:21). But, far from this being the case, they still need instruction, and that in elementary truths.

"Someone to teach you" stands over against "teachers" and points up the contrast. Their knowledge of the faith is minimal when it ought to have been advanced. "The elementary truths" renders an expression that is equivalent to our "ABC." It points to the real beginnings. The Greek actually means something like "the ABC of the beginning of the oracles of God." There can be no doubt as to the elementary nature of the teaching in question. Yet it is not quite clear what "the oracles of God" are.

51

Quite possibly the OT is meant, though some think it is the whole Jewish system. Since the expression is quite general, it seems better to take it of all that God has spoken—i.e., the divine revelation in general.

The verse ends with another strong statement about the plight of the readers. "You need milk" renders an expression that literally means "you have become having need of milk," an expression in which "you have become" is important. Once again the writer is drawing attention to the fact that his readers have moved their position. Always in the Christian life, one either moves forward or slips back. It is almost impossible to stand still. These people had not advanced; so the result was that they had gone back and had "become" beginners. The contrast between milk and solid food is found elsewhere (cf. 1 Cor 3:2, though there the word for "food" is different). "Milk" stands for elementary instruction in the Christian way. "Solid food" is, of course, more advanced instruction, the kind of teaching beginners cannot make much of but which is invaluable to those who have made some progress. What is appropriate at the early stages of the Christian life may cease to be suitable as time goes on.

13 The author explains his reference to milk and solids (the Gr. has a *gar* ["for"], which shows he is giving the reason for his preceding statement). "Anyone" (*pas*) is inclusive (*pas* allows no exception). In other words, the author is saying, "This is the way it is." The Christian occupied with elementary truths is spiritually "still an infant" and must be treated as such. He is "unskilled in the word of righteousness" (RSV), to take a translation a little more literal than NIV. The Greek *apeiros* means "without experience of" and so comes to mean "unskilled." It is uncertain what "word of righteousness" means. The problem is that both "word" and "righteousness" may be taken in more ways than one. "Word" may mean the Christian message, in which case we may wish to see "righteousness" in terms of "the righteousness of God" that is made known and made available in Christ. Or we may see "righteousness" as the right conduct God expects believers to follow. Or the author may be following up the previous metaphor and thinking of the prattling speech of the child (cf. G. Schrenk, "There is a most unusual phrase in Hb. 5:13, where *apeiros logou dikaiosynēs* implies that the infant is incapable of understanding correct, normal speech," TDNT, 2:198). The first of these suggestions scarcely seems called for by the context. Therefore I am inclined to favor the second, though agreeing that the third is quite possible.

14 Mature people (*teleioi*) need solid food. The *teleioi* in the mystery religions were the initiates. It is unlikely, however, that this is its meaning here. "But" (*de*) shows the contrast to infants in v. 13. The reference is clearly to the mature who have "trained themselves." The NT makes considerable use of metaphors from athletics and *gymnazō* means "to exercise naked," "to train." It is not easy to find a good equivalent for *hexis* in this place (NIV, "constant use"). The difficulty is that, apart from this passage, *hexis* seems to denote the quality that results from training, not the training itself ("not the process but the result, the condition which has been produced by past exercise and not the separate acts following one on another" [Westcott, in loc.]). But our uncertainty about the detail does not carry over to the main thrust of the passage. The writer is clearly saying that the mature Christian, the eater of solid food, constantly exercises himself in spiritual perception, and the result is manifest. He can "distinguish good from evil" and, therefore, the implication runs, will not be in danger of doing the wrong thing to which the readers find themselves attracted. Lacking this perception, Christian service will always be immature and partial.

B. Exhortation to Progress

6:1–3

> ¹Therefore let us leave the elementary teachings about Christ and go on to maturity, not laying again the foundation of repentance from acts that lead to death, and of faith in God, ²instruction about baptisms, the laying on of hands, the resurrection of the dead, and eternal judgment. ³And God permitting, we will do so.

Since the readers were still in need of milk, we anticipate that this is what the writer will provide. Instead, he says he will leave elementary things and go on to "maturity." We expect him to introduce this with "despite your condition" or the like. Instead, we get "therefore." The reason for this may lie in the nature of what he calls "the elementary teachings." "Practically every item" in his list "could have its place in a fairly orthodox Jewish community" (Bruce, in loc.). He may have felt that to concentrate on this area would be of no help to those slipping back into Judaism. *Therefore* he went on to "solid food."

1 The writer links himself with his readers in his exhortation to leave elementary things behind and go forward. He sees "repentance from acts that lead to death" as basic. Repentance was the first thing required in the preaching of John the Baptist, Jesus, and the apostles; and it remains basic. Here it is repentance "from dead works," a phrase that has been understood to mean legalistic adherence to Jewish ways (works that could never bring life) or genuinely evil actions (actions that belong to death and not life). The latter seems preferable. Linked with this is the positive attitude of "faith in God." Faith matters immensely to the author. Though in other writings in the NT "faith" usually means faith in Christ, in this epistle it is mostly faith in God. But this means more than a conviction that there is a God. It means trusting in that God in a personal relationship. And it is not so different from faith in Christ as some suggest, because it is basic Christian teaching that God was in Christ and because the author emphasizes the reality of the Incarnation.

2 "Instruction" is in apposition to "foundation" and introduces a fresh group of subjects. "Baptisms" (here *baptismōn*) is a word usually used of purification ceremonies other than Christian baptism (9:10; Mark 7:4), and it is plural (which would be unusual for baptism). Thus it is likely that the word refers to something other than baptism. There were such purification ceremonies, or lustrations, in the Jewish religion as in most other religions of the day. Sometimes there was confusion over ritual washings (John 3:25ff.; Acts 19:1–5). It would thus be one of the elementary items of instruction that converts be taught the right approach to the various "baptisms" they would encounter.

The "laying on of hands" was a widespread practice in antiquity. Among Christians, hands were laid on new converts (Acts 8:17), on Timothy by the presbyterate (1 Tim 4:14), and on Timothy by Paul (2 Tim 1:6). This action was sometimes associated with commissioning for ministry and sometimes with the beginnings of Christian service. It seems to have been connected with the gift of the Spirit at least on some occasions (e.g., Acts 8:17–19). It is Christian beginnings, perhaps with the thought of God's gift of the Holy Spirit, that are in mind here.

"The resurrection of the dead . . . and eternal judgment" were topics that went together and were important for Jews and Christians alike. They form a reminder that this life is not everything. We are responsible people, and one day we shall rise from the dead and give account of ourselves to God. This must have been of importance to new converts in a time when many people thought of death as the end of everything.

3 This verse expresses not only a resolute determination to go ahead on these lines but also a recognition that it is only with the help of God that this can be done. We should take the words not simply as a pious nod in the direction of God but as coming out of the author's realization that without divine aid the plan he was suggesting was impossible.

Notes

1 Φερώμεθα (*pherōmetha*) pictures the Christian as "continually carried along" to maturity. God keeps bearing him up. The preposition ἐπί (*epi*, "upon," "on") is sometimes found after the verb πιστεύειν (*pisteuein*, "to believe"), but it is unusual after the noun. It will point to the fact that faith is not a self-sustaining virtue. Faith rests "on" God.

2 Most MSS read διδαχῆς (*didachēs*, "teaching," "instruction"), but a few important ones have διδαχήν (*didachēn*). With the genitive we have six qualities under the heading "foundation," whereas with the accusative (which is to be preferred) repentance and faith are regarded as foundational, and conjoined with that foundation is teaching about the other four. The word for Christian baptism is βάπτισμα (*baptisma*), but we have βαπτισμός (*baptismos*) here. This latter is used of Christian baptism in some MSS at Col 2:12, but elsewhere it is used only of other lustrations.

C. No Second Beginning

6:4–8

⁴It is impossible for those who have once been enlightened, who have tasted the heavenly gift, who have shared in the Holy Spirit, ⁵who have tasted the goodness of the word of God and the powers of the coming age, ⁶if they fall away, to be brought back to repentance, because to their loss they are crucifying the Son of God all over again and subjecting him to public disgrace.
⁷Land that drinks in the rain often falling on it and that produces a crop useful to those for whom it is farmed receives the blessing of God. ⁸But land that produces thorns and thistles is worthless and is in danger of being cursed. In the end it will be burned.

The writer proceeds to underline the seriousness of apostasy from the Christian faith and, indeed, of any failure to make progress. He does this by pointing to the impossibility of making a second beginning. It is impossible for a Christian to stand still. He either progresses in the faith or slips back. And slipping back is serious; it can mean cutting oneself off from the blessings God offers. The writer is not questioning the perseverance of the saints. As he has done before, he is insisting that only those who continue in the Christian way are the saints.

4 "For" (*gar*, omitted in NIV) indicates the reasonableness of what follows: Had they really fallen away, there would be no point in talking to them. Some see in the reference to being "enlightened" a glance at baptism, for this verb was often used of baptism in the second century. But it is not attested as early as this, and so it is better to interpret the term in the light of the general usage whereby those admitted to the Christian faith are brought to that light that is "the light of the world" (John 8:12; cf. 2 Cor 4:6; 2 Peter 1:19). To abandon the gospel would be to sin against the light they had received.

"The heavenly gift" is not closely defined. Some interpret it as the holy communion, though there seems little reason for this. It would fit well with the verb "tasted," but this verb can be used metaphorically; so the point proves little. The word "gift" (*dōrea*) points to freeness but could be used of any one of a variety of gifts. The thought is of God's good gift and we cannot be more precise than this. The Holy Spirit is active among all believers and for that matter to some extent beyond the church, in his work of "common grace." It is clear that some activity of the Spirit is in mind. Yet once more our author does not define it closely.

5 The people in question have "tasted the goodness of the word of God." While some limit this to the gospel, there seems to be no need and no point in doing this. Any word that God has spoken is a good gift to men, and those the writer has in mind here have come to hear something of God's word to men. They have also experienced something of "the powers of the coming age." The age to come is normally the Messianic Age, and the thought is that powers proper to the coming Messianic Age are in some sense realized now for God's people. "Powers" indicates that that age puts at men's disposal powers they do not have of themselves.

6 "If they fall away" means "fall away from Christianity." The verb *parapiptō* is found only here in the NT, and its meaning is clear. The writer is envisaging people who have been numbered among the followers of Christ but now leave that company. Such cannot be brought back to repentance. Notice that he does not say "cannot be forgiven" or "cannot be restored to salvation" or the like. It is repentance that is in mind, and the writer says that it is impossible for these people to repent. This might mean that the repentance that involves leaving a whole way of life to embrace the Christian way is unique. In the nature of the case, it cannot be repeated. There is no putting the clock back. But it seems more likely that the reference is to a repentance that means leaving the backsliding into which the person has fallen. He cannot bring himself to this repentance. The marginal reading "while they are crucifying the Son of God" is attractive, but in the end it really amounts to a truism and scarcely seems adequate. The tense, however, does convey the idea of a continuing attitude.

It is probable that we should take the verb rendered "are crucifying . . . all over again" (*anastaurountas*) simply as "crucifying." Elsewhere it seems always to have this meaning. The author is saying that those who deny Christ in this way are really taking their stand among those who crucified Jesus. In heart and mind they make themselves one with those who put him to death on the cross at Calvary. *Heautois* ("to themselves"; NIV, "to their loss") points to this inward attitude. The final words of v.6 stress what this attitude means.

There has been much discussion of the significance of this passage. Some think that the author is speaking about genuine Christians who fall away and that he denies that they may ever come back. This view sets the writer of the epistle in contradiction with other NT writers for whom it is clear that the perseverance of the saints is something that comes from God and not from their own best efforts (e.g., John 6:37; 10:27–29). Others think that the case is purely hypothetical. Because the writer does not say that this has ever happened, they infer that it never could really happen and that to put it this way makes the warning more impressive. But unless the writer is speaking of something that could really happen, it is not a warning about anything. Granted, he does not say that anyone has apostatized in this way, nevertheless, he surely means that someone could, and he does not want his readers to do so. A third possibility is that the writer is talking about what looks very much like the real thing but lacks something. The case of Simon Magus springs to mind. He is said to have believed, to have been baptized, and to have continued with Philip (Acts 8:13). Presumably he shared in the laying on of hands and the gift given by it. Yet after all this Peter could say to him, "Your heart is not right before God. . . . you are full of bitterness and captive to sin" (Acts 8:21–23). The writer is saying that when people have entered into the Christian experience far enough to know what it is all about and have then turned away, then, as far as they themselves are concerned, they are crucifying Christ. In that state they cannot repent. (For a good discussion of the various interpretations, see Kent, in loc.)

7 The process is illustrated from agriculture. There is land that frequently drinks in rain and as a result brings forth a crop. The rain comes first. The land does not produce the crop of itself. The spiritual parallel should not be overlooked. The word translated "a crop" (*botanē*) is a general term for herbage; it does not mean any specific crop. "Useful to those for whom it is farmed" means that the beneficiaries are people in general and not only those who actually work on the farm. This land, then, receives God's blessing.

8 We should not miss the point that this is the same land as in v.7. We should probably place a comma at the end of v.7 and proceed thus: "but if it produces . . ." or "but when it produces . . . ." The reference to producing "thorns and thistles" reminds us inevitably of the curse of Genesis 3:17ff.—a curse on that very creation of which it had been said, "God saw all that he had made, and it was very good" (Gen 1:31). This land then, producing only what is worthless, awaits the curse. "Is in danger of being cursed" might give the impression that the land came close to being cursed but just escaped. The author seems rather to be saying that at the moment of which he speaks the curse has not yet fallen, certain though it is. Such a field in the end "will be burned." Some commentators think the writer knew little of agriculture, for the burning of the field was not a curse but rather a source of blessing as it got rid of the weeds and so prepared for a good crop. But whatever his knowledge of farming, he had a valid point. Land that produced nothing but weeds faced nothing but fire. The warning to professing Christians whose lives produce only the equivalent of weeds is plain.

Notes

6 In the verb ἀνασταυρόω (*anastauroō*) the prefix ἀνα (*ana*) is usually taken in the sense of "up," "to lift up on a cross." In other compounds *ana* sometimes signifies "again," and this is why some take the verb here to mean recrucify. But as this sense is not attested elsewhere, it seems better to take it as "crucify."

D. Exhortation to Perseverance

6:9–12

> [9]Even though we speak like this, dear friends, we are confident of better things in your case—things that accompany salvation. [10]God is not unjust; he will not forget your work and the love you have shown him as you have helped his people and continue to help them. [11]We want each of you to show this same diligence to the very end, in order to make your hope sure. [12]We do not want you to become lazy, but to imitate those who through faith and patience inherit what has been promised.

The preceding sections have contained salutary warnings about the dangers of apostasy. The readers have had it made clear to them that they must make progress along the Christian way or suffer disaster. There are no other possibilities. Now the writer goes on to indicate that he has confidence in his correspondents. He has felt it necessary to warn them. But he does not really think they will fall away. So he speaks encouragingly and warmly, at the same time using the occasion to exhort them to go forward.

9 For the only time in the epistle the writer here addresses the readers as "beloved" (*agapētoi;* NIV, "dear friends"). He has a tender concern for his correspondents, even though he has had to say some critical things about them. "We are confident" (which is the first word in the Gr.) carries a note of certainty: "We are sure." He is sure that there are "better" things about them than the kind of disaster he has been speaking about. The writer is fond of the word "better" (see commentary on 1:4). He does not say what these good things are better than, but it is clearly implied that it is the cursing and the like that he has been speaking of. So he goes on and says, "And having salvation" (*echomena sōtērias*). This unusual expression might mean "things that lead to salvation" or "things that follow from salvation." Perhaps we should leave it general as NIV: "things that accompany salvation." The words "even though we speak like this" come last in the Greek and they simply look back. The "we" of course is a plural of authorship and means "I." The writer has been giving some solemn warnings and reminds the readers of them again. But he does not think that in the end they will be caught in the condemnation he refers to.

10 "For" (*gar,* which for some reason NIV does not translate) introduces the grounds for his confidence—a confidence that rests basically on God's constancy. In a masterly understatement the writer refers to God as "not unjust." It is the character of God, the perfectly just judge of all, that gives rise to confidence. This God will not forget what the readers have done. The statement about his remembrance of their work is not an intrusion of a doctrine of salvation by works. But the Christian profession of the readers had been more than formal and they had shown in changed lives what that profession meant. This, the writer is saying, would not go unnoticed with God. He adds, "And the love you have shown him" (lit., "to his name"). "Name" in antiquity summed up all that the person was. The following words show that it is deeds of kindness to men that are in mind. Such deeds, proceeding from loving hearts as they do, demonstrate that the doers have a real affection for God. These Christians have served God's people in the past and they continue with this kind of service. Thus they manifest the love for man that is a proof of real love for God (1 John 4:19–21).

11 "We want" translates a verb that refers to strong desire. The writer was passionately concerned for his friends, a concern that has already appeared in v.9 ("dear friends"; lit., "beloved"), and which we see again in his desire for "each" of them. Not one is excluded. He calls on them to show "this same diligence." The past had set a standard, and he looks for it to be maintained "to the very end." Persistently he brings before them the importance of perseverance. "In order to make your hope sure" renders a somewhat unusual expression (lit., "to the fullness of the hope"). The term *plēro-phoria* can mean "full assurance" (as in 1 Thess 1:5, where NIV has "deep conviction"). But here it is rather the full development of the hope. Notice that in these verses we have love (v.10) and faith (v.12) as well as hope. The three are often joined in the NT (Rom 5:2–5; 1 Cor 13:13; Gal 5:5–6; Col 1:4–5; 1 Thess 1:3; 5:8; Heb 10:22–24; 1 Peter 1:21–22). It was evidently an accepted Christian practice to link just these three. In the twentieth century we would easily think of faith and love for a similar short list. But hope? Clearly it had a greater significance for the early church than it has for us. Hope is important. Probably no movement has ever gripped the hearts of people if it did not give them hope.

12 The Greek does not have the verb "want" (as NIV), but the conjunction *hina* denotes purpose, i.e., "in order that you do not become lazy." The readers are to "imitate" those who get the promises, "imitate" and not simply "follow." Faith is important throughout this epistle, and it is not surprising to have it included here as a most important part of the Christian life. It is probably faith in God, as is usual in this epistle, that is meant here. "Patience," or "longsuffering," points to a quality of being undismayed in difficulties. Faith has a steadfastness about it that sees it through whatever difficulties present themselves.

The verb "inherit" is often used in the NT where there is no strict notion of inheritance, as here. It simply means "to have sure possession of" without specifying the means. It is uncertain whether the allusion is to the great ones of the past (as in ch. 11) or to outstanding contemporaries. Perhaps the present tense tips the scale in favor of those then living. The readers had good examples. Let them follow them.

E. *God's Promise Is Sure*

6:13–20

13When God made his promise to Abraham, since there was no one greater for him to swear by, he swore by himself, 14saying, "I will surely bless you and give you many descendants." 15And so after waiting patiently, Abraham received what was promised.
16Men swear by someone greater than themselves, and the oath confirms what is said and puts an end to all argument. 17Because God wanted to make the unchanging nature of his purpose very clear to the heirs of what was promised, he confirmed it with an oath. 18God did this so that, by two unchangeable things in which it is impossible for God to lie, we who have fled to take hold of the hope offered to us may be greatly encouraged. 19We have this hope as an anchor for the soul, firm and secure. It enters the inner sanctuary behind the curtain, 20where Jesus, who went before us, has entered on our behalf. He has become a high priest forever, in the order of Melchizedek.

Abraham is a splendid example of what the author has in mind. Though that patriarch had God's promise, he had to live for many years in patient expectation with nothing to go on except that God had promised. But that was enough. God is utterly reliable. What he has promised he will certainly perform. But we must wait patiently, for he does it all in his own good time, not in ours.

13 The author is fond of Abraham, whom he refers to ten times, a total exceeded only by Luke (fifteen) and John (eleven). Abraham is the supreme example of one who continued to trust God and obey him even though the circumstances were adverse and gave little support to faith. The NT often speaks of God's promise in connection with this man (Acts 3:25; 7:17; Rom 4:13; Gal 3:8,14,16,18). His greatness and the frequency with which God's promise was linked with his name made him a natural example for the author. It is the fact of the promise rather than its content that the author appeals to—especially to the fact that God confirmed it with an oath. Westcott (in loc.) points out that the oath in itself implies delay in fulfilling the promise. If God had been about to fulfill it immediately, there would have been no place for an oath. So from the first Abraham was faced with the prospect of waiting in hope and faith. God swore the oath by himself, a point mentioned by Philo (*Legum Allegoriae* 3.203). In the Talmud we read, "R. Eleazar said: Moses said before the Holy One, blessed be He: Sovereign of the Universe, hadst Thou sworn to them by the heaven and the earth, I would have said, Just as the heaven and earth can pass away, so can Thy oath pass away. Now, however, Thou hast sworn to them by Thy great name: just as Thy great name endures for ever and ever, so Thy oath is established for ever and ever" (*Berakoth* 32a; the oath is that mentioned in Exod 32:13). So here it is significant that God swore by himself. But for the present the author says no more than that there was no one greater to swear by.

14 The quotation is from Genesis 22:17. (That it was an oath is attested in Gen 22:16.) The few slight changes from the LXX do not affect the sense. "I will surely bless you" reflects the Hebrew infinitive absolute, which conveys the ideas of emphasis and certainty. This is the first occurrence of the word "bless" in this epistle. The author will use it seven times in all, as many as in all the Pauline epistles put together (and exceeded in the NT only by Luke [thirteen times]). Sometimes it is used of people, when it means "invoke blessings on" or sometimes "give thanks." But where God is the subject, the meaning is "bless," "prosper." Here the blessing refers to descendants who would form a great nation, possess the land, and in due course be the source of blessing to others.

15 "So" should not be taken too closely with "waiting patiently." It is not so much "waiting thus" as "thus [confident in God's promise] he waited patiently." Abraham was content to await God's time for the fulfillment of the promise. This meant real patience, because Isaac was not born till twenty-five years after the promise was first given (Gen 12:4; 21:5) and long after Sarah could have been expected to bear children. Abraham's grandchildren were not born for another sixty years (Gen 25:26), only fifteen years before his death (Gen 25:7). The complete fulfillment of the promise, of course, could not take place within his lifetime (a nation cannot be born so quickly). But enough happened for the writer to say, "Abraham received what was promised."

We should possibly bear in mind also John 8:56: "Abraham rejoiced at the thought of seeing my day; he saw it and was glad." In that sense Abraham saw the fuller working out of the promise. But the important thing in the present context is that Abraham had to be patient if he was to see anything in the way of fulfillment. He was patient and he did see it. So the readers are encouraged to be patient and await God's action. He does not go back on his promises. He is completely reliable. But he works in his own way and time, not ours.

16 The importance of the oath is now brought out. When a man swears an oath, he makes a solemn affirmation of the truth of his words before a greater who presumably will punish any misuse of his name if a false statement is made. The Greek here could mean "something greater." Yet NIV is surely right in preferring the masculine "someone greater."

Among people an oath "puts an end to all argument." The writer makes use of the expression *eis bebaiōsin*, which Deissmann calls an "Egyptian legal formula, persistent through hundreds of years" and which he says "is still a technical expression for a legal *guarantee*" (Deiss BS, p. 107). It was widely used in the papyri, and there is no doubt that the writer is making use of a well-known expression to bring out his point that an oath, as commonly understood, is the end of a matter. It is an authoritative word guaranteed by the highest authority.

17 We now turn from human oaths to the oath God swore to Abraham. God had no need to swear an oath. Nevertheless, he did it to make absolutely clear to his servant that his promise would be fulfilled. Abbott-Smith says that the verb NIV translates "wanted" (*boulomenos*) implies "more strongly than *thelō* . . . the deliberate exercise of volition" (s. v.). The operation of God's will is stressed and is further brought out by the reference to "the unchanging nature of his purpose" (where *boulē*, "purpose," is cognate with the word "wanted"). God's will does not change. He has his purpose and he works it out. That was what the oath said.

The word rendered "confirmed" is sometimes translated "interposed" or the like. *Mesiteuō* has the idea of "mediate," which often means "interpose," "stand between." But here the idea is rather that of "stand as guarantor." God appears, so to speak, in two characters, the giver of the promise and then its guarantor. "The only possible translation is 'to guarantee,' 'to vouch for.' In giving the promise, God is as it were one of the parties. But with His oath, and as its Guarantor,. . . He puts Himself on neutral ground and pledges the fulfillment of the promise" (Oepke, TDNT, 4:620). We should not miss the reference to "the heirs." The promise was not confined to Abraham or even to him and his immediate family. Since he was to have a mighty multitude of heirs, it was to all those who follow him, which includes not merely physical Israel but also his spiritual descendants (Gal 3:7). The readers of the epistle must number themselves among those to whom the oath referred.

18 "So that" (*hina*) introduces the purpose God had in swearing the oath. It gave men "two unchangeable things," the promise and the oath. Once God had spoken, it was inconceivable that either should alter. It is impossible for God to lie. At the end of the verse the sense may be as NIV, or we could understand it as "so that . . . we who have fled may have strong encouragement to lay hold on the hope." The word order favors NIV, but Héring, for one, prefers something like the second.

The writer does not specify what we have "fled" from, but the context makes it clear that he is thinking of some aspect of life in a sinful world. So far from clinging to that, he and his readers "take hold of the hope offered." Once again we see the importance of hope. It is the very antithesis of the despair that might grip us if we saw no more than a sinful world. But we do see more. We look forward to the consummation of God's great work of salvation. The word translated "offered" (*prokeimenēs*) pictures hope lying before us, spread out like some inviting prospect; and we are encouraged to go in to it.

19 While the metaphor of the anchor is widely used in antiquity, it occurs only here in the NT. The ship firmly anchored is safe from idle drifting. Its position and safety are sure. So hope is a stabilizing force for the Christian. "Soul" (*psychē*) may be the way to understand it, but the term is often used of the life of man and this seems to be the meaning here. The author is not saying simply that hope secures the "spiritual" aspect of man. He is affirming that hope forms an anchor for the whole of life. The person with a living hope has a steadying anchor in all he does. Westcott takes "firm" (*asphalēs*) to mean that hope "is undisturbed by outward influences" and "secure" (*bebaia*) as "firm in its inherent character" (in loc.). Perhaps we should not tie these qualities too tightly to the two words (which many point out are a standard expression in Gr. ethics). But the two aspects are important, and hope embraces them both.

And there is something more: hope "enters the inner sanctuary." The imagery takes us back to the tabernacle, with its "curtain" shutting off the Most Holy Place. That little room symbolized the very presence of God, but people were not allowed to enter it. But hope can, says the author. The Christian hope is not exhausted by what it sees of earthly possibilities. It reaches into the very presence of God.

20 We return to the imagery of the Day of Atonement, when the high priest entered the Most Holy Place on behalf of the people. Our forerunner, Jesus, has entered the holiest for us. This is something more than the Levitical high priest could do. Though he entered the Most Holy Place and made atonement on behalf of the people, at the end he and they were still outside. But to call Jesus our "forerunner" implies that we will follow in due course.

"On our behalf" indicates that Jesus did something for us. He not only showed the way but also atoned for us. So we come to the thought that he has become "a high priest forever, in the order of Melchizedek." The thought had been introduced in 5:6, but the author had gone on to other things. Now he comes back to that thought and proceeds to develop it.

Notes

14 This is the one place in the NT where we have the oath formula εἰ μήν (*ei mēn*) (classical ἦ μήν, *ē mēn*). This formula in oaths gives the meaning "surely," "certainly" (BAG, s. v.).
18 Some MSS have the article before θεόν (*theon*, "God"), but it should be omitted. The anarthrous form gives the thought "it is impossible for one who is God [one with the nature of God] to lie."

VI. Melchizedek

The writer has mentioned Melchizedek before and has spoken of Jesus as a priest of the Melchizedekian kind, but he has done no more than glance at the theme. Now he develops it. This is an understanding of Christ's work that is peculiar to this epistle, and in the author's hands it is very effective. He uses it to show something of the uniqueness of Christ and something of the greatness of the work he accomplished for humanity. For the Jews of his day, it would have been axiomatic that there was no priesthood other than the Aaronic. We are now shown that the Law itself proves that there is a higher priesthood than that.

A. *The Greatness of Melchizedek*

7:1–10

> [1] This Melchizedek was king of Salem and priest of God Most High. He met Abraham returning from the defeat of the kings and blessed him, [2]and Abraham gave him a tenth of everything. First, his name means "king of righteousness"; then also, "king of Salem" means "king of peace." [3]Without father or mother, without genealogy, without beginning of days or end of life, like the Son of God he remains a priest forever.
> [4]Just think how great he was: Even the patriarch Abraham gave him a tenth of the plunder! [5]Now the law requires the descendants of Levi who become priests to collect a tenth from the people—that is, their brothers—even though their brothers are descended from Abraham. [6]This man, however, did not trace his descent from Levi, yet he collected a tenth from Abraham and blessed him who had the promises. [7]And without doubt the lesser person is blessed by the greater. [8]In the one case, the tenth is collected by men who die; but in the other case, by him who is declared to be living. [9]One might even say that Levi, who collects the tenth, paid the tenth through Abraham, [10]because when Melchizedek met Abraham, Levi was still in the body of his ancestor.

The writer begins with a brief notice of the one incident recorded in the life of Melchizedek, namely his meeting with Abraham as the patriarch returned from the slaughter of the five kings (Gen 14:18–20; Melchizedek is mentioned again only in Ps 110:4). He draws attention to what is known of this man and reaches some important conclusions for Christians. He sees several reasons for regarding Melchizedek as superior: he took tithes from Abraham; he blessed him; he was "without beginning of days or end of life" (v.3); he "is declared to be living" (v.8, in contrast to the Aaronic priests who die); and Levi, the ancestor of the Levitical priests, paid him tithes (being included in Abraham).

1 The writer begins his explanation of the significance of Melchizedek by referring to the incident in Genesis 14:17ff. His minor changes from the LXX do not affect the sense. First he describes Melchizedek as "king of Salem," which may mean "king of Jerusalem" ("Salem" is another name for Jerusalem in Ps 76:2). But it is curious that if the writer thought that Jerusalem was in fact where Melchizedek ministered, he does not mention the fact that Jesus suffered there. Perhaps he was not particularly interested in geography. But it is also possible that he saw Salem as some other place. Westcott (in loc.) says that in Jerome's time Salem was understood to be near Scythopolis; and, again, the LXX of Genesis 33:18 seems to identify Shechem with Salem.

Melchizedek was not only a king but a "priest of God Most High." It was not uncommon for one person to combine the roles of priest and king in antiquity. It is, however, the special characteristics of this man rather than the dual offices that are noteworthy. In Genesis 14:17-18 we read that the king of Sodom, who had suffered at the hands of the kings Abraham had just routed, went out to meet the triumphant patriarch and that Melchizedek brought out bread and wine; but the author passes over both of these facts. He concentrates on those aspects of the incident that will help him make the points he has in mind about the work of Christ. The first of them is that he "blessed him," a point he will return to in v.7.

2 Abraham gave Melchizedek a tenth of everything, i.e., of the spoils from the battle. This is another point that is elaborated later (in vv.4ff.). So far the author is simply identifying Melchizedek with his reference to the incident after the battle. Now he goes on to the significance of Melchizedek's name and title. The name, he says, means "king of righteousness." (This is a translation of the Heb. name; it might be more accurate to render it "my king is righteous," but NIV gives the sense and brings in the noun "righteousness" that features so largely in the NT vocabulary of salvation.)

Then the writer goes on to the title "king of Salem." The place name comes from the same root as *šālôm*, the Hebrew word for "peace," and it may accordingly be translated in this way. The Greek word "peace" (*eirēnē*) has about it the negative idea of the absence of war; in the NT, however, it picks up something of the fuller meaning of the Hebrew *šālôm*, which it regularly translates in the LXX. So *eirēnē* comes to signify the presence of positive blessing, the result of Christ's work for men. We are reminded of the "Prince of Peace" (Isa 9:6; righteousness in v.7 is among the qualities linked with this messianic figure). The combination of righteousness and peace is seen in Psalm 85:10. As used here, the two terms point to distinctive aspects of Christ's saving work.

3 The terms "without father" and "without mother" (*apatōr, amētōr*) are used in Greek for waifs of unknown parentage, for illegitimate children, for people who came from unimportant families, and sometimes for deities who were supposed to take their origin from one sex only. Some scholars hold that Melchizedek is viewed in the last mentioned way and is being pictured as an angelic being. But it seems much more likely that the author is proceeding along the lines that the silences of Scripture are just as much due to inspiration as are its statements. When nothing is recorded of the parentage of this man, it is not necessarily to be assumed that he had no parents but simply that the absence of the record is significant.

What was true of Melchizedek simply as a matter of record was true of Christ in a fuller and more literal sense. So the silence of the Scripture points to an important theological truth. Melchizedek is also "without genealogy," a term the writer apparently coins. Taken together, the three terms are striking, for in antiquity a priest's genealogy was considered all-important. After the Exile, certain priests whose genealogy could not be established "were excluded from the priesthood as unclean" (Neh 7:64). And just as the record says nothing of Melchizedek's genealogy, so it says nothing of his birth or death. This further silence in Scripture points the writer to another truth about Jesus—viz., that his priesthood is without end. He uses the full title of Jesus—"Son of God"—as in 4:14; 6:6; 10:29 ("my son" in 1:5; 5:5). Since the writer does not use it often, we may sense an emphasis on the high dignity of the Son of God. And it is the Son of God who is the standard, not the ancient priest-king. The writer says that Melchizedek is "made like" (*aphōmoiōmenos*) the Son of God, not that the Son of God is like Melchizedek. Thus it is not that Melchizedek sets the pattern and Jesus follows it. Rather, the record about Melchizedek is so arranged that it brings out certain truths that apply far more fully to Jesus than they do to Melchizedek. With the latter, these truths are simply a matter of record; but with Jesus they are not only historically true, they also have significant spiritual dimensions. The writer is, of course, speaking of the Son's eternal nature, not of his appearance in the Incarnation.

4 The author proceeds to bring out the greatness of Melchizedek with an argument the modern mind may find rather curious but which would have been compelling to his contemporaries. In the ancient world, it was generally recognized that there was an obligation to pay tithes to important religious functionaries. This implies a certain subjection on the part of those paying to those to whom the tithe was paid. So it was significant that Abraham paid to Melchizedek "a tenth of the plunder." This last word means literally "the top of the heap" and was used of the choicest spoils of war. From these spoils an offering would be made to the gods as a thanksgiving for victory. Abraham gave a tenth of the very best to Melchizedek. In the Greek text the subject "the patriarch" comes at the end of the sentence, giving it strong emphasis; i.e., "none less than the patriarch."

5-6a Here the meaning of the payment of the tithe is spelled out. Not only was such a payment widely customary but the law required it to be made. The writer speaks of "the descendants of Levi who become priests" as "collecting a tenth from the people." In the law it was provided that the people were to pay tithes to the Levites (Num 18:21, 24). But the Levites similarly paid tithes to the priests (Num 18:26ff.); so it could well be said that the people paid tithes to the priests. In any case there seems to be some evidence that in the first century the priests carried out the whole tithing operation, and the writer may be glancing at contemporary custom. This tithing was done by divine appointment.

The writer is strongly interested in "the law," which he mentions fourteen times. The word can denote law in general or a principle according to which one acts. But it is specially used for the law of Moses, which is the meaning here. The law required tithes to be taken of people of whom the priests were "brothers." There is a sense in which the priests had no inherent superiority. They were kin to those who gave tithes to them. They owed their ability to collect tithes to the provision made in the law and not to any natural superiority. But with Melchizedek it was different. He "did not trace his descent from Levi." Melchizedek was not simply one among a host of brothers. He was a solitary figure of grandeur. And he exacted tithes not simply from his brothers but from Abraham. His greatness stands out.

6b-7 Not only did Melchizedek exact tithes from Abraham, but he also blessed him. The giving of a blessing was a significant act in antiquity. As Calvin puts it, "Blessing is a solemn act of prayer with which one who is endowed with some outstanding public honour commends to God private individuals who are under his care" (in loc). There are senses of the word "bless" in which men "bless" God, i.e., praise him, or in which an inferior prays that God will prosper some superior. But the word is not used in such a way here. It is rather the official pronouncement given by an authorized person. When that happens, there is no denying that it proceeds from a superior: "The lesser person is blessed by the greater."

In the Genesis account Melchizedek makes no claims nor does Abraham concede anything in words. But the patriarch gave up a tenth of the spoils, thus implicitly acknowledging the superior place of Melchizedek. And Melchizedek proceeded to bless Abraham, accepting the implied superiority. The situation is clear to all parties. There is no need to spell it out. And the author is simply drawing attention to what the narrative clearly implies when he brings out the superior status of Melchizedek. Even when Abraham is seen as the one "who had the promises," Melchizedek is superior.

8 NIV is a trifle free in this verse. Rather, it reads, "And, here, mortal ['dying'] men receive tithes, but, there, one of whom it is testified that he lives." Those who receive tithes are not merely capable of dying; they do die. They are seen to die. (The present tenses of both dying and receiving coupled with the "here" at the beginning may be held to indicate that the temple system was still in operation at the time the words were written. Thus they support a date before A.D. 70 for the writing of the epistle.) "There" puts Melchizedek in strong contrast to the Aaronic priests. He is remote from this scene. The writer does not say that Melchizedek lives on but that the testimony about him is that he lives. Once more he is emphasizing the silences of Scripture to bring out his point. Scripture records nothing about the death of Melchizedek. This must be borne in mind when estimating the significance of the incident and the way the priest-king prefigures Christ.

9–10 "One might even say" translates *hōs epos eipein*, an unusual expression (not found elsewhere in the NT or LXX) that "serves to introduce a statement which may startle a reader, and which requires to be guarded from misinterpretation" (Westcott, in loc). The characteristic of Levi (and his descendants) was not that of paying but of receiving tithes. Of course, there is something of the "in-a-manner-of-speaking" about Levi's collecting of tithes just as there is in his paying of them, because he collects them not in person but through his descendants. But the startling thing is that he should be said to pay tithes at all.

When Abraham paid Melchizedek a tithe, the author sees Levi as paying it, for "Levi was still in the body of his ancestor." This is a way of speaking we find here and there in the Bible when the ancestor includes the descendants. So it was said to Rebekah, not two children but "two nations are in your womb" (Gen 25:23). Again, Paul can say, "In Adam all die" (1 Cor 15:22). Levi was thus included in the payment of the tithe (and, of course, all the priests who descended from him and whom the Hebrews esteemed so highly). The author wants his readers to be in no doubt about the superiority of Christ to any other priests and sees the mysterious figure of Melchizedek as powerfully illustrating this superiority.

Notes

1 The full name "God Most High" is rare apart from the Melchizedek incident (but see Ps 78:35). But the title "Most High" (עֶלְיוֹן, *ʿelyôn*) is quite often used as a title for God.
3 "Forever" translates εἰς τὸ διηνεκές (*eis to diēnekes*), which occurs only in Hebrews in the NT (four times). It does not necessarily indicate duration without any end but rather duration which lasts through the circumstances indicated in the particular case. Here, however, no

limit is expressed or implied and the expression thus indicates that Melchizedek's priesthood goes right on without cessation.

5 "Descended from Abraham" is rather "come out from the loins of Abraham." Ὀσφῦς (osphys, "the waist, "loins") is used of the place where the belt is (Mark 1:6) and hence a number of metaphorical uses emerge, mostly concerned with preparation for activity ("girding up the loins," etc.). It is also used of the place of the reproductive organs and thus, as here, with reference to a man's descendants.

9 "One might even say" renders ὡς ἔπος εἰπεῖν (hōs epos eipein) which BDF refers to as "the so-called infinitive absolute after ὡς" and which "is fairly common in Attic in certain formulae" (par.391a). Héring rejects the meaning "so to speak" in favor of "to give the real point"(in loc.).

B. *The Royal Priesthood of Melchizedek and of Christ*

7:11-14

> [11]If perfection could have been attained through the Levitical priesthood (for on the basis of it the law was given to the people), why was there still need for another priest to come—one in the order of Melchizedek, not in the order of Aaron? [12]For when there is a change of the priesthood, there must also be a change of the law. [13]He of whom these things are said belonged to a different tribe, and no one from that tribe has ever served at the altar. [14]For it is clear that our Lord descended from Judah, and in regard to that tribe Moses said nothing about priests.

For the Jew there was an air of finality about the law; it was God's definitive word to men. Also, there was for the Jew the presumption that the Aaronic priesthood was superior to that of Melchizedek, for the law came later than Melchizedek and could be thought to be God's way of replacing all previous priesthoods. But the author points out that the priesthood of Melchizedek was spoken of in Psalm 110, well after the giving of the law. That God spoke through David about the Melchizedekian priesthood, while the Aaronic priesthood was a going concern, shows that the priests of the line of Aaron could not accomplish what a priesthood aimed at. And because the priesthood and the law went together, that meant a change in the law as well. The author sees it as significant that Jesus did not come from the priestly tribe of Levi but from the royal tribe of Judah. This fits in with the fact that Jesus' priesthood is of the order of Melchizedek and that he was king as well as priest.

11 Here "perfection" means the condition in which men are acceptable to God. The work of the priests of the line of Levi aimed at bringing about this acceptability, but our author tells us that they failed. That the psalmist speaks of another priest shows that the Levitical priests had not accomplished what they aimed at. The words in parenthesis show that the law and the priesthood were closely connected. Moffatt translates, "It was on the basis of that priesthood that the Law was enacted for the People."

We ought not think of the law and the priesthood as two quite separate things that happened to be operative at the same time among the same people. The priesthood is the very basis of the law. Without that priesthood it would be impossible for the law to operate in its fullness. Thus the declaration by the psalmist (v.17) that there would be another priest was devastating. He looked for a priest "in the order of

Melchizedek, not in the order of Aaron." The Aaronic priesthood was not succeeding and thus had to be replaced by a more effective priesthood.

12 The connection between the priesthood and the law means that a change in the one involves a change in the other. The author is speaking of more than a transference of the office of priest from one person to another. He is speaking of a change from one kind of priesthood to another. Priesthood like that of Melchizedek differs fundamentally from that after the order of Aaron. Christ is not another Aaron; he replaces Aaron with a priesthood that is both different and better. And with the Aaronic priesthood went the law that had been erected with that priesthood as its basis. Lacking that priesthood, that law had to give way. It had lost its basis. So the author says there *must* be a change of law.

13 The change in the law is seen in that Jesus did not belong to the tribe recognized by the law as the priestly tribe. His tribe was "different," which may mean no more than that it was another than the priestly tribe or that that tribe was of a different nature. It was a nonpriestly tribe. In fact, it was a royal tribe. From this tribe no one "has ever served at the altar." There is a change of tense from the perfect in the word translated "belonged" to an aorist in that rendered "served." Zuntz comments, "The differentiation is excellent; it intimates that no one of the tribe of Judah *had ever attended* to the altar (*prosesche*) and that Jesus '*has permanently a share in*' (*meteschēke,* 'belongs to') that tribe" (cited by Bruce, in loc.).

David and Solomon, who were of the tribe of Judah, are said to have offered sacrifice (2 Sam 6:12–13, 17–18; 24:25; 1 Kings 3:4; 8:62ff.). But two things should be said about this. In the first place, it is possible that these kings did not do the actual ceremonial. (It is unlikely that Solomon personally offered 22,000 oxen and 120,000 sheep.) David and Solomon may have "offered" in the sense that they provided the sacrificial victims, leaving priests to perform the liturgical function. And in the second place, even if these kings did sometimes perform the actual offering, this was occasional and not their regular function. The author is speaking of the regular ministrations of a priest at the altar, and this none but the sons of Aaron did in the OT period.

14 "For" introduces the explanation of the preceding. The author calls Jesus "our Lord" again only in 13:20. Mostly his use of the term "Lord" (*kyrios*) is for the Father, but there is no doubt as to whom he means here. His verb "descended" (*anatetalken*) is unusual in this sense; and Buchanan can go as far as to say, "In none of the Old Testament usages of the verb *anatellein* was it employed to mean a 'descendant' of a certain tribe or family" (in loc.). *Anatellein* means "rise," "spring up" and may be used of the rising of a star or of the springing up of a shoot from the roots of a plant. The author may have in mind the rising of a star or, more likely, the OT prophecies about the Messiah being a shoot from the root of David (Jer 23:5 uses the cognate noun for this purpose). Here in v. 14 Jesus is said to come "from Judah," this and Revelation 5:5 being the only places outside the nativity stories to say explicitly that this was his tribe. And to this tribe Moses had nothing to say about priests; the law did not envisage priests from any tribe other than Levi. That is what made the priesthood like that of Melchizedek so unusual.

Notes

---

11 There is dispute about the unexpected ἐπ᾽ αὐτῆς (*ep' autēs*). We might have anticipated περὶ αὐτῆς (*peri autēs*) or ἐπ᾽ αὐτήν (*ep' autēn*). Some take it in the sense of περὶ αὐτῆς (*peri autēs*), "about it," but it seems better to understand it as "on the basis of it" (with BAG; BDF, par. 234 [8]; NIV;etc.).

Νομοθετέω (*nomotheteō*) means "to make laws" and the passive here will have the sense "to be furnished with laws" (A-S, s.v.).

12 Ἱερωσύνη (*hierōsynē*) "priesthood" is used only in this ch. in the NT (vv. 12, 24). There does not seem special significance in this, but the word is certainly unusual.

13 Ἕτερος (*heteros*) strictly means "the other of two," and our author may be eliminating from his thinking all priesthoods but these two. But the word also sometimes means "different," and this may be his meaning.

C. Christ's Priesthood Superior Because of:

1. His life

7:15–19

> ¹⁵And what we have said is even more clear if another priest like Melchizedek appears, ¹⁶one who has become a priest not on the basis of a regulation as to his ancestry but on the basis of the power of an indestructible life. ¹⁷For it is declared:
>
> > "You are a priest forever,
> > in the order of Melchizedek."
>
> ¹⁸The former regulation is set aside because it was weak and useless ¹⁹(for the law made nothing perfect), and a better hope is introduced, by which we draw near to God.

The author pursues his theme of the superiority of Christ. He sees him as superior because of his life, the divine oath, the permanence of his priesthood, and his sacrifice. First, he indicates the importance of the fact that Christ is not limited by death as the Levitical priests were.

15 What it is that is "even more clear" is not said (there is nothing in the Gr. equivalent to NIV's "what we have said"). Westcott thinks it is the ineffectiveness of the Levitical priesthood; Moffatt, that it is the abrogation of the law. More likely the expression is general and is meant to include both—possibly also that Jesus came not from Levi but from Judah. It is the appearance of a priest "like Melchizedek" that is the decisive factor.

16 This priest is distinguished by the quality of his life. "A regulation as to his ancestry" renders an expression that is literally "a law of a fleshly commandment." This includes his ancestry, but it may well be wider. It includes all that is "fleshly" about the law. As Robinson puts it, the command "is one which belongs to the realm of man's physical nature, and bears only indirectly on his spiritual being" (in loc.). By contrast, Christ's priesthood depends on "the power" (which means more than "authority") "of an indestructible life." There is a special quality about the life of

Christ. Neither does it end nor can it end (cf. the description of him as "the prince" or "author of life,'" Acts 3:15).

17 "For" introduces the clinching testimony of Scripture. The passage cited gives the reason for the foregoing. It is quoted verbatim as in 5:6 (where see commentary). It establishes the special character of Christ's priesthood because of no other priest could it be said that his life was "indestructible." Though it could be said that the Aaronic priesthood was "a priesthood that will continue for all generations" (Exod 40:15), no individual priest is "forever."

18 The opening words might more literally be rendered "For there is an annulling of a foregoing commandment," where "annulling" is a legal term that points to the complete cancellation of the commandment in question. "Regulation" refers as in v. 16, to the whole law. The Levitical system in its entirety is set aside by the coming and the work of Christ. At the same time, "former" (*proagousēs*) implies a connection. The Levitical system was not simply earlier in time; it also prepared the way for the coming of Christ. But it had to give way because it was weak and unprofitable. It could not give men strength to meet all the needs of life. It could not bring men salvation.

19 The parenthesis underlines the defects of the law. The writer does not explain what he means by "made perfect" (see comments on 2:10), but clearly he has in mind something like "made fit for God." The law did not give people complete and lasting access to the presence of God. It had its merits, but it did not satisfy their deep needs. For the writer's use of "better," see comments on 1:4; and for his use of "hope," see comments on 3:6; 6:11. The thought of what is better is characteristic of Hebrews, and hope is central to the Christian way. Notice that the hope is said to be better than the regulation or commandment, not better than the hope associated with the commandment. Law and gospel stand in contrast. The gospel is "better" because it enables people to "draw near to God." It was this that the old way could not bring about, but the new way can.

2. The divine oath

7:20–22

> 20And it was not without an oath! Others became priests without any oath, 21but he became a priest with an oath when God said to him:
>
> > "The Lord has sworn
> > and will not change his mind:
> > 'You are a priest forever.' "
>
> 22Because of this oath, Jesus has become the guarantee of a better covenant.

The argument is now developed with reference to the oath that established the priesthood after the order of Melchizedek. There was no such oath when the Aaronic priesthood was set up, which means that this priesthood lacks the permanence so characteristic of the priesthood after the order of Melchizedek. There was always something conditional about Aaron's priesthood.

20–21 The oath declares the purpose of God in an absolute fashion. It allows of no qualification on account of human weakness or sinfulness or anything else. So the writer contrasts the priesthood that has the security of the divine oath to that which lacked it. Christ is contrasted with the Levitical priests, and the importance of the oath is stressed. It was not simply that an oath was sworn at the same time he was made priest but that the oath was the very essence of what was done. That is the point of the argument. The psalm is quoted once more, this time beginning a little earlier to include the reference to the swearing of the oath and the assurance that the Lord will not change his mind. The new priesthood is permanent. There is no question of its ever being done away.

22 "Guarantee" translates a word found only here in the NT (*engyos*) and it brings before us an unusual idea. The old covenant was established, as Bruce (in loc.) points out, with a mediator (Gal 3:19) but with no one to guarantee that the people would fulfill their undertaking. But Jesus stands as a continuing guarantor and that in two directions. He guarantees to men that God will fulfill his covenant of forgiveness, and he guarantees to God that those who are in him are acceptable.

This is the writer's first use of the term "covenant" (*diathēkē*), a word whose importance for him may be gauged from the fact that he uses it no fewer than seventeen times, whereas in no other NT book is it found more than three times. In nonbiblical Greek it denotes a last will and testament, but in the LXX it is the normal rendering of the Hebrew *berît* ("covenant"). It is agreed that in NT *diathēkē* mostly means "covenant." It also seems, however, that now and then the meaning "testament" is not out of mind (e.g., 9:16). The author may have chosen this word rather than *synthēkē*, the usual word for "covenant," because the latter might suggest an agreement made on more or less equal terms. By contrast, there is something absolute about a will. One cannot dicker with the testator. And in like manner man cannot bargain with God. God lays down the terms. (See further my *Apostolic Preaching of the Cross* 3rd ed. [Grand Rapids: Eerdmans, 1965] ch.2).

Notes

20 The periphrastic perfect tense εἰσὶν γεγονότες (*eisin gegonotes*, "became," NIV) is unusual and may be meant to indicate a continuing state. Christ's priesthood lasts eternally whereas theirs terminates, but within that framework there is a certain element of continuance.
21 Ὁ δέ (*ho de*, "but he") sets Christ in contrast to the Levitical priests, answering as it does to the οἱ μέν (*hoi men*, "they") of the previous verse. So also μετά (*meta*, "with") stands over against χωρίς (*chōris*, "without").
22 There is no "oath" in the text, but NIV gives the sense, as κατὰ τοσοῦτο (*kata tosouto*) answers to καθ' ὅσον (*kath' hoson*) in v.20.

3. *Its permanence*

7:23-25

> ²³Now there were many of those priests, since death prevented them from continuing in office; ²⁴but because Jesus lives forever, he has a permanent priesthood. ²⁵Therefore he is able to save completely those who come to God through him, because he always lives to intercede for them.

It matters to the author that Christ's life was different in quality from other lives. He has emphasized this in vv.15ff. and he comes back to it with the thought that the permanence of Christ's priesthood makes it superior to the Levitical priesthood. His life is such that there is no need and no place for a successor.

23-24 Once more the Levitical priests are set in contrast to Christ. They had to be numerous because like all men they died, and successors were needed to keep the priesthood functioning. Josephus says that there were eighty-three high priests from Aaron to the destruction of the temple in A.D. 70 (Antiq. XX, 227 [x.1]; the Tal says there were eighteen during the first temple and more than three hundred during the second, *Yoma* 9a).

Death was inevitable for the Aaronic priests and it meant the cessation of their exercise of the high priesthood. But with Christ it is different. He remains forever and thus his priesthood never has to be continued by another. The word rendered "permanent" (*aparabatos*) is found nowhere else in the NT. It is often understood to mean "without a successor," but this meaning does not seem to be demonstrated. The word means "that cannot be transgressed," or, as Abbott-Smith puts it, "*inviolable*, and so unchangeable" (s.v.). Christ lives through eternity, and his priesthood lives with him. The quality of his life means a quality of priesthood that cannot be matched by the Levitical priests.

25 From Christ's unchanging priesthood the author draws an important conclusion about the salvation Christ accomplishes. The verb "to save" (*sōzō*) is used absolutely, which means that Christ will save in the most comprehensive sense; he saves from all that humanity needs saving from. The expression rendered "completely" (*eis to panteles*) is an unusual one, used again in the NT only in Luke 13:11 of the woman who could not straighten herself "completely" ("at all," NIV). This may well be the sense of it here, too. Christ's salvation is a complete deliverance, no matter what the need of the sinner. Some take the word *panteles* in a temporal sense and see it as scarcely differing from "forever" or "always." There is more to be said for the former meaning, though the latter is not impossible. The verb "is able" (*dynatai*) refers to power. Christ's inviolable priesthood, a priesthood that can never be put away, means that he has the capacity (as others have not) of bringing a complete salvation to all who approach God through him.

At the end of the verse we find that Christ intercedes for those who come to him (cf. Rom 8:34). This is sometimes made the vehicle of strange theories, such as the one that says that Christ is always pleading his sacrifice in heaven while worshipers on earth do the same thing in the Holy Communion. It must be stressed that there is no thought of Christ as a humble suppliant. Rather, he is supreme and his very presence in heaven in his character as the one who died for mankind and rose again is itself an intercession. As Snell puts it, "We must be careful not to infer from this verse, or from the last phrase of 9:24, that the author thought of our Lord as having to maintain a kind of continuous liturgical action in heaven for our benefit . . . the meaning is that our Lord's presence in heaven, *seated* at God's right hand, and awaiting the full manifestation of his already achieved victory, itself constitutes his effective intercession for us" (in loc.).

Notes

24 Μένειν (*menein*, "remain"; NIV, "lives") takes up παραμένειν (*paramenein*, "remain with"; NIV, "continuing") of the previous verse: the Levitical priest could not "remain with" men but he does "remain."

4. His better sacrifice

7:26–28

26Such a high priest meets our need—one who is holy, blameless, pure, set apart from sinners, exalted above the heavens. 27Unlike the other high priests, he does not need to offer sacrifices day after day, first for his own sins, and then for the sins of the people. He sacrificed for their sins once for all when he offered himself. 28For the law appoints as high priests men who are weak; but the oath, which came after the law, appointed the Son, who has been made perfect forever.

This section of the study is rounded off with a glowing description of Christ as our High Priest, better qualified than the Levitical priests, and one who offered a better sacrifice than they did.

26 NIV omits the important word "for" (*gar*) that links this proposition to the preceding one. It is because Christ is what he is that he intercedes as he does. "Meets our need" is literally "is fitting for us" (*hēmin eprepen*). Even our human sense of the fitness of things is able to recognize Christ's suitability for his saving work.

There are two Greek words for "holy," one (*hagios*) refers to the quality of separateness, of belonging to God, and the other (*hosios*) signifies rather the character involved in that separation. *Hosios* is used here. He is also "blameless" (*akakos*, "without evil," "innocent") and "pure" (*amiantos*). "Pure" contains the thought of being undefiled, and there may be a contrast between the ritual purity the Levitical high priest must be careful to maintain and the complete moral purity of Jesus.

There is probably another contrast in the words "set apart from sinners," for the Levitical high priest was required to leave his home seven days before the Day of Atonement and live in such a manner as to ensure that he avoided ritual defilement (M *Yoma* 1.1). But Jesus' separation was not ritual. Some think the words refer to his spotless character and think he is being contrasted with sinful men. It is more likely that we should take the words closely with the following. His work on earth is done. He has accomplished his sacrifice. He has been "exalted above the heavens." This makes him the perfect intercessor.

27 There is a problem in the reference to offering sacrifices "day after day" for, while there were daily sacrifices in the temple, the high priest was not required to offer them personally; and the sacrifices that did demand his personal action, those on the Day of Atonement, took place once a year not once a day, a fact the author well knows (9:7,25; 10:1). Some have thought that we should understand the words to mean not that the high priest offered every day but that he felt the need to offer every day. Others think that Christ's high priestly office, unlike that of the Levitical high priests which involved repeated offerings, is fulfilled daily by his one sacrifice. Such solutions

have their attraction. Yet it is not easy to reconcile them with the actual words used. Bruce (in loc.) reminds us that it was always possible for the high priest, as for other people, to commit inadvertent sin, which required the offering of a sin offering (Lev 4:2–3) and that thus the high priest needed to offer daily (to ensure his fitness for ministry). We should also bear in mind that Leviticus requires the high priest to offer the cereal offering each day (Lev 6:19–23; notice that it is "the son [not all the priests] who is to succeed him [Aaron] as anointed priest" who is required to offer this offering [v.22]). This was regarded as expiatory (Lev R 3:3).

Jesus stands in contrast to the earthly priests. He has no need to offer for his own sins because he has none (4:15). And he has no need to keep offering for the sins of the people, for his one sacrifice has perfectly accomplished this. They were sinful men and had to provide for the putting away of their own sin before they were in a fit condition to do anything about the sins of the people. What they did for themselves, they then proceeded to do for others. But Christ's offering is different. There is none for himself. And for others, he offered "once for all" (*ephapax*). There is an air of utter finality about this expression. It is characteristic of the author that he introduces the thought of Christ's sacrifice but does not elaborate. He will return to the thought later and develop it.

28 Here the contrast between men with all their infirmities and the Son with his eternal perfection is further brought out. "The law" brings us back to the law of Moses, the law of divine origin indeed, but the law that necessarily operates among men with all their weakness. And when the law appoints high priests, they must be limited as all men are limited. There is no other possibility. The "weakness" (*astheneia*) refers to "the frailty to which all human flesh is heir" (BAG, s.v.). Priests are not made from some super race but from ordinary men, with all the frailty that characterizes ordinary men.

"But" introduces the contrast: the oath makes the difference. This, we are reminded, "came after the law" and so cannot be thought of as superseded by it. The oath has the last word, not the law. And the oath appointed the Son. Actually Psalm 110, which speaks of the oath, does not mention the Son, who is referred to in Psalm 2. But the author sees both psalms as referring to Jesus; so he has no difficulty in applying terminology taken from the one to a situation relating to the other. And the Son "has been made perfect forever." He has been made perfect through those sufferings (2:10) that bring people to God.

Notes

26 We should notice the transition from the perfect participle κεχωρισμένος (*kechōrismenos,* "set apart from") to the aorist γενόμενος (*genomenos,* "having been"; untranslated in NIV). Christ continues in his state of separation, after the single event of his exaltation.

VII. A New and Better Covenant

Throughout the OT period the relationship of the people of God to their God was characteristically viewed in terms of covenant. Indeed, it would not be too much to say that covenant was fundamental to the thinking and outlook of the men of the old way. "It included every aspect of the relation of Israel to Yahweh" (Robinson, MNT, *Hebrews*, p. 112). It is accordingly something radically new and daring to maintain that this whole system has been done away and replaced by a new covenant. And central to the new covenant is the death of Jesus, the sacrifice that established the new covenant. The demonstration of what all this means spells out the end of the Mosaic system. The author shows that once the Christian way is understood, there is no place for the old system.

A. Christ's "More Excellent" Ministry

8:1–7

> [1]The point of what we are saying is this: We do have such a high priest, who sat down at the right hand of the throne of the Majesty in heaven, [2]and who serves in the sanctuary, the true tabernacle set up by the Lord, not by man.
> [3]Every high priest is appointed to offer both gifts and sacrifices, and so it was necessary for this one also to have something to offer. [4]If he were on earth, he would not be a priest, for there are already men who offer the gifts prescribed by the law. [5]They serve at a sanctuary that is a copy and shadow of what is in heaven. This is why Moses was warned when he was about to build the tabernacle: "See to it that you make everything according to the pattern shown you on the mountain." [6]But the ministry Jesus has received is as superior to theirs as the covenant of which he is mediator is superior to the old one, and it is founded on better promises.
> [7]For if there had been nothing wrong with that first covenant, no place would have been sought for another.

The author leads on from his treatment of the priesthood after the order of Melchizedek to emphasize the point that Christ's ministry far surpasses that of the Levitical priests. The readers of the epistle would be familiar with this priesthood, and the writer wants it to be clear that Jesus has a ministry far excelling it.

1 The problem in this verse is whether we should understand *kephalaion* in the sense of "the chief point" or "to sum up." While the word could have either meaning, here it seems that something like "the chief point" is required. The words that follow are not a summary of what has gone before (nor do they summarize the argument that is to be developed). The present participle *legomenois* (NIV, "what we are saying") does not suit a summary, and the same must be said of the introduction of new material (e.g., "the true tabernacle" [v.2]). The writer is rather picking out the principal point and proceeding to develop it. There is also something of an ambiguity with "such," which might be taken with the preceding ("such as we have just described") or with the following ("such that he sat down . . ."). The stress on his high place perhaps favors the latter. We have, then, a high priest who is so great that he took his seat at God's right hand. "The Majesty in heaven" is a reverent way of referring to God, and to be at his right hand is to be in the place of highest honor (see comments on 1:3). The posture of sitting points to a completed work. "Heaven" can be used in a variety of ways, but here it clearly means the dwelling place of God.

2 "The sanctuary" renders *tōn hagiōn*, which might mean "of holy men," but in this context almost certainly means "of holy things," i.e., the sanctuary. NIV has taken the noun *leitourgos* ("minister," "servant") and made it into a verb—"who serves."

The word is used of one who engages in any one of a variety of forms of public service. In the Bible, however, it seems to be confined to the service of God, though it includes what is done by pagan officials (Rom 13:6). It is used also of angels (1:7) and of men (Rom 15:16; Phil 2:25). It speaks of Christ in his capacity as servant, which is striking, as it immediately follows the reference to his high place in heaven.

The "tabernacle" takes us back to the wilderness days. The word means no more than "tent" and could be used of tents that people lived in. But it was also used of the tent used for worship during the wilderness wanderings (e.g., Exod 27:21). That earthly tent corresponds to a heavenly reality, and it is in the heavenly reality that Christ's ministry is exercised. "True" (*alēthinos*) means true "in the sense of the reality possessed only by the archetype, not by its copies" (BAG, s.v.). This is further brought out with the statement that the Lord pitched it, not man. Sin is dealt with in the way and in the place determined by God.

3 The author has already said in 5:1 that high priests are appointed to offer sacrifices. "For" (which NIV omits) links the argument to the preceding. Christ is ministering in the real tabernacle because to offer sacrifice is of the essence of being high priest. So the writer finds it "necessary" that Christ have something to offer. The Greek has no verb here and some understand the phrase in the sense of "it *is* necessary." NIV is, however, surely right. The author is referring to one offering made once for all, not a continuous offering always being made in heaven. Christ is eternally High Priest, for he never loses his status. But to say that he is eternally offering is quite another thing and one to which this epistle lends no support. It is characteristic of the author that he does not say what is offered at this point; having introduced the subject, he will explain it more fully later (9:14; cf. also 7:27).

4 We must be clear that Christ's priesthood is not one of this earth (though his offering of himself took place here). There are divinely appointed earthly priests, and Jesus has no place among them. On earth Jesus was a layman. He performed no priestly functions in any earthly sanctuary. Those functions were performed by the priests to whom God had entrusted them. Christ's priestly functions must obviously, then, be exercised elsewhere, in the true sanctuary in heaven.

5 The earthly priests serve in a sanctuary they value highly, though it is no more than "a copy and shadow of what is in heaven." There has been much discussion as to how "Platonic" this idea is. Some remind us that Plato thought of heavenly "ideas" as the archetypes of all things earthly. They think that the author has used the thought of an earthly sanctuary as no more than the imperfect actualization of a Platonic heavenly sanctuary. Others point out that the idea of heavenly counterparts of earthly objects was widespread. For example, we read of the heavenly temple in the Testament of Levi 5:1 and in Wisdom of Solomon 9:8, which says, "Thou hast given command to build a temple on thy holy mountain, and an altar in the city of thy habitation, a copy of the holy tent which thou didst prepare from the beginning."

There can be no question but that there is enough of the heavenly counterpart concept in Jewish sources for us to maintain that the author need not have been dependent on Plato. However, he does not say that the earthly was an exact copy of the heavenly, as the rabbis apparently did. There is a good deal to be said for the idea that his language is that of the Alexandrian modification of Platonism. This does not mean that he is using the distinction out of strong philosophic views but that he is using popular terminology with such associations. His main thought accords with the OT model, though he adds the idea that the earthly is but imperfect. It is the heavenly that is real. Inevitably the ministry of the Levitical priests was defective; they could serve only the "copy and shadow." So we are reminded of the Lord's words to Moses that he must make everything "according to the pattern shown [him] on the mountain" (Exod 25:40). The rabbis often appealed to the Mosaic example (see SBK pp. 702–4). For example, they said, "An ark of fire and a table of fire and a candlestick of fire came down from heaven; and these Moses saw and reproduced" (Tal *Menahoth* 29a; the passage goes on to affirm that Moses did this "after their pattern" and not merely "according to the fashion thereof").

6 The ministry of priests in a sanctuary made according to the heavenly pattern is obviously one of great dignity. But the author's point is that Jesus' ministry in the heavenly archetype is of incomparably greater dignity and worth. He chooses to bring this out by using a comparison of the two covenants. Jesus is the mediator of a better covenant. "Mediator" is a legal term for one who arbitrates between two parties. The thought is that Christ mediates between men and God; it is he who establishes the new covenant (for this latter term see comments 7:22). This new covenant is better than the old because it is "founded on better promises." Calvin reminds us that "the same salvation" was promised to the ancients (in loc.). But the new covenant is explicitly based on the forgiveness of sins, as the author goes on to show; and the better promises may be held to refer to the concentration on spiritual things in the new covenant (there is a good deal about possessing the land and the like in the old covenant) and in its unconditional nature.

7 The author brings out the superiority of the new covenant by referring to the supersession of the old one. If there had been "nothing wrong" with the old covenant, there would have been no place for the new. That the new covenant has now been established is itself evidence that the old one was not adequate. (For the line of argument, cf. 7:11ff.) The old covenant was lacking not so much in what its terms spelled out as in the fact that it was weak and unable to bring men to God (cf. 7:18f.; Rom 7:10f.).

Notes

1 "Heaven" is plural (οὐρανοῖς, *ouranois*), as in seven instances out of the ten in Hebrews. But there seems to be no distinction between singular and plural in this epistle (we have the plural in 9:23 and the singular in 9:24 with no apparent change in meaning). The preference for the plural probably does not indicate a belief in a plurality of heavens but is a stylistic feature. In Rev the singular is used in every case but one, whereas in Eph the word is always plural.
2 "The Lord" is ὁ κύριος (*ho kyrios*). In this epistle the form with the article seems usually to mean Christ, whereas that without the article means the Father. It is hard to see a reason for the variation here and in v.11.

B. *The Old Covenant Superseded*

8:8–13

⁸But God found fault with the people and said:

> "The time is coming, declares the Lord,
>   when I will make a new covenant
> with the house of Israel
>   and with the house of Judah.
> ⁹It will not be like the covenant
>   I made with their forefathers
> when I took them by the hand
>   to lead them out of Egypt,
> because they did not remain faithful to my covenant,
>   and I turned away from them,
>   declares the Lord.
> ¹⁰This is the covenant I will make with the house of Israel
>   after that time, declares the Lord.
> I will put my laws in their minds
>   and write them on their hearts.
> I will be their God,
>   and they will be my people.
> ¹¹No longer will a man teach his neighbor,
>   or a man his brother, saying, 'Know the Lord,'
> because they will all know me,
>   from the least of them to the greatest.
> ¹²For I will forgive their wickedness
>   and will remember their sins no more."

¹³By calling this covenant "new," he has made the first one obsolete; and what is obsolete and aging will soon disappear.

This long quotation from Jeremiah 31:31–34 makes the point that the old covenant under which Israel has had its religious experience is now superseded by a new covenant. The author's interest is in the fact that under the new covenant forgiveness of sins is brought about. As soon as he comes to the words about forgiveness, he breaks off his quotation.

8 The writer proceeds to show that a place was indeed sought for a new covenant. He begins by telling us that God found fault with the men of old, and this leads to the quotation from Jeremiah 31:31ff., which differs only slightly from the LXX reading. The Greek says only "he says." But NIV is correct in inserting "God" as subject. It is the author's habit to ascribe what is found in Scripture to God. "I will make" (*synteleso*) is not the usual word for making a covenant but one with a meaning like "I will bring a new covenant to accomplishment" (BAG, s.v.). There may be the thought that the covenant is all of God. Men do not bargain with God and come to an acceptable compromise. In any covenant with God, it is God who lays down the terms (for "covenant," cf. comments on 7:22). The prophet looks for the unification of "the house of Israel" and "the house of Judah." They had long been separated when Jeremiah wrote, but his vision was large enough to take in both and to look for the day when they would be one.

9 The new covenant is contrasted with the old one. Calvin points out that the prophet does not say, "I will renew the covenant which has failed by your fault," but "he says expressly that it will be different" (in loc.). It will not be simply the old one patched up and renewed. The differences will be those mentioned in the following verses, especially the way the new covenant brings forgiveness of sins. But first the kindness and the love of God are brought out by the reference to taking the people "by the hand" to bring them out of Egypt. The metaphor is that of a father or mother taking a little child by the hand to lead him safely to the place where he is going (cf. Hos 11:1–4). Egypt had been a place of slavery. Yet God had brought Israel out of it to set up the old covenant. But Israelites lacked perseverance. The emphatic pronouns set "they" and "I" over against each other. They refused to remain faithful but found no less a one than God ranged against them. "I turned away from them" is a strong expression (*emelēsa autōn*), with a meaning like "I ignored them" (Buchanan, in loc.) or perhaps "I abandoned them" (NEB).

10 From the failures of the past, Jeremiah turns his vision to the future. Again he sees a united people as he thinks of the covenant being made with "the house of Israel." It will be made "after that time," which clearly refers to the future but does not locate it with any precision. The repeated "declares the Lord" keeps before the reader the truth that a divine and not a human act is in mind. The first point is that the new covenant is inward and dynamic: it is written on the hearts and minds of the people. A defect in the old had been its outwardness. It had divinely given laws, indeed; but it was written on tablets of stone (Exod 32:15–16). The people had not been able to live up to what they knew was the word from God. It remained external. Jeremiah looked for a time when people would not simply obey an external code but would be so transformed that God's own laws would be written in their inmost beings. We should probably not distinguish too sharply between "minds" and "hearts," for in poetic parallelism such expressions are close in meaning. But if there is a difference, "hearts" is the more inclusive term, standing for the whole of the inner life.

The second point in the new covenant is that there will be a close relationship between the God who will be "their God" and the people who, he says, will be "my people." There is nothing really new in the terms of this promise, for in connection with the old way it was said, "I will take you as my own people, and I will be your God" (Exod 6:7). But Bruce is certainly correct in saying, "While the 'formula' of the covenant remains the same from age to age, it is capable of being filled with fresh meaning to a point where it can be described as a *new* covenant. 'I will be your God' acquires fuller meaning with every further revelation of the character of God" (in loc.). The life, death, resurrection, and ascension of Jesus mean that God has acted decisively to save a people. The God who saves people in Christ is the God of his redeemed in a new and definitive way. And when people have been saved at the awful cost of Calvary, they are the people of God in a way never before known.

11 The third significant feature of the new covenant is that all who enter it will have knowledge of God. There will be no need for a person to instruct his neighbor. The word rendered "neighbor" (*politēs*) means a "citizen" (as in Luke 15:15), and thus a "fellow-citizen." Jeremiah moves from the wider relationship in the community to the narrower relationship in the family and says that in neither case will there be the need for exhorting anyone to know God. For "from the least of them to the greatest," all will know God. This does not mean that in the conditions of the new covenant there will be no place for a teacher. There will always be the need for those who have advanced in the Christian way to pass on to others the benefit of their knowledge. Rather, the meaning is that the knowledge of God will not be confined to a privileged few. All those in the new covenant will have their own intimate and personal knowledge of their God.

12 The fourth significant thing about the new covenant is that in it sins are forgiven. "For" shows the important point that it is God's forgiveness that is the basis of what has gone before. It is because sins are really dealt with that the blessings enumerated earlier become possible. And those sins really are dealt with. God's wrath no longer rests on the sinner and God does not bear his sins in mind. They are completely forgotten. We might get some of the force of all this by reflecting that the men of Qumran saw themselves as the men of the new covenant. But for them that meant looking forward to a day when the corrupt priesthood in Jerusalem would be deposed and replaced by those they regarded as the true priests and when the whole temple ritual with its never-ceasing round of sacrifices would be carried on in the way they approved in a kind of ritualist's paradise! For the writer of this epistle, there was no more sacrifice. The one sacrifice that avails has been offered once and for all. Therefore sin has been completely and finally dealt with; it is a problem no longer.

13 The author picks out the word "new" (cf. v. 8) and sees it as making his essential point. It implies that something else is "old" and that the old is to be replaced. When God speaks of a "new" covenant, then, it means that the old one is obsolete. And that in turn means that it is close to disappearing. It is not something people should go back to with nostalgia. The words used of it emphasize that it is ineffective, unable to meet people's needs, outworn.

The idea of the new covenant is not confined to this epistle. It is implied in the narratives of the institution of the Lord's Supper in the first two Gospels (Matt 26:27–28; Mark 14:23–24). What is the meaning of "covenant" in these passages unless the new covenant is in mind? And it is explicit in Luke's longer narrative (Luke 22:20) and in Paul's account (1 Cor 11:25). Paul also saw Christian ministers as "ministers of a new covenant" (2 Cor 3:6). The new covenant is thus one of the strands in the NT teaching about what Christ has done for us. While it emphasizes radical novelty, we should not overlook the fact that it also points to continuity. The new arrangement retains the term "covenant" and it is established on the basis of sacrifice. It refers to the fulfillment of what is superseded rather than outright opposition to it.

Notes

8 The verb for "making" the covenant is συντελέω (*synteleō*) used only here in the NT in this sense. The usual word is διατίθημι (*diatithēmi*) (8:10; 10:16; Acts 3:25), but ποιέω (*poieō*) (8:9) and ἐντέλλομαι (*entellomai*, "command") (9:20) are also used. The thought conveyed is that God is in charge. He dictates the terms.
10 It is not certain whether we should take ἐπὶ καρδίας (*epi kardias*, "on their hearts") as genitive singular or accusative plural. The corresponding word in the original is singular, which favors the singular here. But most take the similar expression in 10:16 to be plural. The sense is not greatly affected.

C. *The Old Sanctuary and Its Ritual*

9:1-10

> [1]Now the first covenant had regulations for worship and also an earthly sanctuary. [2]A tabernacle was set up. In its first room were the lampstand, the table and the consecrated bread; this was called the Holy Place. [3]Behind the second curtain was a room called the Most Holy Place, [4]which had the golden altar of incense and the gold-covered ark of the covenant. This ark contained the gold jar of manna, Aaron's rod that had budded, and the stone tablets of the covenant. [5]Above the ark were the cherubim of the Glory, overshadowing the place of atonement. But we cannot discuss these things in detail now.
> [6]When everything had been arranged like this, the priests entered regularly into the outer room to carry on their ministry. [7]But only the high priest entered the inner room, and that only once a year, and never without blood, which he offered for himself and for the sins the people had committed in ignorance. [8]The Holy Spirit was showing by this that the way into the Most Holy Place had not yet been disclosed as long as the first tabernacle was still standing. [9]This is an illustration for the present time, indicating that the gifts and sacrifices being offered were not able to clear the conscience of the worshiper. [10]They are only a matter of food and drink and various ceremonial washings—external regulations applying until the time of the new order.

The author proceeds to bring out the superiority of the new covenant by pointing to the significance of the way of worship in the old one. Interestingly, he concentrates his attention not on the temple but on the long-vanished tabernacle, which would have had a wider appeal to Jews than the temple had. The temple was accessible only to those in Jerusalem; but wherever Jews were, their Scriptures told them all about the tabernacle. And in any case it was the synagogue rather than the temple that was the center of worship for most Jews. Even in Palestine there were some, like the men of Qumran, who repudiated the temple. But the tabernacle was different. The attention it received in Scripture meant that wherever Jews were it was known and esteemed. It is also not unimportant that the account of the setting up of the old covenant is recounted in Exodus 24, while the description of the tabernacle follows in the very next chapter. So when the author wants to show the greatness of the new covenant, it is natural for him to draw attention to the ineffectiveness of the old as reflected in the way the tabernacle was set up and used.

1 The writer has no noun with his adjective "first," but NIV is almost certainly correct in inserting "covenant." Buchanan argues on grammatical grounds that we should read "the first Tent" (in loc.). Few, however, have followed him. The thrust of the argument at this point is to contrast the old and the new covenants. It is true that this involves the "Tent," but it means much more. The author is contrasting two whole ways of approach to God. Some press the past tense "had" as though it means that the temple had been destroyed. Yet this is illegitimate. The writer is not talking about the temple but about the old covenant that has been superseded now that Jesus has established the new one. But the old one, the writer points out, had been set up with a full set of regulations for worship and the like. The method of worship was not left haphazard but was divinely prescribed. The old way must be seen as originating in the divine initiative. Then the new is its fulfillment, not its contradiction.

The old way not only had regulations but also a sanctuary described as "earthly" (*kosmikon*). The adjective is unusual and in its only other NT occurrence signifies "worldly" (Titus 2:12). NIV is certainly correct here. The meaning is not that the sanctuary is worldly in the bad sense but simply that it belonged to this world in contrast to the heavenly sanctuary where Jesus ministers (v.11). The first covenant, then, was established with its due regulations for worship and its holy place of this earth where worship could be carried on. The author will go on to stress the "earthly" nature of it all.

2 NIV uses the traditional term "tabernacle," no doubt to remind readers of the wilderness sanctuary of the Israelites of old. But the word is the ordinary word for "tent" and it is thus translated elsewhere (e.g., NEB, JB, TEV). Usually it is described as a tent with two compartments. Here, however, the writer speaks instead of two tents (there is nothing in the Gr. to correspond to NIV's "room"; that "tent" is to be supplied with "first" is clear from the specific use of this word in v.3, where NIV has translated *skēnē* by "room").

The term rendered "was set up" (*kateskeuasthē*) is not the usual word for the pitching of a tent but has rather the meaning of "prepare." It may be used not only of the erection of a building but also of its furnishings and equipment. This is in mind here as is shown by the list of furnishings that follows. In the first tent there was "the lampstand," i.e., the seven-branched lampstand (Exod 25:31ff.; 37:17ff.; Solomon's temple had ten lampstands [1 Kings 7:49], but our author is referring to the tabernacle, not the temple).

"The table and the consecrated bread" is a hendiadys for "the table of the consecrated bread." There were twelve loaves, each baked from two-tenths of an ephah of fine flour, arranged in two rows of six, pure frankincense being put with each row. Every Sabbath day Aaron was bidden to set them up, and it was prescribed that they were to be eaten only by the priests (Lev 24:5–9). Scripture does indeed record an exceptional occasion when they were eaten by David and his men (1 Sam 21:1–6), and Jesus referred to the incident (Mark 2:25–26). The loaves were called "the continual bread" (Num 4:7), a name that brings out the fact that there were always to be such loaves in the Holy Place. They were put on a table specially constructed for the purpose (Exod 25:23–30; 37:10–16). The tent in which these objects were placed was called "the Holy Place."

3 The "second curtain" is that which screened off the Most Holy Place from the Holy Place (Exod 26:31–33; 36:35–36; Lev 24:3). It is called the "second" to distinguish it from the curtain between the outer court and the Holy Place (Exod 26:36–37; 36:37–38). Behind this curtain was a tent (*skēnē*) called the "Most Holy Place" (*Hagia Hagiōn*). This was the very special place where God dwelt between the cherubim; and, as the author will presently emphasize, it was never to be entered by anyone other than the high priest, and by him only on the Day of Atonement.

4 The author says some things about the furnishings of the Most Holy Place. There are problems about the expression translated "the golden altar of incense." The word *thymiatērion* denotes something connected with the burning of incense (*thymiama*), and in the LXX it is always used of a censer. Some (e.g., KJV, RV, Snell) favor this meaning here. But the word is also used by Symmachus, Theodotion, and others of the altar on which incense was offered (Exod 30:1–10); and most agree that this is the meaning here. There seems no reason for referring to the censer and much reason for referring to the far more significant altar.

A further problem arises from the fact that the author appears to locate this altar inside the Most Holy Place, though its place was really "in front of the curtain" (Exod 30:6). Indeed, it *had* to be outside the Most Holy Place, for it was in daily use (Exod 30:7–8). Some have thought that this altar was in the Most Holy Place (2 Baruch 6:7). But it seems more likely that the author has in mind the intimate connection of the incense altar with the Most Holy Place. So it "belonged to the inner sanctuary" (1 Kings 6:22), as is shown by its situation "in front of the curtain that is before the ark of the testimony—before the atonement cover [mercy seat] that is over the Testimony" (Exod 30:6).

On the Day of Atonement, the high priest was to offer incense, using coals of fire from this altar (Lev 16:12–13). Notice the warning "so that he will not die" (Lev 16:13). The incense was indeed important. We should also notice that the writer does not say that his altar was "in" the Most Holy Place but only that that Place "had" it. It is true that the same verb covers the ark that was undoubtedly inside the veil, but the indefinite term may be significant. Montefiore comments, "In any case our author does not actually commit himself to the view that the altar of incense is situated in the sanctuary: he merely says that it belonged to the sanctuary" (in loc.).

There is no question that the "gold-covered ark of the covenant" was in the Most Holy Place (Exod 25:10ff.; 26:33; 40:21). That is to say, it was there in the time of the tabernacle. It was placed in the Most Holy Place in the temple of Solomon (1 Kings 8:6); but evidently it was taken out for some reason, and the last time it appears is when Josiah told the priests to put it into the temple (2 Chron 35:3). According to the rabbis, the ark disappeared at the time of the early prophets (Mishnah, *Yoma* 5:2; *Shekalim* 6:1f.); and there was a tradition that Jeremiah hid it (2 Macc 2:4ff.).

The author goes on to inform us that the ark contained "the golden jar of manna" (cf. Exod 16:33–34). MT does not say what the jar was made of, but LXX says it was golden. Aaron's rod that had budded was also there (Num 17:1–11). Neither of these is said in the OT to be "in" the ark; rather, they were "in front of" it (Exod 16:34; Num 17:10). We are told in 1 Kings 8:9 that in Solomon's temple there was nothing in the ark but the tables of stone. But the author is not concerned with the temple. He is writing about the tabernacle, and it is possible that a different arrangement held there; though, if that was so, we have no information about it. Also in the ark were "the stone tablets of the covenant" (cf. Exod 25:16; 31:18; Deut 9:9ff.; 10:3ff.). They represented the permanent record of the terms of the old covenant and were kept in the most sacred place.

5 Above the ark were "the cherubim of the Glory." The exact form of these is not known, but most interpreters hold that they had bodies of animals. They were certainly winged (Exod 25:18–20; 37:7–9). Moreover, they were especially associated with the presence of God (Ps 80:1; 99:1), which is why they are here called the cherubim "of the Glory" (NEB, "of God's glory"; others, however, prefer the sense "the glorious cherubs," JB). They overshadowed the lid of the ark, which is here called "the place of atonement." The justification for this translation is that on the Day of Atonement this object was sprinkled with the blood of the sin offering whereby sins were atoned. The word is from the word group meaning "propitiate," and it may be that there is a recognition that it was the place where God's wrath against sin was put away. But as our author is taking the term from the LXX, we cannot press the point. As with the other articles mentioned, details of its construction are given in the account of the tabernacle (Exod 25:17ff.; 37:6ff.). Doubtless the writer would have

been glad to dwell on the significance of all these objects. He points out, however, that it is not the time for him to do this. His argument proceeds on other lines.

6 From the sanctuary the author moves to the ritual. He is particularly interested in what was done on the Day of Atonement, and he uses the limitations attached to the high priest's entry into the Most Holy Place to bring home the inferiority of the whole Levitical system. But he begins with the ministry of the lower priests. When the tabernacle system was established, the priests did their work in "the first tent" ("outer room," NIV). This included such things as burning incense (Exod 30:7–8), setting out the holy loaves (Lev 24:8–9), and trimming the lamps (Exod 27:20–21; Lev 24:3–4). There was a sharp distinction between the duties and place of service of the priests and those of the Levites (Num 18:1–7).

7 "But" (*de*) marks the contrast. We move from the priests to the high priest and from ministry in the Holy Place to that in the Most Holy Place. Into "the inner room" (i.e., "second tent," v.3) only the high priest might go and then "only once a year." The reference is to the ceremonies of the Day of Atonement (Lev 16). We should understand "once" to mean "on one day," because the high priest made more than one entrance into the room beyond the curtain. He certainly went in twice (Lev 16:12, 15), and a third entrance may be meant for the sprinkling of the blood of the bull (Lev 16:14). The rabbis thought there were four entrances of the high priest into the Most Holy Place, the three just mentioned and a final one to retrieve the ladle and the fire pan he had left there when he offered the incense (M *Yoma* 5:1, 3, 4; 7:4).

To go into the Most Holy Place was dangerous; so the high priest had to safeguard himself by offering blood in the prescribed manner. The rabbis were conscious of the danger and spoke of the high priest as praying when he came out the first time, "but he did not prolong his prayer lest he put Israel in terror" (*Yoma* 5:1). They also said that when he emerged safely from the hazards of the Day, he made a feast for his friends (*Yoma* 7:4). His offering was "for himself and for the sins the people had committed in ignorance." Being a sinner himself, he had to atone for himself before he could minister on behalf of others. The sins "committed in ignorance" point to the truth that there is ignorance that is culpable. Sins of this kind do matter, and we should be on our guard against minimizing their seriousness. In Ecclesiasticus 23:2 the son of Sirach asks not to be spared discipline for these sins of ignorance (he uses the same word that appears here), lest they multiply and bring him low.

8 The author sees the Holy Spirit as using the pattern of the tabernacle to teach important truths. The limited access into the Most Holy Place was meant to bring home the fact that ordinary men had no direct access to the presence of God. NIV is almost certainly correct in its translation, "the way into the Most Holy Place." Yet we should notice that *hagiōn*, which is usually taken as neuter ("holy things" and thus "the Holy Place") might be masculine. In that case the meaning would be "the way for the saints." Now while we should probably not accept this translation, it does point us to the fact that it is the saints who are to travel the way. This was was not revealed while "the first tabernacle was still standing." Some take "the first tabernacle" to mean the Holy Place (as in v.6), but this yields a difficult sense. It seems much more likely that the writer means the whole tabernacle ("the way into the Most Holy Place was not disclosed while the Holy Place still stood" would be strange). The final words do not bear on the problem of whether the temple was still standing. The author is saying that people get direct access to God through the finished work of Christ and that before that work was accomplished there was no such access.

9 "This is an illustration" ("All this is symbolic," NEB). But the precise application of the symbolism is not quite clear. Bruce (in loc.) points out that "the present time" might mean "the time then present" (i.e., in OT days the way to God was not yet revealed) or "the time now present" (i.e., "the real meaning of the tabernacle can only now be understood, in the light of the work of Christ"). In either case the writer is contrasting the limited access that was all that could be obtained in OT days with the free access to the presence of God that Christ has made possible for his people. The trouble with the sacrificial offerings of the old covenant was that they could not "clear the conscience of the worshiper." The reference to conscience is significant. The ordinances of the old covenant had been external. They had not been able to come to grips with the real problem, that of the troubled conscience. This does not mean, of course, that no OT saint ever had a clear conscience, but he did not obtain it by the sacrifices as such.

10 The externality of the old way is brought out from another viewpoint. It concerned only matters like "food and drink and various ceremonial washings." There is no problem about the mention of food, for there were some strict food laws (Lev 11). But drink is not so prominent. Priests were to abstain from alcoholic drinks while engaged in their ministry (Lev 10:8–9) and there were limitations on the Nazarites (Num 6:2–3). No one was allowed to drink from an unclean vessel, one into which a dead animal had fallen (Lev 11:33f.). And, of course, there were libations accompanying some of the sacrifices (e.g., Num 6:15, 17; 28:7f.). There were several ceremonial lustrations in the OT, such as those performed by the priests in their ministry (Exod 30:20), and a variety of washings for defiled people (Lev 15:4–27; 17:15–16; Num 19:7–13). All such things the author dismisses as "external regulations." They have their place, but only "until the time of the new order." Though he does not explain this, the drift of his argument shows that he has in mind the new covenant Christ brought. It replaced all the merely external regulations of the old way.

Notes

2 Unexpectedly we have ἡ πρόθεσις τῶν ἄρτων (hē prothesis tōn artōn, "the setting out of the loaves") where we might have had οἱ ἄρτοι τῆς προθέσεως (hoi artoi tēs protheseōs) as in Matt 12:4. The expression is used figuratively to denote the table on which the bread was set out. Ἅγια (Hagia) is taken by NIV, probably rightly, as a neuter plural, "holy things," and thus "the Holy Place." But Montefiore sees it as feminine singular, pointing out that the use of this adjective without the article in such a sense is unparalleled and, further, that our author uses this expression of the Most Holy Place, not the Holy Place. He prefers to take it in the sense "this Tent is called Holy." This is possible, but NIV is to be preferred.

3 This is the one example in the NT of μετά (meta) with the accusative in the local sense, "behind."

4 JB has a note that our author "may be following a different liturgical tradition, or the sense may be that the place of the altar of incense was immediately in front of the curtain of the inner sanctuary."

6 "Regularly" translates διὰ παντὸς (*dia pantos*), which according to Westcott denotes "the continuous, unbroken permanence of a characteristic habit, while πάντοτε marks that which is realised on each several occasion" (in loc.).

D. The Blood of Christ

9:11–14

> ¹¹When Christ came as high priest of the good things that are already here, he went through the greater and more perfect tabernacle that is not man-made, that is to say, not a part of this creation. ¹²He did not enter by means of the blood of goats and calves; but he entered the Most Holy Place once for all by his own blood, having obtained eternal redemption. ¹³The blood of goats and bulls and the ashes of a heifer sprinkled on those who are ceremonially unclean sanctify them so that they are outwardly clean. ¹⁴How much more, then, will the blood of Christ, who through the eternal Spirit offered himself unblemished to God, cleanse our consciences from acts that lead to death, so that we may serve the living God!

The argument moves a stage further as the author turns specifically to what Christ has done. The sacrifices of the old covenant were ineffectual. But in strong contrast Christ made an offering that secures a redemption valid for all eternity. In the sacrifices, a good deal pertained to the use of blood. So in accord with this, the author considers the significance of the blood of animals and that of Christ.

11–12 The MSS are divided as to whether we should read "the good things that are already here" or "the good things that are to come." The resolution of the point is not easy. On the whole it seems that NIV is correct in preferring the former. Scribes would be tempted to alter the past into the future, but scarcely the reverse. All the more would they do this in view of the similar expression in 10:1 and the frequency of the verb (*mellō*) that expresses the future in this epistle. The author does not explain what the "good things" are, but the expression is evidently a comprehensive way of summing up the blessings Christ has won for his people. The past tense points us to the Cross and all it means. At the same time, we should bear in mind Héring's point that the aorist is probably ingressive and means "The good things have begun to come into existence." There is more to come than we now see. Because the new covenant has been established, the past tense is fitting. Yet the full realization of what this means is yet to come.

There is another difficult problem in the meaning of the "greater and more perfect tabernacle" (v.11) and with it the meaning of "through" (*dia*), which relates to this tabernacle. Also, in the same Greek sentence (v.12) *dia* relates negatively to the blood of animals and positively to the blood of Christ. Many commentators see a reference to heaven in "a greater and more perfect tabernacle"; and still others think of Christ's flesh, his glorified body, or his people (cf. 3:6). Some suggestions seem negated by the words "not man-made, that is to say, not a part of this creation" (v.11). Perhaps we should take notice of the similar expression in v.24, where the author is saying that it was by means of the heavenly sanctuary, and by means of his own blood (not that of animals), that Christ entered the holiest of all, into the presence of God. This is an emphatic way of saying that he has won for his people an effective salvation and that this has nothing to do with earthly sacrifices.

Some translations import the idea of Christ as taking his blood into heaven, e.g.,

RSV, "taking not the blood of goats and calves but his own blood" (similar are TEV, JB). This is quite unwarranted. The Greek does not say this. The translation is objectionable because it implies that Christ's atoning work was not completed on the cross but that he still had to do some atoning act in heaven like the earthly high priest who took the blood into the Most Holy Place on the Day of Atonement. In this epistle, what Christ did on the cross was final. It needs no supplement. There may be another glance at the Day of Atonement ceremonies in the listing of "goats and calves," for these were the animals used on that day. "Once for all" (*ephapax*) is an emphatic expression underlining the decisive character of Christ's saving work. There can be no repetition. "Redemption" (*lytrōsis*) is the process of setting free by the payment of a ransom price, in this case the death of Jesus.

13 The author turns again to the Levitical sacrifices. In them he finds the power to effect an external purification, a cleansing from ritual defilement. He refers to the blood "of goats and bulls," which means much the same as that of "goats and calves" in v.12 (the calf now being seen as a young adult). "The ashes of a heifer" point to the ceremony for purification described in Numbers 19:1–10. A red heifer was killed, the carcass was burned (together with "cedar wood, hyssop and scarlet wool"), and the ashes used "in the water of cleansing; it is for purification from sin." When anyone was ceremonially unclean because of contact with a dead body or even by entering a tent where a dead body lay (Num 19:14), he was made clean by the use of these ashes. The verb "sanctify" is often used of the moral and spiritual process of "sanctification." Here, however, a ritual matter is plainly in mind. The Levitical system is not dismissed as useless. It had its values and was effective within its limits. But those limits were concerned with what is outward.

14 The "how much more" argument stresses the incomparable greatness of Christ and his work for us. "The blood of Christ" means Christ's death regarded as a sacrifice for sin. Though some have suggested that we should see in references to "the blood" allusions to life rather than death, this does not seem soundly based. The word "blood" points to death (see my *Apostolic Preaching of the Cross*, 3rd ed. [Grand Rapids: Eerdmans, 1965], ch. 3). In this context "blood" is not death in general but death seen as a sacrifice. Christ offered himself in sacrifice to God. "Unblemished" (*amōmos*) is the word used technically of animals approved for sacrifice, animals without defect of any kind. The idea of Christ as an offering to God is not popular these days and can, of course, be stated in a crude and totally unacceptable way. But we must never forget that atonement must be seen in the light of God's demand for uprightness in a world where people sin constantly. No view of atonement can be satisfactory that does not regard the divine demand.

There is a problem in the way we should understand "the eternal Spirit." Spelled with capital "S," it appears to be another name for the Holy Spirit (cf. NIV, KJV, RSV, JB, et al.). But the Holy Spirit is not elsewhere referred to in this way. Thus many commentators, feeling that such a reference would be out of place here, prefer to see the "spirit" as Christ's own spirit. For example, Snell sees the words as possibly "a rather odd way of saying that he put his whole human self into it," but he prefers the meaning "by virtue of his own Personal nature as being Spirit" (in loc.). Probably most modern commentators take the words in some such way. Bruce (in loc.), however, points out that we ought to see the "Servant of the Lord" imagery behind this whole passage and he reminds us that the Servant is introduced in Isaiah with "I will put my Spirit on him" (Isa 42:1). Just as the prophet sees the Servant as accomplishing his entire ministry in the power of the divine Spirit, so we should see Christ as winning men's salvation by a mighty act performed in the power of the Spirit of God.

Yet, despite the modern disinclination to see a Trinitarian reference here, it does seem as though something of the kind is needed if we are to do justice to the writer's thought. While Christ's own spirit is involved in his sacrifice, the divine Spirit is involved, too. It seems that the writer has chosen this unusual way of referring to the Holy Spirit to bring out the truth that there is an eternal aspect to Christ's saving work.

Christ, then, offered himself in sacrifice, the aim being to "cleanse our consciences." It is important to be clear that Christ's saving work operates on quite a different level from that of the Levitical sacrifices. These were but external and material, as the author repeatedly emphasizes. But Christ was concerned with the sins that trouble the consciences of men. So his sacrifice was directed to the cleansing of conscience, something the sacrifices under the law could never do (10:2). NIV speaks of a cleansing "from acts that lead to death," where the Greek is more literally "from dead works." This might mean "either those which end in death or which are the fruits of death" (Calvin, in loc.). So far from engaging in works of that kind, those purified by Christ "serve the living God" (see comments on 3:12). The Christian way is positive, not negative.

Notes

11–12 Διά (*dia*) is used with σκηνῆς (*skēnēs*, "tent") and in the same sentence with both examples of αἵματος (*haimatos*, "blood"). It is not easy to see why it should be used with different meanings in expressions so close; so a meaning like "by means of" is favored. But many favor "through" in the case of the tabernacle and "by means of" in the later places.

13 "Outwardly clean" translates πρὸς τὴν τῆς σαρκὸς καθαρότητα (*pros tēn tēs sarkos katharotēta*) "to the purifying of the flesh."

E. *The Mediator of the New Covenant*

9:15–22

> [15]For this reason Christ is the mediator of a new covenant, that those who are called may receive the promised eternal inheritance—now that he has died as a ransom to set them free from the sins committed under the first covenant.
> [16]In the case of a will, it is necessary to prove the death of the one who made it, [17]because a will is in force only when somebody has died; it never takes effect while the one who made it is living. [18]This is why even the first covenant was not put into effect without blood. [19]When Moses had proclaimed every commandment of the law to all the people, he took the blood of calves, together with water, scarlet wool and branches of hyssop, and sprinkled the scroll and all the people. [20]He said, "This is the blood of the covenant, which God has commanded you to keep." [21]In the same way, he sprinkled with the blood both the tabernacle and everything used in its ceremonies. [22]In fact, the law requires that nearly everything be cleansed with blood, and without the shedding of blood there is no forgiveness.

The author has introduced the thought of the death of Christ and proceeds to develop it. This death is the means of redeeming people from the plight they found themselves in as the result of their sin. It brings them an eternal inheritance. With a play on the double meaning of *diathēkē* (both "a covenant" and "a testament"), the author goes on to bring out the necessity for the death of Christ just as the death of the testator is required if a will is to come into force.

15 "For this reason" may refer to the preceding: because Christ really cleanses from dead works by his blood, he mediates the new covenant. But it is also possible that the words look forward: Christ mediates the new covenant so that the called might receive the inheritance. "Those who are called" preserves the divine initiative, as does "promised." Both expressions remind us of the freeness of salvation and of God's will to bless his people. "Inheritance" originally denoted a possession received through the will of someone who died; then it came to denote anything firmly possessed without regard to the way it was obtained. "Eternal" points to the fact that the believer's possession is no transitory affair. The salvation Christ won is forever.

Christ's death is viewed, then, as "a ransom," the price paid to set free a slave or a prisoner or a person under sentence of death. While the idea of redemption is widespread in the ancient world, the actual word used here (and the most common one in the NT) is a rare word—a fact that may point to the conviction that the redemption Christians know is not simply another redemption among many. It is unique. And this redemption avails for those who sinned under the old covenant as well as for those who are embraced in the new covenant. The author insists that the sacrifices offered under the old covenant cannot take away sins. So it is left to Christ to offer the sacrifice that really effects what the old offerings pointed to but could not accomplish.

16 The argument is not easy to follow in English because we have no single word that is the precise equivalent of *diathēkē*. This Greek word denotes something like an authoritative laying down of what is to be done and is the normal word for a last will and testament. But it is also suited to covenants God makes with people. These are not the result of a process of negotiation in which God talks things over with people and they come to a mutually acceptable arrangement. God lays down the terms. The result is a covenant characterized by the same kind of finality as we see in a testament. (One cannot dicker with a testator!) The author moves easily from the idea of covenant to that of testament. It might help us follow him if we render the first clause in v. 15 (with NEB) as "he is the mediator of a new covenant, or testament." This gives two translations for the one Greek word but helps us retain something of the continuity of thought. The death of the testator is necessary for a *diathēkē* (taking the term in the sense "testament") to come into effect. The will may be perfectly valid but it does not operate till death takes place.

17 The point is emphasized. The author uses a technical legal term to indicate that the will is "in force" only (as Moffatt puts it in loc.) "in cases of death." "It never takes effect" makes use of another legal term. It is only the death of the testator that brings the provisions of a will into force.

18 From this the author reasons to the necessity for Christ's death. It was not, so to speak, an option God happened to prefer. The writer will go on to show from the Law that for sin to be forgiven the rule is that blood must be shed. But first he argues that the necessity for death if a *diathēkē* is to be effective (it is plainly needed in the case of a testament), applies just as much when a covenant is in mind. This kind of *diathēkē* also demands that blood be shed if it is to be "put into effect."

19 When the first covenant was made, Moses did two things. First, he "proclaimed every commandment of the law to all the people." That is to say, he set out the terms and conditions of the covenant; he made plain the requirements the covenant laid on the people so they were left in no doubt as to what covenant membership demanded of them. They were now God's people, and that meant they must obey God's laws.

Second, Moses performed certain ritual actions. In what follows the author includes some details not mentioned in Exodus 24. There Moses threw blood on the altar and on the people and read the book to the people. But there is no mention of the water, scarlet wool, hyssop, or the sprinkling of the book. Water and scarlet (whether wool or other material is not said) and hyssop were used in the rite of cleansing healed lepers (Lev 14:4–6; cf. 49–51). Hyssop is mentioned also in connection with the Passover (Exod 12:22) and the cleansing rites associated with the ashes of the red heifer (Num 19:6, 18). It was the natural thing to use hyssop in cleansing (Ps 51:7). The sprinkling of the scroll is not mentioned in Exodus 24. But the book was written by men, and thus it must be cleansed of any defilement they might have conveyed to it. While we do not know where this information came from, there is nothing improbable about any of it.

20 The author has changed the LXX's "Behold, the blood of the covenant" to "This is the blood of the covenant" (which may be meant as a reminiscence of the words used by Jesus at the Last Supper [Mark 14:24]). The verb, too, is different, and the change to "commanded" is highly suitable in the case of a covenant where God lays down the terms. This is no negotiated instrument.

21 "In the same way" does not imply "at the same time." When the covenant was made, the tabernacle had not been constructed. But the cleansing with blood that marked the solemn inauguration of the covenant marked also the solemn inauguration of the place of worship when that took place in due course. Perhaps we are meant to see the dedication of the tabernacle as a kind of renewal of the covenant. Certainly there is continuity. The sprinkling with blood at the consecration of the tabernacle is not specifically mentioned in the OT. It is, however, attested also by Josephus, who says that Aaron's garments, Aaron himself, and apparently the tabernacle and its vessels were sprinkled with blood (Antiq. III, 205–6 [viii. 6]). Under the old covenant sprinkling with blood was the accepted way of cleansing.

22 Cleansing, then, meant blood, though the qualification "nearly [*schedon*] everything" shows that the author is well aware that there were exceptions. Thus the worshiper who was too poor to offer even little birds might instead make a cereal offering (Lev 5:11–13). Some purification could be effected with water (e.g., Lev 15:10), and there might be purification of metal objects by fire and "the water of impurity" (Num 31:22–23). On one occasion gold made atonement for the warriors (Num 31:50), while on another occasion incense atoned (Num 16:46). But such ceremonies were all exceptional. As a whole the Levitical system looks constantly for blood as the means of putting away sin and impurity. The author does not ask why this should be so, though it is clearly the teaching of the OT, as the rabbis also recognized (see, for example, Tal *Yoma* 5a).

Notes

---

16 It is not said that he who makes the testament must die but that his death must be "brought forward" (φέρεσθαι, *pheresthai*). Bruce cites P Oxy ii.244 for the verb used in the technical sense "be registered" and Wettstein for the meaning "be produced as evidence" (in loc.).

17 There is a problem in the use of μήποτε (*mēpote*) with an indicative. The best suggestion seems to be that the expression should be taken as a question expecting the answer no; i.e., "Does it ever take effect while the testator lives?"

19 After μόσχων (*moschōn*, "calves"), a number of MSS add καὶ τῶν τράγων (*kai tōn tragōn*, "and goats"). Some argue that the longer reading is to be preferred, the words being left out by scribes because they do not occur in Exod 24. This is possible, but it seems better to take the shorter reading as original. The reference to goats may have been added because "calves and goats" was a common expression or because goats were so prominent in the Day of Atonement ritual.

22 Αἱματεκχυσία (*haimatekchysia*, "shedding of blood") is not attested before this time, and the writer may have coined the word himself.

F. *The Perfect Sacrifice*

9:23–28

> 23It was necessary, then, for the copies of the heavenly things to be purified with these sacrifices, but the heavenly things themselves with better sacrifices than these. 24For Christ did not enter a man-made sanctuary that was only a copy of the true one; he entered heaven itself, now to appear for us in God's presence. 25Nor did he enter heaven to offer himself again and again, the way the high priest enters the Most Holy Place every year with blood that is not his own. 26Then Christ would have had to suffer many times since the creation of the world. But now he has appeared once for all at the end of the ages to do away with sin by the sacrifice of himself. 27Just as man is destined to die once, and after that to face judgment, 28so Christ was sacrificed once to take away the sins of many people; and he will appear a second time, not to bear sin, but to bring salvation to those who are waiting for him.

From the sanctuary and what is needed to purify it the author turns to the sacrifice that perfectly cleanses, a sacrifice that was offered once and for all. That one sacrifice, once offered, has effectively put away sin. And the author looks forward briefly to the time when our Lord will come back again, this time not to do anything in connection with sin (all that is necessary has been done) but to bring salvation.

23 "It was necessary" points to something more than expediency or the selection of one among a number of possible courses of action. There was no other way. "Therefore" (rather than "then"; the Greek is *oun*) introduces the necessary inference. The writer has made it clear that blood must be shed in purification according to the law. Specifically the rule is that "without the shedding of blood there is no forgiveness" (v.22). This cannot be ignored as merely Jewish, for the Mosaic system was set up by divine command.

It is true, the author reasons, that the Mosaic system was concerned only with "the copies of the heavenly things"; it was taken up with the external. But the fact that God commanded the system to be set up means that there must be something analogous in it to the way the forgiveness that would really put away sin was brought about. What is stressed is that where atonement really matters—i.e., in the heavenly sphere—better sacrifices are needed than were provided under the old system.

There is a problem in seeing in what sense things in heaven—where God is (v.24)—need purification. Some deny outright that they need it, regarding the expression as a way of referring to God's people. Thus Bruce (in loc.) reminds us that the author tells us repeatedly that it is people's consciences that need to be cleansed; and so the author can speak of God's people as his dwelling, his house (cf. 3:6). Others make essentially the same point and hold that it is not something material but spiritual that is seen as needing cleansing—a fact meaning that Christ's work is effective in the spiritual life of men, not in some material sanctuary. The difficulty with such interpretations is that, while what they say is true, "the heavenly things themselves" is a strange way of referring to men and women here on earth. Other commentators see in v.23 a reference to Satan's rebellion and think of that as somehow defiling heaven so that heaven itself needs cleansing. Still others think of purification in the sense in which it is used here as meaning not so much the removal of impurity as a consecratory or inaugural process. This, they feel, is not out of place with "the heavenly things" any more than with an earthly sanctuary. Akin to that is the view that the earthly sanctuary needed cleansing, not so much because it was unclean, as because it was the place where sinners were restored. So with heaven.

On the whole, it seems best to recall that in the NT there are references to "the spiritual forces of evil in the heavenly realms" (Eph 6:12); the "rulers of this age" (1 Cor 2:8); the "powers" like "height" and "depth" (Rom 8:38–39), as well as "angels" and "demons." Such references seem to indicate wickedness beyond this earth. And when Christ performed his atoning work, he "disarmed the powers and authorities, . . . triumphing over them by the cross" (Col 2:15). It was God's will "through him to reconcile to himself all things, whether things on earth or things in heaven, by making peace through his blood, shed on the cross" (Col 1:20). This strand of teaching is not prominent in Hebrews. Nevertheless, the language used here seems to accord with it better than with other views. The author is fond of the word "better" (see comments on 1:4), but it is unexpected for him to use the plural "sacrifices," since he is insistent that there was but one sacrifice and that Christ suffered "once for all" (v.26). Probably we should take "sacrifices" as the generic plural that lays down the principle fulfilled in the one sacrifice.

24 Christ's work for mankind was done where it really counted. "For" introduces an explanation of what precedes. We have already had the idea that Christ's ministry was not in a sanctuary that is "man-made" (v.11), and here we come back to it. Not in such sanctuaries can the Atonement be made that really deals with sin. Here such a sanctuary is described as a "copy" (*antitypa*) of the true one. The word *typos* "type" is ambiguous and may mean the original or a copy. Thus *antitypos*, "corresponding to the *typos*," is also ambiguous. It may mean the fulfillment of what is foreshadowed in the type, as in 1 Peter 3:20–21, where the Flood is no more than a foreshadowing and baptism the *antitypos*, the significant thing. Here it seems the other way around. The *antitypos* is the copy, the shadow, of the real thing that is in heaven. The earthly antitype points us to the heavenly reality, "the true one."

What he entered is "heaven itself." The word for "heaven" is usually plural in this epistle. Here, however, it is singular. There seems no difference in meaning. The important point is that heaven itself is regarded as the true sanctuary, not some structure within it to which the earthly tabernacle corresponded. "Now" points to present activity. After his atoning work done once for all, Christ now appears before God. We are not fit to stand before God and plead our case, and in any event we are on earth and not in God's heaven. But Christ is there in our stead and in his capacity as the one who died as a better sacrifice (v.23) for sins.

25 "Nor" carries on the negative at the beginning of v.24: "Christ did not enter a man-made sanctuary . . . nor did he . . . offer himself again and again." While there is nothing in the Greek corresponding to NIV's "did he enter heaven," the words seem required. The author is concerned in this verse to repudiate the idea that Christ might have made an offering from time to time in the manner of the high priests. It was basic to their ministry to offer sacrifices repeatedly, just as it was basic to Christ's ministry that he did not do so. The reference in v.25 to entering "the Most Holy Place every year" shows that the sacrifices mainly in mind are those of the Day of Atonement.

Two things call for comment. The first is the clear implication that only Christ's offering can put away sin. The sins of those who lived in old times were dealt with by Christ's one offering. The reasoning is that if that offering had not been sufficient, Christ would have had to offer himself "again and again." That is to say, no other offering is in view when it is a matter of really putting sin away. The other point is that when the high priest entered the Most Holy Place he did so "with blood that is not his own." The superiority of Christ's offering is seen in that he does not press into service some external means, like the blood of some noncooperating, noncomprehending animal. He uses his own blood and with it makes the one sufficient offering.

26 What is implied in v.25 is made explicit here. "Then" is perhaps not the best translation of *epei*, which, as often, introduces an elliptical construction, with a meaning like "for [if it were different]" or, as BAG (s.v.) puts it, "for otherwise he would have had to suffer many times." Again, the implication is that there is no other way of dealing with sin than Christ's own offering of himself. If his one offering was not enough, he would have had to suffer over and over. "Suffer," of course, is used in the sense of "suffer death." The reference to "creation" carries the idea right back to the beginning. No one would ever have been saved without the offering made by Christ.

"Now" (*nyni*) is not temporal; this is an example of its use "introducing the real situation after an unreal conditional clause or sentence, *but, as a matter of fact*" (BAG, s.v.). Once again the author emphasizes the decisive quality of Christ's sacrifice with his "once for all." It matters a great deal to the author that Christ made the definitive offering and that now that it has been made there is no place for another. Many take "at the end of the ages" to mean that the author thought he was living in the last days and that Christ would return very speedily to bring this world to an end. So his sacrifice on the cross was made in the world's last days. But whatever he thought about the imminence of the end of all things, the author says little about it. We should probably understand the words here rather in the sense of "the consummation of the ages," or perhaps with NEB, "at the climax of history." If we take it in the sense of "the close of the age," it would mean that the first coming of Christ—and more particularly his offering of himself on the cross—ushered in the final state of affairs.

It is a common thought of the NT writers that God's decisive action in Christ has altered things radically. The Messianic Age has come—the age that all the preceding ages have led up to.

The purpose of Christ's coming was "to do away with sin." Here the expression *eis athetēsin* is a strong one, signifying the total annulment of sin. The word "is used in a technical juristic sense" (Deiss BS, pp. 228–29) with the meaning "to annul" or "cancel." Sin, then, is rendered completely inoperative and this was done "by the sacrifice of himself." It is the self-offering of Christ that is the decisive thing. For the author this is the truth that must be grasped.

27 This phase of the argument is rounded off with a reference to the one death men die and the one death Christ died. There is a finality about both but very different consequences. Men are "destined to die once." This is not something within their control. A condition of life here on earth is that it ends in death. The "once for all" (*hapax*) so often used of Christ's sacrifice is here used of man's death. There is a finality about it that is not to be disputed. But if it is the complete and final end to life on earth, it is not, as so many in the ancient world thought, the complete and final end. Death is more serious than that because it is followed by judgment. Men are accountable, and after death they will render account to God.

28 "So" introduces a correspondence with the "just as" at the beginning of the previous verse. The passive "was sacrificed" is interesting because it is much more usual for the author to say that Christ offered himself (cf. v.26). Some see the thought here that Christ's enemies were in a sense responsible for his death, but it seems more likely that it is the divine purpose that is in mind. Once more we have the adverb "once-for-all" (*hapax*) applied to the death of Christ. This means a good deal to the author, and he comes back to it again and again.

It is a little difficult to follow NIV in this verse, for an expression meaning "to bear sins" is here rendered "to take away the sins" while later in the verse "not to bear sin" is the translation of an expression that signifies "apart from sin" and has nothing to do with the bearing of sin at all. Sin-bearing is a concept found in the NT only here and in 1 Peter 2:24, but it is quite frequent in the OT, where it plainly means "bear the penalty of sin." For example, the Israelites were condemned to wander in the wilderness for forty years as the penalty for their failure to go up into the land of Canaan: "For forty years—one year for each of the forty days you explored the land—you will suffer for your sins" (Num 14:34; cf. Ezek 18:20, et al.). Many see here an echo of the fourth Servant Song: "He will bear their iniquities" (Isa 53:11); "he bore the sin of many" (Isa 53:12). So the author is saying that Christ took upon himself the consequences of the sins of the many (cf. Mark 10:45).

But this is not the whole story. Christ will come back a second time and then he will not be concerned with sin. The thought is that sin was dealt with finally at his first coming. There is nothing more that he should do. The second time he will come "to bring salvation." There is a sense in which salvation has been brought about by Christ's death. But there is another sense in which it will be brought to its consummation when he returns. Nothing is said about unbelievers. At this point the writer is concerned only with those who are Christ's. They "are waiting for him," where the verb *apekdechomai* expresses the eager looking for the Lord's coming so characteristic of the NT.

Notes

---

24 Ἅγια (*hagia,* "holy things") is used in the sense "sanctuary" as in 8:2 and elsewhere.

After "the true one" NIV omits "but." The Greek is ἀλλ' (*all*'), the strong adversative, which sets the following in firm contrast to the preceding. The adversative idea comes out in the NIV translation, however.

"For us" renders ὑπὲρ ἡμῶν (*hyper hēmōn*). The preposition in such contexts signifies "on behalf of" or "in the place of."

26 The ἐπεί (*epei,* "since," "then") construction is classed under "the imperfect (without ἄν) in expressions of necessity, obligation, duty, possibility, etc." This "denotes in classical something which is or was actually necessary, etc., but which does not or did not take place" a construction which "is retained in the NT" (BDF, par.358[1]).

"The end of the ages" ἐπὶ συντελείᾳ τῶν αἰώνων (*epi synteleia tōn aiōnōn*) is found in this form here only, though there are some similar expressions in Matt 13:39, 40, 49; 24:3; 28:20.

On ἁμαρτία (*hamartia,* "sin") BAG (s.v.) has the following note: In Hebrews "sin appears as the power that deceives men and leads them to destruction, whose influence and activity can be ended only by sacrifices."

G. *The Law a Shadow*

10:1-4

> [1]The law is only a shadow of the good things that are coming—not the realities themselves. For this reason it can never, by the same sacrifices repeated endlessly year after year, make perfect those who draw near to worship. [2]If it could, would they not have stopped being offered? For the worshipers would have been cleansed once for all, and would no longer have felt guilty for their sins. [3]But those sacrifices are an annual reminder of sins, [4]because it is impossible for the blood of bulls and goats to take away sins.

The preceding sections have brought out the efficacy of the blood of Jesus as a prevailing sacrifice, and now stress is laid on the once-for-all character of that sacrifice. First, the author contrasts the substance and the shadow. He sees the ancient system that meant so much to the Jews as no more than an unsubstantial, shadowy affair. The real thing is in Christ. To leave Christ in favor of Judaism would be to forsake the substance for the shadow. The sacrificial system practiced by the Jews could not deal effectually with sin. Since it was no more than a shadow, that was quite impossible.

1 "The law" means strictly the law of Moses, but here it stands for the whole OT, with particular reference to the sacrificial system. This is dismissed as no more than "a shadow" (*skia*). The word is used in conjunction with "copy" (*hypodeigma*) in 8:5 and in opposition to "body" (*sōma*) in Colossians 2:17. It points to something unsubstantial in opposition to what is real. This is not the Platonic thought of a copy of the heavenly "idea" but rather that of a foreshadowing of what is to come. Here the contrast is with "image" (*eikōn*), which is surprising, as *eikōn* normally means "a *derived* likeness and, like the head on a coin or the parental likeness in a child, implies an archetype" (A-S, s.v.).

NIV renders a Greek expression meaning "the image itself of the things" as "the realities themselves." Perhaps those exegetes are right who see a metaphor from painting (e.g., Calvin, in loc.). The "shadow" then is the preliminary outline that an artist may make before he gets to his colors, and the *eikōn* is the finished portrait. The author is saying that the law is no more than a preliminary sketch. It shows the shape of things to come, but the solid reality is not there. It is in Christ. The "good things that are coming" are not defined, but the general term is sufficient to show that the law pointed forward to something well worthwhile.

There is a problem in the second half of v.1. Should we take the expression *eis to diēnekes*, rendered as "endlessly," with what precedes it in the Greek (as NIV) or with what follows, as NEB: "It provides for the same sacrifices year after year, and with these it can never bring the worshippers to perfection for all time [*eis to diēnekes*]"? Technically, the former is possible, but there are reasons for preferring NEB here. The expression *eis to diēnekes* marks "an act which issues in a permanent result" (Westcott, in loc.), a meaning we see when it is repeated in v.12 (where NIV has "for all time") and v.14 (NIV, "forever"). The Greek word order also favors NEB (Montefiore [in loc.] thinks that this, along with vv.12, 14, "forbids" taking the word otherwise).

The author is saying, then, that the Levitical sacrifices continue year by year, but they are quite unable to bring the worshipers into a permanent state of perfection. The yearly sacrifices mark another reference to the Day of Atonement ceremonies— ceremonies of which the author makes a good deal of use. "Can never" points to an inherent weakness of the old system: the animal sacrifices are quite unable to effect the putting away of sin. The yearly repetition repeats the failure. The same rites that were unavailing last year are all that the law can offer this year. There is an inbuilt limitation in animal sacrifice. "Make perfect" is used, of course, in a moral and spiritual sense.

2 The rhetorical question emphasizes the truth that the very continuity of the sacrifices witnesses to their ineffectiveness. Incidentally, the way it is put seems to accord more naturally with a situation in which the sacrifices were still being offered in the temple than with one in which they had ceased. This may be a pointer to the date of the epistle. Had the sacrifices really dealt with sins, the author reasons, the worshipers would have been cleansed and that would have been that. There would have been no need and no place for repeating them (cf. 9:9). The very necessity for repetition shows that the desired cleansing has not been effected. "An atonement that needs constant repetition does not really atone; a conscience which has to be cleansed once a year has never been truly cleansed" (Robinson, in loc.). The translation "would no longer have felt guilty for their sins" obscures the reference to "conscience." It may be that this rendering gives much the right sense, but we should not miss this further reference to conscience, which means so much in this epistle (see 9:9, 14; 10:2, 22; 13:18; in the NT only 1 Cor uses the term more often). A really effectual atonement would mean the permanent removal of the worshipers' sins. There would be no need for anything like the annual Day of Atonement ceremonies.

3 The strong adversative "but" (*all'*) puts the truth in sharp contrast with false estimates of what sacrifices might do. Perhaps the flavor of the Greek word *anamnēsis* is better caught with "remembrance" instead of "reminder"; i.e., "in them is a remembrance of sins." *Anamnēsis* is used in the NT only in the accounts of the institution of the Lord's Supper (Luke 22:19; 1 Cor 11:24–25) and here. Where the Bible has the idea of remembrance, as Bruce points out (in loc.), action appears to be involved. When people remember sins, they either repent (Deut 9:7) or else persist in sin (Ezek 23:19). When God remembers sin, he usually punishes it (1 Kings 17:18; Rev 16:19); when he pardons, he can be said not to remember sin (Ps 25:7). The author then is using an expression that reminds us that Jesus said, "Do this in remembrance of me" (Luke 22:19), as he established a covenant in which the central thing is that God says, "[I] will remember their sins no more" (Jer 31:34). The Day of Atonement ceremonies each year reminded people of the fact that something had to be done about sin. But the ceremonies did no more than that.

4 The yearly ceremonies were ineffective because "it is impossible for the blood of bulls and goats to take away sins." The word "impossible" is a strong one. There is no way forward through the blood of animals. "Take away" (*aphaireō*) is used of a literal taking off, as of Peter's cutting off the ear of the high priest's slave (Luke 22:50), or metaphorically as of the removal of reproach (Luke 1:25). It signifies the complete removal of sin so that it is no longer a factor in the situation. That is what is needed and that is what the sacrifices could not provide.

Notes

1 Instead of οὐκ αὐτὴν τὴν εἰκόνα (*ouk autēn tēn eikona*, "not the image itself"), P46 reads καὶ τὴν εἰκόνα (*kai tēn eikona*, "and the image"), which solves some problems by making the text read, "For the law, having a shadow and the image of the good things. . . ." But support for this reading is slight and the construction of the sentence seems to imply that εἰκών (*eikōn*, "image") is contrasted with σκιά (*skia*, "shadow"), not joined with it as of similar meaning. It seems an attempt to remove a difficulty and should be rejected.

Another textual problem is whether to take the singular δύναται (*dynatai*, "it can") or the plural δύνανται (*dynantai*, "they can"). NIV is almost certainly correct in favoring the singular, for the plural involves leaving νόμος (*nomos*, "law") as a *nominativus pendens*, which the author normally avoids.

Εἰς τὸ διηνεκὲς (*eis to diēnekes*) is found in NT only in 7:3; 10:1, 12, 14. A-S derives the adjective from διήεγκα (*diēnenka*), the aorist of διαφέρω (*diapherō*), and gives it the meaning "unbroken, continuous." The present expression he sees as meaning "continually, perpetually, forever" (s.v.). Westcott distinguishes it from εἰς τὸν αἰῶνα (*eis ton aiōna*, "forever") in that "it expresses the thought of a continuously abiding result. The former phrase looks to the implied absence of limit while εἰς τὸ διηνεκές affirms uninterrupted duration in regard to some ruling thought" (in loc.).

Προσέρχομαι (*proserchomai*) has a curious distribution. It is found in NT eight-seven times, of which no less than fifty-two are in Matt, ten in Luke, ten in Acts, and then seven in Heb. It occurs but once in all the Pauline corpus and similarly once in all the Catholic Epistles. The word means "approach," "draw near," and may be used of drawing near to God (7:25; 11:6) or to the throne of grace (4:16). Here, as in v.22, we have the absolute use, with "God" understood. The participle "those who draw near" means "the worshipers."

2 We must understand an ellipsis after ἐπεί (*epei*) to give the meaning "since [if it were not so]," "otherwise," "if it could."

H. *One Sacrifice for Sins*

10:5–18

⁵Therefore, when Christ came into the world, he said:

"Sacrifice and offering you did not desire,
but a body you prepared for me;
⁶with burnt offerings and sin offerings
you were not pleased.
⁷Then I said, 'Here I am—it is written about me
in the scroll—
I have come to do your will, O God.' "

⁸First he said, "Sacrifices and offerings, burnt offerings and sin offerings you did not desire, nor were you pleased with them" (although the law required them to be made). ⁹Then he said, "Here I am, I have come to do your will." He sets aside the first to establish the second. ¹⁰And by that will, we have been made holy through the sacrifice of the body of Jesus Christ once for all.
¹¹Day after day every priest stands and performs his religious duties; again and again he offers the same sacrifices, which can never take away sins. ¹²But when this priest had offered for all time one sacrifice for sins, he sat down at the right hand of God. ¹³Since that time he waits for his enemies to be made his footstool, ¹⁴because by one sacrifice he has made perfect forever those who are being made holy.
¹⁵The Holy Spirit also testifies to us about this. First he says:

¹⁶"This is the covenant I will make with them
after that time, says the Lord.

I will put my laws in their hearts,

and I will write them on their minds."

¹⁷Then he adds:

"Their sins and lawless acts
I will remember no more."

¹⁸And where these have been forgiven, there is no longer any sacrifice for sin.

It is the author's habit to clinch his argument by appealing to Scripture. In the preceding sections, however, he has been arguing without such appeals. Now he rounds off this stage of his theme by showing that the Bible proves the correctness of the position he has advocated. Animal sacrifices could not take away the sins of the people. But it was the will of God that sin be atoned for. Christ's perfect sacrifice of himself fulfills God's will as animal sacrifices could never do. This the author sees foretold in Psalm 40. Then, as he goes on to bring out something of the utter finality of the offering of Christ, he returns to the quotation from Jeremiah he had used in chapter 8 to initiate his discussion of the new covenant. His argument up till now has been the negative one that the animal sacrifices of the old covenant were unavailing. Now he says positively that Christ's sacrifice, which established the new covenant, was effectual. It really put away sin. And it was foreshadowed in the same passage from Jeremiah.

5–7 The inferential conjunction "therefore" (*dio*) introduces the next stage of the argument: Because the Levitical sacrifices were powerless to deal with sin, another provision had to be made. The writer does not say who the speaker is nor whom he spoke to, but TEV gives the sense of it with "When Christ was about to come into the world, he said to God. . . . " The words of the psalm are regarded as coming from Christ and as giving the reason for the Incarnation. The preexistence of Christ is assumed. The quotation is from Psalm 40:6–8 (LXX, Ps 39:7–9), with some variations that, however, do not greatly affect the sense. This psalm is not quoted elsewhere in the NT, and this reminds us once more that the writer of this epistle has his own style of writing and his own way of viewing Holy Writ.

In the passage quoted, the LXX reads "a body you prepared for me," whereas the Hebrew has "ears you have dug for me." Some MSS of the LXX, it is true, read "ears." Moreover, some scholars hold that this reading is original and that the reading "body" arose from accidental error in the transmission of the text. But it seems more probable that the LXX gives an interpretative translation (with "ears" substituted in some MSS by scribes who knew the Hebrew). Some see a reference to the custom of piercing the ear of a slave who did not wish to avail himself of the opportunity to be set free, preferring to remain enslaved to his master for life (Exod 21:6; Deut 15:17). But the language makes this unlikely. It is more probable that the LXX translators are giving us a somewhat free rendering. They may wish to express the view that the body is the instrument through which the divine command, received by the ear, is carried out (so, for example, Westcott). Or, taking the part for the whole, they may be reasoning that "the 'digging' or hollowing out of the ears is part of the total work of fashioning a human body" (Bruce, in loc.). The verb "prepare" is an unusual one to use of a body, but in this context it is both intelligible and suitable.

The words "sacrifice" and "offering" are both quite general and might apply to any sacrificial offering, whereas the "burnt offering" and the "sin offering" are both specific. Actually, in the Hebrew the first two are a trifle more precise and may be differentiated as the sacrifice of an animal (*zebah*) and the cereal offering (*minhāh*). The four terms taken together are probably meant as a summary of the main kinds of Levitical sacrifice. The classification is not exhaustive, but the ones listed sufficiently indicate the main kinds of sacrifices under the old covenant.

The psalmist says that God did not "will" (so rather than "desire," *ēthelēsas*) or "take pleasure in" such offerings. This does not mean that the offerings were against the will of God or that God was displeased with them. The meaning rather is that, considered in themselves as simply a series of liturgical actions, they were not the product of the divine will nor did they bring God pleasure. They might have done so if they had been offered in the right spirit, by penitent people expressing their state of heart by their offerings. But the thrust of the quotation emphasizes the importance of the will.

"Then" means "in those circumstances" rather than "at that time." Since sacrifice as such did not avail before God, other action had to be taken. That action means that Christ came to do the will of God. In his case, there was no question of a dumb animal being offered up quite irrespective of any desires it might have. He came specifically to do the will of God, and his sacrifice was the offering of one fully committed to doing the will of the Father.

The reference to the "scroll" is not completely clear, but probably the psalmist meant that he was fulfilling what was written in the law. The author sees the words as emphasizing that Christ came to fulfill what was written in Scripture. The words that immediately follow in the psalm are "your law is within my heart," and they show what this expression implies. The author uses the word "will" (*thelēma*) five times, always of the will of God. It was important to him that what God wills is done. Christ came to do nothing other than the will of God.

8 "First," that is, "above," "as he said above," refers to what came earlier, not to what was spoken first of all. It is not clear why the references to sacrifices are all plural here. In v.5 both "sacrifice" and "offering" are singular and while "burnt offerings" in v.6 is plural, in most MSS of the LXX it is singular, as is the underlying Hebrew throughout. Probably all we can say is that the plural makes it all very general. Multiply them how you will and characterize them how you will, God takes no pleasure in sacrifices as such. Indeed, this is so even though the law requires them to be offered and the law is from God. Westcott sees a significance in the absence of the article "the" with "law" (*nomos*), which indicates to him that the stress is on the character of the sacrifices as legal rather than Mosaic (in loc.). But even if the grammatical point be sustained, it is not easy to see how this helps.

We should see the statement concerning the necessity of sacrifice as another illustration of the attitude consistently maintained by the author that the OT system is divinely inspired but preliminary. He holds it to be effective but only within its own limited scope. The sacrifices were commanded in God's law and therefore must be offered. But they were not God's final will nor God's answer to the problem of sin. They were partial and they pointed the way. Even though they came as part of the law, we are to recognize their limitation.

9 "He said" (*eirēken*) is perfect, whereas "I said" (*eipon*) in v.7, to which it refers, is aorist; the change of tense emphasizes the permanence of the saying ("the perfect of a completed action = the saying stands on record," Moffatt, in loc.). The words about doing the will of God are there for all time. On this occasion the omission of the parenthesis means that they stand out in their simplicity and strength. The verb "sets aside" (*anairei*) is used only here in Hebrews. It means "take away" and is used sometimes in the sense of taking away by killing, that is, murdering, and this shows that it is a strong word. It points to the total abolition of the former way. By contrast the second way is "established," "made firm." Neither "the first" nor "the second" is defined, but clearly the way of the Levitical sacrifices and the way of the sacrifice of Christ are being set over against each other. These are not complementary systems that may exist side by side. The one excludes the other. No compromise is possible between them.

10 We must translate *en ho thelēmati* in some such way as "by that will." But the preposition *en* is "in," and it may be that our author sees the sanctified as "in" the will of God. That will is large enough and deep enough to find a place for them all. We should notice a difference between the way the author uses the verb "to sanctify" (NIV, "made holy") and the way Paul uses it. For the apostle, sanctification is a process whereby the believer grows progressively in Christian qualities and character. In Hebrews the same terminology is used of the process by which a person becomes a Christian and is therefore "set apart" for God. There is no contradiction between these two; both are necessary for the fully developed Christian life. But we must be on our guard lest we read this epistle with Pauline terminology in mind. The sanctification meant here is one brought about by the death of Christ. It has to do with making people Christian, not with developing Christian character. It is important also to notice that it is the offering "of the body" of Christ that saves.

Some exegetes have been so impressed by the emphasis on doing the will of God over against the offering of animal sacrifice that they suggest that the actual death of Jesus mattered little. What was important, they say, is the yielded will, the fact that Jesus was ready to do his Father's will at whatever cost to himself. The death was incidental; the will was primary. But this is not what the author is saying. The will is certainly important, and unless we see this we misunderstand the author's whole position. Yet it is also important to realize that the will of God in question was that "the body of Jesus Christ" be offered. Calvary, not Gethsemane, is central, important though the latter certainly was. The contrast is not between animal sacrifice and moral obedience. It is between the death of an uncomprehending animal and the death in which Jesus accepted the will of God with all that it entails.

The offering of Jesus' body was made "once for all." Here again we have the emphatic *ephapax*. It matters immensely that this one offering, once made, avails for all people at all times. This contrasts sharply with the sacrifices under the old covenant as the author has been emphasizing. But it contrasts also with other religions. Héring (in loc.), for example, points out that this distinguishes Christianity from the mystery religions, where the sacrifice of the god was repeated annually. In fact, there is no other religion in which one great happening brings salvation through the centuries and through the world. This is the distinctive doctrine of Christianity.

11 The author brings out the finality of Jesus' sacrifice from another angle as he considers once more the continuing activity of the Levitical priests. Actually he does not confine the continual activity to those priests, for he uses the quite general expression "every priest." It is characteristic of the activity of a priest that he stands and ministers day by day. But of course the writer has the Levitical priests especially in mind. And it is true of them (as of other priests) that they keep offering sacrifices that can never take sins away. Standing is the posture appropriate to priestly service, and in the tabernacle or temple the priests of Aaron's line never sat during the course of their ministry in the sanctuary.

The word translated "performs his religious duties" (*leitourgōn*) is that from which we derive our word "liturgy." Originally it meant "perform a public service" and was used of a wide variety of activities. In the Bible, however, it is confined to service of a religious character. Here it clearly applies to all the services a priest performs. Yet despite all their activity, priests cannot deal with the basic problem—that of removing sin.

12 Jesus' work is contrasted to that of priests. He offered one sacrifice—just one alone (there is emphasis on "one"). Then he sat down. The author mentioned this before (e.g., 1:3; 8:1), but he put no emphasis on it. Now he stresses Jesus' posture, contrasting it to that of the Levitical priests, and the contrast brings out an important point for understanding the work of Christ. Levitical priests stand, for their work is not done but goes on. Christ sits, for his work is done. Sitting is the posture of rest, not of work. That Christ is seated means that his atoning work is complete; there is nothing to be added to it. The expression "for all time" (*eis to diēnekes*) is so situated in the Greek that it can be taken either with "offered" (as NIV) or with "sat down" (as Moffatt, in loc.). There is no grammatical reason for either course, but on the whole it seems best to take it with the words about offering. This seems more consistent with the way the author is unfolding his thought.

We should notice further that to be seated at God's right hand is to be in the place of highest honor. Even angels are not said to have attained to this; they stand in God's presence (Luke 1:19). When Jesus claimed this place for himself, the high priest tore his robe at what he regarded as blasphemy (Mark 14:62–63). The author is combining with the thought of a finished work the idea that our Lord is a being of the highest dignity and honor.

13 His work accomplished, the Lord now waits. The remaining words of this verse are a quotation from Psalm 110:1, with slight alterations to fit the grammatical context. The "enemies" are not defined, and the meaning appears to be that Christ rests until in God's good time all evil is overthrown. In other parts of the NT we read of God's enemies as being defeated at the end time (notably in Rev), but this is not a feature in Hebrews; and we have no means of knowing precisely what enemies he has in mind. There is possibly a hint of warning to the readers—viz., they should take care that they are not numbered among these enemies.

14 Once more the writer emphasizes that Christ has offered one offering that saves men. Clearly this is of the utmost importance for him. So he comes back to it again and again. The conjunction "because" introduces the reason for the statement in v.13. As in v.12, "one" is in an emphatic position; the perfecting of the saints came by one offering and by one alone. The writer does not say that Christ's sacrifice perfects the people but that Christ does this. His salvation is essentially personal. We have seen a number of times that the author is fond of the idea of "perfecting." He applies it to Christ (see comments on 2:10) and also to his people. The process of salvation takes people who are far from perfect and makes them fit to be in God's presence forever. It is not temporary improvement he is speaking of but improvement that is never ending.

As in v.10, the author uses the concept of sanctifying, or making holy, to character-ize the saved. The present tense (*hagiazomenous*, "those being made holy") poses a small problem that has been solved in more than one way. Some see it as timeless; others think of it as indicating a continuing process of adding to the number of the saved, others again of those who in the present are experiencing the process of being made holy. The last-mentioned view is not likely to be correct because, as we have noticed, the idea of sanctification as a continuing process does not seem to appear in Hebrews. But either of the other two views is possible. Those Christ saves are set apart for the service of God and that forever. The writer, then, is contemplating a great salvation, brought about by one magnificent offering that cannot and need not be repeated—an offering that is eternal in its efficacy and that makes perfect the people it sanctifies.

15–17 The writer consistently regards God as the author of Scripture and, as we have seen, ascribes to God words uttered by Moses and others. He does not often speak of the Holy Spirit as responsible for what is written. (See 3:7 and here; in 9:8 he sees the arrangement of the tabernacle, which of course is recorded in Scripture, as due to the Spirit.) But this is consistent with the writer's general approach, and we should not be surprised at it here. The Spirit, he says, "testifies." The choice of word implies that there is excellent testimony behind what he has been saying about Christ. There is a small grammatical problem because the quotation is introduced with "First he says," though there is nothing to follow this up. NIV supplies the lack with "Then he adds" in v.17; and this seems to be the sense of it, even though there is nothing in the Greek corresponding to these words.

Once more the writer quotes from Jeremiah 31:33ff. (words he quoted at length in 8:7ff.). This time he does not begin his quotation so early (in ch. 8 it began at Jer 31:31), and there is a big gap (with the omission of the end of Jer 31:33 and most of 34). The reason for this appears to be that he quotes enough to show that it is the "new covenant" passage he has in mind and then goes straight to the words about forgiveness. Since his real interest lies here, he omits all else. The quotation has a considerable number of minor differences from the LXX, though none that greatly affects the sense. But there are so many of them that most commentators think the writer is here quoting from memory and giving the general sense of Jeremiah's words. The effect of all this is to emphasize the fact that Christ has established the new covenant and that he has done so by providing for the forgiveness of sins.

18 This short verse emphatically conveys the utter finality of Christ's offering and the sheer impossibility of anything further. Where sins have been effectively dealt with, there can be no further place for an offering for sin. The author sees this as established by Scripture, and this is consistent with his normal use of the OT. He cites the Bible to show that since the new covenant is established, there is no room for any further sacrifice. This is the word of the prophet and must be accepted by any who see the OT as Scripture. So, the author reasons, now that the new covenant spoken of by the prophet is a reality, the prophetic word itself rules out the possibility of any further sacrifice.

Notes

5 Προσφορά (prosphora) is found nine times in the NT, five of them in this chapter (vv.5, 8, 10, 14, 18). The word means originally "the act of bringing" and thus "what is brought," or "offering." Here it is practically equivalent to "sacrifice."

6 This is one of the few cases in which the verb εὐδοκέω (eudokeō, "be pleased") takes a direct object (v.8; Matt 12:18).

7 Κεφαλίς (kephalis), here only in NT, is a diminutive of κεφαλή (kephalē) and it is used for such things as the capital of a column. It is often said that its use here comes from its application to the little knobs at the end of the sticks on which scrolls were wound. Though this is not improbable, Westcott points out that no example of this usage of κεφαλίς (kephalis) is cited (in loc.). Be that as it may, here the word must mean "scroll." The genitive of the articular infinitive, τοῦ ποιῆσαι (tou poiēsai, "to do"), normally denotes purpose, as here.

13 This is the one occurrence of λοιπός (loipos) in Hebrews (55 times in NT). The word means "remaining" and the neuter singular is used adverbially with or without the article in the sense of "from now on," "in the future," "henceforth" (BAG [s.v.] translates here as "then waiting"). From the time that Christ sat down, his saving work completed, he waited.

15 Some regard ἡμῖν (hēmin) as a dative of advantage, "bears witness for us" rather than "to us." But the difference is not great.

I. The Sequel—The Right Way

10:19-25

[19]Therefore, brothers, since we have confidence to enter the Most Holy Place by the blood of Jesus, [20]by a new and living way opened for us through the curtain,

that is, his body, [21]and since we have a great priest over the house of God, [22]let us draw near to God with a sincere heart in full assurance of faith, having our hearts sprinkled to cleanse us from a guilty conscience and having our bodies washed with pure water. [23]Let us hold unswervingly to the hope we profess, for he who promised is faithful. [24]And let us consider how we may spur one another on toward love and good deeds. [25]Let us not give up meeting together, as some are in the habit of doing, but let us encourage one another—and all the more as you see the Day approaching.

We have now concluded the solid doctrinal section that constitutes the main section of the epistle. As Paul often does, the writer of Hebrews exhorts his readers on the basis of the doctrine he has made so clear. Because the great teachings he has set forth are true, it follows that those who profess them should live in a manner befitting them. There are resemblances between the exhortation in this paragraph and that in 4:14–16. But we must not forget that the intervening discussion has made clear what Christ's high priestly work has done for his people. On the basis of Christ's sacrifice, the writer exhorts his readers to make the utmost use of the blessing that has been won for them.

19 The address "brothers" is affectionate, and the writer exhorts them on the basis of the saving events. "Therefore" links the exhortation with what has preceded it. These saving events give the Christian a new attitude towards the presence of God. Nadab and Abihu died while offering incense (Lev 10:2), and it had become the custom for the high priest not to linger in the Most Holy Place on the Day of Atonement lest people be terrified (M *Yoma* 5:1). But Christians approach God confidently, completely at home in the situation created by Christ's saving work. They enter "the Most Holy Place," which, of course, is no physical sanctuary but is, in truth, the presence of God. And they enter it "by the blood of Jesus," i.e., on the basis of his saving death.

20 The way to God is both "new" and "living." It is "new" because what Jesus has done has created a completely new situation, "living" because that way is indissolubly bound up with the Lord Jesus himself. The writer does not say, as John does, that Jesus is the way (John 14:6), but this is close to his meaning. This is not the way of the dead animals of the old covenant or the lifeless floor over which the Levitical high priest walked. It is the living Lord himself. This way to God he "dedicated" (NIV, "opened"; the word is that used of dedicating the old covenant with blood, 9:18), which hints again at his sacrifice of himself. The "curtain" goes back once more to the imagery of the tabernacle, for it was through the curtain that hung before the Most Holy Place that the high priest passed into the very presence of God.

There is a problem as to whether we take "that is, his flesh" (NIV, "body") with "curtain," which is the more natural way of taking the Greek, or whether we take it with "way." The difficulty in taking it with "curtain" is that it seems to make the flesh of Christ that which veils God from men. There is a sense, however, in which Christians have always recognized this, even if in another sense they see Christ's body as revealing God. As a well-known hymn puts it, "Veiled in flesh the Godhead see." The value of this way of looking at the imagery of the curtain is that it was by the rending of the veil—the flesh being torn on the cross—that the way to God was opened. The author is saying in his own way what the Synoptists said when they spoke of the curtain of the temple as being torn when Christ died (Matt 27:51; Mark 15:38;

Luke 23:45). The flesh (NIV, "body") here is the correlate of the blood in v.19. The alternative is to see in the equation of "flesh" and "way" the thought that the whole earthly life of Jesus is the way that bring us to God. This is not impossible, but the grammar favors the former view.

21 The term "great priest" is a literal rendering of the Hebrew title we know as "high priest" (see, e.g., Num 35:25, 28; Zech 6:11). We have had references to Jesus as "a son over God's house" (3:6) and as a high priest. Now the two thoughts are brought together. The author does not forget Jesus' high place. He has taken a lowly place (cf. the reference to his flesh, v.20), and he has died to make a way to God for men. But this assumption of the role of a servant should not blind us to the fact that Jesus is "over" God's household. Once again we have the highest Christology combined with the recognition that Jesus rendered lowly service.

22 Now come three exhortations: "Let us draw near," "Let us hold unswervingly" (v.23), and "Let us consider" (v.24). The contemplation of what Christ has done should stir his people into action. First, we are to draw near to God "with a sincere heart." The "heart" stands for the whole of the inner life of man, and it is important that as God's people approach him, they be right inwardly. It is the "pure in heart" who see God (Matt 5:8). In view of what Christ has done for us, we should approach God in deep sincerity. The "full assurance of faith" stresses that it is only by trust in Christ, who has performed for us the high priestly work that gives access to God, that we can draw near at all.

The references to the sprinkled hearts and the washed bodies should be taken together. The washing of the body with pure water is surely a reference to baptism, despite the objection of Calvin, who sees it as meaning "the Spirit of God" (in loc.). But the thing that distinguished Christian baptism from the multiplicity of lustrations that were practiced in the religions of the ancient world was that it was more than an outward rite cleansing the body from ritual defilement. Baptism is the outward sign of an inward cleansing, and it was the latter that was the more important. So here it is mentioned first. The sprinkling of the hearts signifies the effect of the blood of Christ on the inmost being. Christians are cleansed within by his shed blood (cf. the sprinkling of the priests, Exod 29:21; Lev 8:30).

23 The second exhortation is to hold fast the profession of hope. The author has already used the verb *katechō* in urging his readers to "hold on to" their confidence and their glorying in hope (3:6) and the beginning of their confidence (3:14). With a different verb (*krateō*), he has told them to "hold firmly" to the confession (4:14). Now he wants them to retain a firm grasp on "the confession of the hope," or, as NIV puts it, "the hope we profess." This is an unusual expression, and we might have expected "faith" rather than "hope" (this is actually the reading in a few MSS). But there is point in referring to hope. It has already been described as an "anchor for the soul" (6:19). Westcott comments, "Faith reposes completely in the love of God: Hope vividly anticipates that God will fulfill His promises in a particular way" (in loc.). Christians can hold fast to their hope in this way because behind it is a God in whom they can have full confidence. God is thoroughly to be relied on. When he makes a promise, that promise will infallibly be kept. He has taken the initiative in making the promise, and he will fulfill his purposes in making it.

24 The third exhortation is to consider one another. This is the only place where the author uses the expression "one another" (*allēlous*), though it is frequently found in the NT. He is speaking of a mutual activity, one in which believers encourage one another, not one where leaders direct the rest as to what they are to do. The word rendered "spur" is actually a noun, *paroxysmos*, which usually has a meaning like "irritation" or "exasperation." It is most unusual to have it used in a good sense, and the choice of the unusual word makes the exhortation more striking.

Christians are to provoke one another to love (*agapē*), a word found again in Hebrews only in 6:10. It is the characteristic NT term for a love that is not self-seeking, a love whose paradigm is the Cross (1 John 4:10). This is a most important Christian obligation, and believers are to help one another attain it. It is interesting that this kind of love is thus a product of community activity, for it is a virtue that requires others for its exercise. One may practice faith or hope alone, but not love. (For the conjunction of faith, hope, and love, see comments on 6:11.) The readers are to urge one another to "good deeds" as well as to love. The contemplation of the saving work of Christ leads on to good works in the lives of believers. The expression is left general, but the writer selects as especially important love and (in the next verse) the gathering together of believers—an interesting combination.

25 Though NIV might give the impression that this is a fourth exhortation, this is not so. The construction is a participial one, carrying on the thought of the previous verse, not giving up "meeting together." "Some" were doing this. The word is quite general, and we have no way of knowing who these abstainers were. Though it would be interesting to know whether they were from the same group as the readers, we know no more than that the early church had its problems with people who stayed away from church. It was a dangerous practice because, as Moffatt says, "Any early Christian who attempted to live like a pious particle without the support of the community ran serious risks in an age when there was no public opinion to support him" (in loc.). The attitude may mean that the abstainers saw Christianity as just another religion to be patronized or left alone. They had missed the finality on which the author lays such stress.

The writer goes on to suggest that Christians ought to be exhorting one another, and all the more as they see "the Day" getting near. Some think this Day was that of the destruction of Jerusalem, signs of which may have been evident even as this letter was being written. But it is more in accordance with NT usage to see a reference to the Day of Judgment, though, as many commentators point out, it must have been difficult for Christians in those early days to separate the two. The main thing, however, is that the writer is stressing the accountability of his readers. They must act toward their fellow believers as those who will give account of themselves to God.

Notes

19 The construction παρρησίαν εἰς τὴν εἴσοδον (*parrēsian eis tēn eisodon*, "confidence to enter") is unusual, and Héring refers to it as "rather strained." Εἰς (*eis*) apparently denotes the end or aim, "confidence leading to."

23 Strictly ἀκλινῆ (*aklinē*, "unswervingly") refers to ὁμολογίαν (*homologian*, "confession"), but NIV and most translations transfer it to those who do the confessing, a reasonable procedure, for it is the people who must hold unwaveringly to the confession.

25 "Meeting together" here is ἐπισυναγωγή (*episynagōgē*), a very unusual word used again in the NT only at 2 Thess 2:1. Some argue that the ἐπί (*epi*) is important and means "in addition." They think that some Jewish Christians worshiped in the synagogue and also in the Christian "episynagogue." In that case, ceasing to attend the "episynagogue" would leave them simply as Jews. But this is reading a lot into the prefix, and the word does not seem to be used in this way elsewhere. The Jews held firmly to the importance of meeting together; there is a well-known saying of Hillel's, "Keep not aloof from the congregation" (M *Aboth* 2:5). There is also a less-well-known one in which he says that God said, "To the place that I love, there My feet lead me: if thou wilt come into My House, I will come into thy house; if thou wilt not come to My House, I will not come to thy house" (Tal *Sukkah* 53a).

J. The Sequel—the Wrong Way

10:26-31

> [26]If we deliberately keep on sinning after we have received the knowledge of the truth, no sacrifice for sins is left, [27]but only a fearful expectation of judgment and of raging fire that will consume the enemies of God. [28]Anyone who rejected the law of Moses died without mercy on the testimony of two or three witnesses. [29]How much more severely do you think a man deserves to be punished who has trampled the Son of God under foot, who has treated as an unholy thing the blood of the covenant that sanctified him, and who has insulted the Spirit of grace? [30]For we know him who said, "It is mine to avenge; I will repay," and again, "The Lord will judge his people." [31]It is a dreadful thing to fall into the hands of the living God.

The issues are serious. While the writer continues to express confidence that his friends will do the right thing, he leaves them in no doubt as to the gravity of their situation and the terrible consequences of failing to respond to God's saving act in Christ. God is a God of love. But he is implacably opposed to all that is evil. Those who persist in wrong face judgment.

26 It is clear that the writer has apostasy in mind. He is referring to people who "have received the knowledge of the truth," where "truth" (*alētheia*) stands for "the content of Christianity as the absolute truth" (BAG, s.v.), as it frequently does in the NT. The people in question, then, know what God has done in Christ; their acquaintance with Christian teaching is more than superficial. If, knowing this, they revert to an attitude of rejection, of continual sin (cf. the present participle *hamartanontōn* rendered "keep on sinning"), then there remains no sacrifice for sins. Such people have rejected the sacrifice of Christ, and the preceding argument has shown that there is no other. If they revert to the Jewish sacrificial system, they go back to sacrifices that their knowledge of Christianity teaches them cannot put away sin (v.4). The writer adopts no pose of superiority, but his "we" puts him in the same class as his readers. While he emphasizes the danger of others, he does not forget that he too is weak and liable to sin.

27 Far from any sacrifice to put away the sins of the apostates, "only a fearful expectation of judgment" awaits such people. The nature of this expectation is not defined, and the fact that the fate of these evil persons is left indefinite makes the warning all the more impressive. The adjective *phoberos* ("fearful") is unusual; it occurs elsewhere in the NT only in v.31 and 12:21 and conveys the idea of "frightening." The judgment of the person still bearing his sins is a terrible one. The writer describes it as "raging fire" (possibly borrowed from Isa 26:11), which is a vivid expression for "the fire of judgment that, with its blazing flames, appears like a living being intent on devouring God's adversaries" (BAG, p. 338). The word "enemies" (*hypenantious*) shows that the apostates were not regarded as holding a neutral position. They have become the adversaries of God.

28–29 An argument from the greater to the lesser brings out the seriousness of the situation. To despise the law of Moses was a very serious matter, but this is more serious still. The law of Moses was held by Jews to be divinely given: anyone who rejected it rejected God's direction. When this happened, no discretion was allowed: the man must be executed. In such a serious matter the charge had to be proved beyond doubt. The testimony of one witness was not sufficient; there had to be two or three. But when there were the required witnesses to say what the man had done, then justice took over. There was no place for mercy. He must be executed (Deut 17:6; 19:15).

The writer invites the readers to work out for themselves how much more serious is the punishment of the man who apostatizes from Christ. It must be more severe than under the old way because Jesus is greater than Moses (3:1ff.); the new covenant is better than the old, founded on better promises (8:6) and established by a better sacrifice (9:23).

There are three counts in the indictment of the apostate. First, he has "trampled the Son of God under foot." It is most unusual to have the verb *katapateō* used with a personal object (elsewhere in the NT it is the literal treading under the feet of things that the verb denotes). "To trample under foot" is a strong expression for disdain. It implies not only rejecting Christ but also despising him—him who is no less than "the Son of God."

The second count is that the apostate takes lightly the solemn shedding of covenant blood. "The blood of the covenant" is an expression used of the blood that established the old covenant (Exod 24:8; cf. Heb 9:20) and also of the blood of Jesus that established the new covenant (Matt 26:28; Mark 14:24; cf. also Luke 22:20; 1 Cor 11:25). The author regards it as a dreadful thing to take lightly the shedding of the blood of one who is so high and holy and whose blood moreover is the means of establishing the new covenant that alone can bring men near to God. The apostate regards that blood as "a common thing" (*koinon*). That is to say he treats the death of Jesus as just like the death of any other man. The word "common" can also be understood over against the holy and it thus comes to mean "unhallowed." So NIV has the translation "an unholy thing." This stands out all the more sharply when it is remembered that that blood has "sanctified" him. The person who accepts Christ's way is set apart for God by the shedding of Christ's blood. As elsewhere in this epistle, the idea of being sanctified refers to the initial act of being set apart for God, not the progressive growth in grace it usually means in the other NT writings. To go back on this decisive act is to deny the significance of the blood, to see it as a common thing.

The third count in the indictment of the apostate is that he has "insulted the Spirit of grace." The author does not often refer to the Holy Spirit, being occupied for the most part with the person and the work of the Son. Nevertheless, he esteems the person of the Spirit highly as this passage shows. It also implies that he saw the Spirit as a person, not an influence or a thing, for it is only a person who can be insulted. His word for "insulted" is *enybrizō*, from *hybris*, which Westcott sees as "that insolent self-assertion which disregards what is due to others. It combines arrogance with wanton injury" (in loc.). In the NT there is a variety of ways of referring to the Spirit, but only here is he called "the Spirit of grace" (cf. Zech 12:10). The expression may mean "the gracious Spirit of God" or "the Spirit through whom God's grace is manifested." Willful sin is an insult to the Spirit, who brings the grace of God to man.

30 The appeal to knowledge ("we know") reminds us of Paul who is fond of appealing to his readers' understanding. The author calls God "him who said" words of Scripture. He uses this word for "said" (*eipon*) six times, four of them being with quotations from Scripture. He is sure that God speaks to men. The author's first quotation here is from Deuteronomy 32:35. It agrees exactly neither with the MT nor the LXX, though it is quoted in the same form in Romans 12:19. It is unlikely that either the Deuteronomy or Romans passage is dependent on the other, and much more probably the authors were both using a Greek text form that happens not to have survived. We usually speak of "the" LXX as though there was but one translation of the OT into Greek, but it is highly probable that there were a number of such translations.

The quotation here emphasizes that vengeance is a divine prerogative. It is not for men to take it into their own hands. But the emphasis is not on that. It is rather on the certainty that the Lord will act. The wrongdoer cannot hope to go unpunished because avenging wrong is in the hands of none less than God. The second quotation, from Deuteronomy 32:36, agrees with the LXX (see also Ps 135[134]:14). It leaves no doubt whatever about the Lord's intervention, for he is named and so is his activity.

The word "judge" may mean "give a favorable judgment" as well as "condemn." In both Deuteronomy 32:36 and Psalm 135:14, it is deliverance that is in mind; and both times RSV, for example, translates it as "vindicate." But in the OT God does not vindicate his people if they have sinned. Vindication implies that they have been faithful in their service and that God's intervention recognizes this. But where they have not been faithful, that same principle of impartial judgment according to right demands that intervention bring punishment. It is this that the author has primarily in mind. That a man claims to be a member of the people of God does not exempt him from judgment. God judges all. Let not the apostate think that he, of all people, can escape.

31 The sinner should not regard the judgment of God calmly. It is "a dreadful thing" to fall into God's hands ("dreadful" renders the word *phoberos*, which is translated "fearful" in v.27—i.e., it is frightening). David chose to fall into God's hands (2 Sam 24:14; 1 Chron 21:13; cf. Ecclus 2:18). But David was a man of faith; he committed himself in trust to God, not man. It is different with one who has rejected God's way. He must reckon with the fact that he will one day fall into the hands of a living, all-powerful deity. Such a fate is a daunting prospect, not to be regarded with equanimity.

Notes

27 The word ἐκδοχή (*ekdochē*), found here only in the NT, usually seems to mean "receiving from or at the hands of another" (LSJ, s.v.). The context here shows that a meaning like NIV's "expectation" is required, but this is not found elsewhere. Héring commends Spicq's translation "prospect," adding, "The question is less of a psychological fact than of an objective future which is drawing nearer" (in loc.).

The expression rendered "raging fire" (πυρὸς ζῆλος, *pyros zēlos*) is more literally "zeal of fire." "Zeal" may be used in a good sense or in the bad sense of "jealousy," "envy." To Montefiore its use here "suggests the passionate jealousy of wounded love" (in loc.).

K. *Choose the Right*

10:32–39

32Remember those earlier days after you had received the light, when you stood your ground in a great contest in the face of suffering. 33Sometimes you were publicly exposed to insult and persecution; at other times you stood side by side with those who were so treated. 34You sympathized with those in prison and joyfully accepted the confiscation of your property, because you knew that you yourselves had better and lasting possessions.

35So do not throw away your confidence; it will be richly rewarded. 36You need to persevere so that when you have done the will of God, you will receive what he has promised. 37For in just a very little while,

"He who is coming will come and will not delay.
38But my righteous one will live by faith.
And if he shrinks back,
I will not be pleased with him."

39But we are not of those who shrink back and are destroyed, but of those who believe and are saved.

As he has done before, after a section containing stern warnings, the author expresses his confidence in his readers and encourages them to take the right way. He reminds them of the early days of their Christian experience. Then they had experienced some form of persecution and had come through it triumphantly. This should teach them that in Christ they had blessings of a kind they could never have had if they had given way to persecution.

32 "But" (which NIV omits) sets the following section over against the preceding one. The author does not class his friends among those who go back on their Christian profession. He begins by inviting them to contemplate the days just after they had become Christians. The verb translated "received the light" (*phōtisthentes*) was sometimes used in the early church in reference to baptism. But it is difficult to find it used with this meaning as early as this, and in any case it is not required by the context. It is the enlightenment the gospel brought that is in mind. This had resulted in some form of persecution that the readers had endured in the right spirit. There should be no going back on that kind of endurance now. The word rendered "contest" (*athlēsis*) is used of athletic competition and is, of course, the term from which we get our word "athletics." It became widely used of the Christian as a spiritual athlete and so points to the strenuous nature of Christian service. On this occasion, the athletic performance had been elicited by a period of suffering they had steadfastly endured.

33–34 This suffering is further explained. "Sometimes . . . at other times" (so also RSV) is often taken to mean that the one group of people had had two experiences.

But it seems more likely that we should take it to mean two groups: "Some of you . . . others of you." The first group had been subjected to verbal attack ("insult") and also to other forms of trouble (*thlipsis* points to severe pressure and thus to trouble or "persecution" of various kinds). The word "publicly exposed" (*theatrizomenoi*) is not a common one; its connection with *theatron* "a theatre" makes it clear that it connotes publicity. The readers had been made a spectacle by being exposed to insult and injury.

The second group had suffered by being associates of the former group. This is explained as sympathizing with prisoners. In the world of the first century the lot of prisoners was difficult. Prisoners were to be punished, not pampered. Little provision was made for them, and they were dependent on friends for their supplies. For Christians visiting prisoners was a meritorious act (Matt 25:36). But there was some risk, for the visitors became identified with the visited. The readers of the epistle had not shrunk from this. It is not pleasant to endure ignominy, and it is not pleasant to be lumped with the ignominious. They had endured both. Attempts have been made to identify the persecution behind these words, but there is not enough information for such attempts to be successful. None of them had been killed (12:4), a fact that rules out Jerusalem, where James had been put to death quite early (Acts 12:2), and Rome after the Neronian persecution. We have no means of knowing what the persecution referred to was.

In addition to identifying with prisoners, the readers had had the right attitude to property. There is a question whether the word rendered "confiscation" (*harpagē*) means official action by which the state took over their goods, or whether it points rather to mob violence. A third possibility is the readers' voluntary surrender of their goods to some Christian community when they joined it (as Buchanan holds possible). But the word *harpagē* makes this unlikely. It is also an unlikely term for the action of officials (unless they were acting in a very "unofficial" manner; the scope for petty officialdom to tyrannize over Christians was immense). On the whole, it looks like mob violence or the like. The readers had taken this in the right spirit. It would not be a surprise if they endured all this with fortitude, but that they accepted it "joyfully" is another thing altogether. So firmly had their interest been fixed on heavenly possessions that they could take the loss of earthly goods with exhilaration.

The reason for their cheerful attitude is not quite clear. NIV gives a very plausible understanding of the Greek. But "yourselves" might be the object and not the subject of the verb, in which case it means "knowing that you had yourselves as a better and lasting possession." This would be in the spirit of Luke 21:19: "By standing firm you will save yourselves." Whichever way we take it, the possession (the word is singular in the Gr.) was both better and longer lasting. The possession in Christ is not subject to petty depredations like the earthly possessions of which they had been robbed. It is an abiding possession.

35 "So" connects what follows with what precedes. There is a reason for the conduct suggested. "Throw away" (*apoballō*) seems a fairly vigorous verb and perhaps conveys the thought of a reckless rejection of what is valuable. Because the earlier conduct of the readers showed that they knew the value of their possession in Christ, the writer can appeal to them not to discard it. As Christians they had a confidence that was based firmly on Christ's saving work and that would be the height of folly to throw away. What they had endured for Christ's sake entitled them to a reward. Let them not throw it away. The NT does not reject the notion that Christians will receive rewards, though, of course, that is never the prime motive for service.

36 The Greek has the equivalent of "you have need of perseverance"; the word *hypomonē* denotes an active, positive endurance or steadfastness. Christianity is no flash in the pan. "Need" means something absolutely necessary, not merely desirable. This leads to the thought that doing the will of God has its recompense. The author has spoken of Christ as occupied with doing the will of God (vv. 7ff.). Now he makes the point that Christ's people must similarly be occupied in doing that will. He describes the result in terms of receiving the promise, and this safeguards against any doctrine of salvation by works. God's good gift is in mind, and it is secured—though not merited—by their continuing to the end.

37–38 Now the writer encourages his readers by drawing their attention to passages in Scripture that point to the coming of God's Messiah in due course. The "very little while" (cf. Isa 26:20) points to a quite short period. The argument is that the readers ought not let the "very little while" rob them of their heavenly reward. The writer goes on to a quotation from Habakkuk 2:3–4, but he makes a few significant changes from the LXX. The first of them is to precede his quotation with the definite article so that it is "the," not "a," coming one. In other words, the reference to the Messiah is unmistakable (cf., e.g., Matt 11:3; 21:9; John 11:27 for this expression used of the Messiah). The rabbis could interpret this passage messianically as when it was held to teach people patience and warn them against calculating the date when the Messiah would come: "Blasted be the bones of those who calculate the end. For they would say, since the predetermined time has arrived, and yet he has not come, he will never come. But (even so), wait for him, as it is written, *Though he tarry, wait for him*" (Tal *Sanhedrin* 97b).

The author has reversed the order of the clauses. He thus finishes with the words about shrinking back, and this enables him to apply them immediately to his readers. We should notice also a difference between the Hebrew and the Greek of this quotation. In the original Hebrew the point is that the faithful must await God's good time for the destruction of their enemies, the Chaldeans. This cannot be hastened, and they must patiently await it. Meanwhile, the faithful man is preserved by his trust in God. In the LXX, however, it is not so much for the fulfillment of the vision that the prophet waits as for a person, a deliverer. If someone appears and draws back, he is not God's deliverer. The author is using the LXX to bring out the truth that Christ will come in due course. In the intervening time, the readers must patiently await him. .

The words about the "righteous one" living by faith are used again in Romans 1:17 and Galatians 3:11. In those passages the emphasis appears to be on how the man who is righteous by faith will live, whereas here the author seems to be using the words to convey the meaning that the person God accepts as righteous will live by faith. Paul is concerned with the way a man comes to be accepted by God; the author is concerned with the importance of holding fast to one's faith in the face of temptations to abandon it.

The mention of faith (*pistis*) leads us into the most sustained treatment of the subject in the NT. The term is mentioned again in the next verse and then throughout chapter 11. The first point made is that faith and shrinking back are opposed to each other.

The passage does not say from what the shrinking back is. In the context, however, it must relate to proceeding along the way of faith and salvation. The quotation from Habakkuk makes it clear that God is not at all pleased with the one who draws back. It is important to go forward in the path of faith.

39 The chapter closes with a ringing affirmation of confidence in which the writer identifies himself with his readers. He takes no position of superiority but sees himself as one with them. He sees two possibilities: on the one hand, drawing back and being destroyed; on the other hand, persevering in faith to salvation. The end result of shrinking back he sees as total loss (*apōleia*). But that will not be the fate of his readers. Far from being lost, they will go on in faith and be saved.

Notes

34 The reading δεσμίοις (*desmiois*, "prison") should be accepted, even though it is not read by many MSS. Δεσμοῖς (desmois, "bonds") is read by a few MSS, but it is hard to accept. Most MSS have inserted μου (*mou*, "my"), perhaps under the influence of the view that Paul was the author.

37 The expression translated "just a very little while" is μικρὸν ὅσον ὅσον (*mikron hoson hoson*), which is sufficiently unusual for us to identify it with the words of Isa 26:20 with some confidence.

38 The author puts μου (*mou*, "my") after δίκαιός (*dikaios*, "righteous one"), though there are some MSS that omit it (which seems to be an assimilation to the quotations in Rom 1:17; Gal 3:11, neither of which has the possessive). In this he follows the "A" text of the LXX, while the "B" text places it after πίστεως (*pisteōs, "faith"*). There is no reason for thinking that our author has put the pronoun there himself.

VIII. Faith

The preceding section introduced the thought of faith, and the subject is now continued in one of the classic treatments of the topic. In a passage of great eloquence and power, the author unfolds some of his thoughts on this most important subject for Christians. He is sometimes criticized for failing to convey the idea of warm personal faith in Jesus Christ that means so much to Paul. Such criticisms are, however, beside the point. Granted that the author does not follow the thoughts of Paul, yet what he says is both true and important in its own right. Nor is it of any less value because it is not what another would have said had he written at the same length on the same subject. The writer does not contrast faith with works as Paul sometimes does, nor does he treat it as the means of receiving justification. Instead, he treats faith not so much with reference to the past (what God has done in Christ) as to the future. He sees faith as that trust in God that enables the believer to press on steadfastly whatever the future holds for him. He knows that God is to be relied on implicitly. So the writer's method is to select some of the great ones in the history of the people of God and to show briefly how faith motivated all of them and led them forward, no matter how difficult the circumstances. The result is a great passage that not only encouraged his readers but also has encouraged hosts of Christians through the ages.

A. *The Meaning of Faith*

11:1-3

> [1]Now faith is being sure of what we hope for and certain of what we do not see. [2]This is what the ancients were commended for. [3]By faith we understand that the universe was formed at God's command, so that what is seen was not made out of what was visible.

The chapter begins with some general observations on the nature of faith. They do not constitute a formal definition; rather, the writer is calling attention to some significant features of faith. Then he proceeds to show how faith works out in practice.

1 In the Greek the verb "is" (*estin*) is the first word. Faith is a present and continuing reality. It is not simply a virtue sometimes practiced in antiquity. It is a living thing, a way of life the writer wishes to see continued in the practice of his readers. Faith, he tells us, is a *hypostasis* of things hoped for. The term has evoked lively discussion. Sometimes it has a subjective meaning, as in 3:14 where NIV translates it as "confidence." But it may also be used more objectively, and KJV understands it that way in this passage by translating it as "substance." This would mean that things that have no reality in themselves are made real (given "substance") by faith. But this does not seem to be what the writer is saying. Rather, his meaning is that there are realities for which we have no material evidence though they are not the less real for that. Faith enables us to know that they exist and, while we have no certainty apart from faith, faith does give us genuine certainty. "To have faith is to be sure of the things we hope for" (TEV). Faith is the basis, the substructure (*hypostasis* means lit. "that which stands under") of all that the Christian life means, all that the Christian hopes for.
There is a further ambiguity about the word *elenchos*, which usually signifies a "proof" or "test." It may be used as a legal term with a meaning like "cross examining" (LSJ, s.v.). Some take it here as "test" and some see its legal use, while many prefer to understand it in much the same sense as the preceding expression (e.g., NIV). This may well be the right way to take it, though "test" is far from impossible. The meaning would then be that faith, in addition to being the basis of all that we hope for, is that by which we test things unseen. We have no material way of assessing the significance of the immaterial. But Christians are not helpless. They have faith and by this they test all things. "What we do not see" excludes the entire range of visible phenomena, which here stand for all things earthly. Faith extends beyond what we learn from our senses, and the author is saying that it has its reasons. Its tests are not those of the senses, which yield uncertainty.

2 "The ancients" more strictly means "the elders" (*hoi presbyteroi*), a term that may be used of age or dignity. Here it refers to the religious leaders of past days and means much the same as "the forefathers" in 1:1. These men had witness borne to them (*emartyrēthēsan*) on account of their faith. As this chapter unfolds, the writer will go on to bring out some of that testimony and link the heroes of old specifically with faith. This is an example of a type of literature that recurs in antiquity. A well-known example is the passage in Ecclesiasticus, which begins, "Let us now praise famous men" (44:1–50:21). But this chapter in Hebrews is distinguished from all others by its consistent emphasis on faith. Other writers see a variety of reasons for the success of those they describe. Here in Hebrews one thing and one thing only is stressed—faith. Single-mindedly the author concentrates on that one splendid theme.

3 "By faith" runs through the chapter with compelling emphasis. For the most part it is attached to the deeds of the great ones of previous generations. Here, however, the writer and his readers are involved in the "we." Faith is a present reality, not exclusively the property of past heroes. Faith gives us convictions about creation. Belief in the existence of the world is not faith, nor is it faith when men hold that the world was made out of some preexisting "stuff." (In the first century there were people who did not believe in God but who held to some kind of "creation.") But when we understand that it was the Word of God ("God's command," NIV) that produced all things, that is faith. The emphasis on God's word agrees with Genesis 1, with its repeated "And God said." The point is emphasized with the explicit statement that the visible did not originate from the visible. For the author the visible universe is not sufficient to account for itself. But it is faith, not something material, that assures him that it originated with God. His view is none the less certain because it is based on faith, and he does not qualify his statement as though any doubt were possible. This world is God's world, and faith assures him that God originated it.

Notes

1 On ὑπόστασις (hypostasis, "confidence"), MM (s.v.) note a variety of uses of the word in the papyri and conclude: "These varied uses are at first sight somewhat perplexing, but in all cases there is the same central idea of something that underlies visible conditions and guarantees a future possession." They suggest that we translate here "Faith is the titledeed of things hoped for." This translation may not commend itself, but the word as used here does seem to point to certainty.

B. The Faith of the Men Before the Flood

11:4–7

4By faith Abel offered God a better sacrifice than Cain did. By faith he was commended as a righteous man, when God spoke well of his offerings. And by faith he still speaks, even though he is dead.
5By faith Enoch was taken from this life, so that he did not experience death; he could not be found, because God had taken him away. For before he was taken, he was commended as one who pleased God. 6And without faith it is impossible to please God, because anyone who comes to him must believe that he exists and that he rewards those who earnestly seek him.
7By faith Noah, when warned about things not yet seen, in holy fear built an ark to save his family. By his faith he condemned the world and became heir of the righteousness that comes by faith.

The author proceeds to demonstrate the universality of faith in those God approves. He selects a number of men and women universally regarded among the Jews as especially outstanding (though we cannot always see why he has chosen one and not another). He begins by looking to remote antiquity and showing that faith was manifested in the lives of certain great men who lived before the Flood.

4 The first example of faith is Abel, who brought God a more acceptable sacrifice than did his brother Cain (Gen 4:3–7). Bruce (in loc.) canvasses a number of opinions as to the reasons for the superiority of Abel's offering: it was living, whereas Cain's was lifeless; it was stronger, Cain's weaker; it grew spontaneously, Cain's by human ingenuity; it involved blood, Cain's did not. But all such suggestions seem wide of the mark. Scripture never says there was anything inherently superior in Abel's offering. It may be relevant that there are some references to Abel as being a righteous man (Matt 23:35; 1 John 3:12), while the author of Hebrews insists on the importance of Abel's faith. Abel was right with God and his offering was a demonstration of his faith.

Once again, NIV's "commended" represents the passive of the verb "to witness": "it was witnessed" or "testified" that he was righteous (cf. v.1). This is explained as that God "bore witness" to (NIV, "spoke well of") his offerings. This indicates the importance the author attached to Abel's sacrifice offered in faith, for very rarely is God said to have borne witness. The meaning may be either that on the basis of Abel's sacrifice God testified to his servant or that God bore witness about the gifts Abel offered. We should probably accept NIV's "And by faith he still speaks," though the Greek is simply "through it," where "it" might refer either to "sacrifice" or to "faith." Whichever way we resolve this problem, the main point is that Abel is not to be thought of as one long-since dead and of no present account. He is dead, but his faith is a living voice.

5 In Jewish apocalyptic thought, Enoch was a very popular figure, and several books are ascribed to him. But in the NT he figures only in Luke 3:37, Jude 14, and here. The Hebrew OT says nothing of the manner of his departure from this life, only that God "took" him (Gen 5:24). But the author follows LXX in speaking of him as "transferred," which indicates that he did not die, a truth made explicit in the words "he did not experience death."

The passive of the verb "to find" (*heuriskō*) is sometimes used with the meaning "no longer be found, despite a thorough search = *disappear*" (BAG, s.v.). The author follows this up with the active *metethēken* (lit., "God transferred him") instead of the passive *metetethē* he used previously, a change that brings out the divine initiative. There is an air of permanence about the use of the perfect of this verb. There was no going back on it. For the fourth time in this chapter NIV avoids translating the verb *martyreō* with "witness" or "testify," preferring "he was commended." But this must be understood to mean that testimony was borne to him, the content of the testimony being that he was "one who pleased God" (Gen 5:22, 24, LXX).

6 Though the OT does not say that Enoch had faith, the author goes on to explain why he can speak of it so confidently. It is impossible to please God without faith, and Enoch pleased God. Thus it is clear that he had faith. Notice that the author lays it down with the greatest of emphasis that faith is absolutely necessary. He does not say simply that without faith it is difficult to please God; he says that without faith it is impossible to please him! There is no substitute for faith. He goes on to lay down two things required in the worshiper ("anyone who comes to him" renders the participle of the verb *proserchomai*, used, as in 10:1, of one who comes near in worship). First, he must believe that God exists. This is basic. Without it there is no possibility of faith at all. But it is not enough of itself. After all, the demons can know that sort of faith (James 2:19). There must also be a conviction about God's moral character, belief "that he rewards those who earnestly seek him." As Barclay puts it,

"We must believe, not only that God exists, but also that God cares" (in loc.). Without that deep conviction, faith in the biblical sense is not a possibility.

7 Attention moves to Noah. He was "warned," a verb that is used frequently of divine communications, the pronouncements of oracles, and the like. Noah was not acting on a hunch or on merely human advice. It was the voice of God that carried conviction to him. The warning concerned things "not yet seen," i.e., events of which there was no present indication, nothing that could be observed. At the time Noah received his message from God, there was no sign of the Flood and related events. His action was motivated by faith, not by any reasoned calculation of the probabilities based on the best available evidence.

In the expression "holy fear" (*eulabētheis*), some put the emphasis on "holy" and some on "fear." While it is true that this verb may convey the notion of fear, it is not easy to see it in this context. The author is not telling us that Noah was a timid type but that he was a man of faith. He acted out of reverence for God and God's command. So he "built" (*kateskeuasen*) an ark. Though the verb may be used of preparing or building in a variety of senses, it is a "favorite word for construction of ships" (BAG, p. 419) and so is relevant to this reference to the ark. The purpose of building the ark was "to save his family" (lit., "for the salvation of his house"). In the NT the noun "salvation" (*sōtēria*) usually refers to salvation in Christ. Here, however, as in a few other places, it is the more general idea of salvation from danger—deliverance from disaster—that is in mind. Noah's faith led to the preservation of his entire household during the Flood.

There is a problem here similar to that in v.4, and NIV solves it exactly the same way. The Greek relative pronoun *di' hēs* ("through which"; NIV, "by") might refer back either to "faith," "ark," or "salvation." NIV inserts "faith" and removes the ambiguity. This is probably the correct way to understand the passage, though we should bear in mind that some notable exegetes think that the ark is meant (e.g., Calvin). Westcott (in loc.) refers it to the ark as the outward expression of faith. Noah's faith in action was a condemnation of the men of his day who failed to respond to the example of that godly man and presumably to the reasons he gave for his conduct. (Noah must have told them why he was doing such an extraordinary thing as building an ark there on dry land.) Upright conduct will always stand in condemnation of wickedness (cf. Matt 12:41–42; Luke 11:31–32; 1 John 3:12).

"The world" signifies the totality of mankind of that day who did not obey God. "Heir" is used in the sense of "possessor," not strictly of one who enters a possession as a result of a will. Here in v.7 we have the author's one use of the term "righteousness" in the Pauline sense of the righteousness that is ours by faith. In the Bible Noah was the first man to be called righteous (Gen 6:9). He was right with God because he took God at his word; he believed what God said and acted on it.

Notes

3 NIV is surely correct in understanding τοὺς αἰῶνας (*tous aiōnas*) as "the universe," though we should bear in mind that the term strictly means "the ages." The author prefers to use a word that has a time reference.

4 The use of πλείονα (*pleiona*) of Abel's sacrifice has puzzled commentators. Usually it is taken in the sense of "better" and support for such an understanding may be found in passages such as Luke 12:23: "Life is more than food" (cf. Luke 11:31–32). But some conjecture that there was an early textual error with ΗΔΕΙΟΝΑ being misread as ΠΛΕΙΟΝΑ. This is possible, but there is no MS evidence to support such a reading. If such a corruption did occur, it must have been very early. Some prefer to take the expression literally and think of Abel as giving God "more" in the literal sense. Some such sense as in NIV seems right.

In the second occurrence of the word "God," some MSS read the dative τῷ θεῷ (*tō theō*) instead of the genitive τοῦ θεοῦ (*tou theou*). With this reading the meaning is that Abel bore witness to God on the basis of his gifts. But the reading should probably be rejected. It is not strongly supported in the MSS, and it looks like an attempt to make a hard reading easier. Héring further points out that it demands an unusual sense for the preposition ἐπί (*epi*), "by his offerings" (in loc.).

C. The Faith of Abraham and Sarah

11:8–19

8By faith Abraham, when called to go to a place he would later receive as his inheritance, obeyed and went, even though he did not know where he was going. 9By faith he made his home in the promised land like a stranger in a foreign country; he lived in tents, as did Isaac and Jacob, who were heirs with him of the same promise. 10For he was looking forward to the city with foundations, whose architect and builder is God.

11By faith Abraham, even though he was past age—and Sarah herself was barren—was enabled to become a father because he considered him faithful who had made the promise. 12And so from this one man, and he as good as dead, came descendants as numerous as the stars in the sky and as countless as the sand on the seashore.

13All these people were still living by faith when they died. They did not receive the things promised; they only saw them and welcomed them from a distance. And they admitted that they were aliens and strangers on earth. 14People who say such things show that they are looking for a country of their own. 15If they had been thinking of the country they had left, they would have had opportunity to return. 16Instead, they were longing for a better country—a heavenly one. Therefore God is not ashamed to be called their God, for he has prepared a city for them.

17By faith Abraham, when God tested him, offered Isaac as a sacrifice. He who had received the promises was about to sacrifice his one and only son, 18even though God had said to him, "It is through Isaac that your offspring will be reckoned." 19Abraham reasoned that God could raise the dead, and figuratively speaking, he did receive Isaac back from death.

The great progenitor of the race and his wife are now singled out as examples of faith. The Jews prided themselves on their descent from Abraham, and the great patriarch is mentioned a number of times in the NT as one who had faith and who acted on his faith (Acts 7:2–8; Rom 4:3; Gal 3:6; James 2:23). It is in line with this that the author gives more space to Abraham than to any other individual on his list. He sees Abraham as an excellent example of what he has in mind, for the author does not see faith as making a good guess based on the best human estimate of the possibilities. Abraham's faith accepted God's promises and acted on them even though there was nothing to indicate that they would be fulfilled. He "went, even though he did not know where he was going." This faith is seen in his acceptance of the promise of a child when Sarah was old and even more in his readiness to sacrifice that child—the one through whom the promise was to be fulfilled—when God commanded. Consistently, Abraham believed God and acted on his faith. He obeyed God implicitly, though there was nothing tangible he could rely on.

8 Abraham is mentioned ten times in Hebrews, a total exceeded only by Luke (fifteen) and John (eleven). The author of Hebrews shows a strong interest in this patriarch. "When called" translates a present participle that indicates a very prompt obedience. "He obeyed the call while (so to say) it was still sounding in his ears" (Westcott, in loc.). His prompt obedience took him out to a region as yet unknown to him but which he would later receive "as his possession" (*klēronomia;* strictly, "inheritance"). The last half of this verse is a classical statement of the obedience of faith. Men like to know where they are going and to choose their way. But the way forward can be obscure. Abraham was one who could go out, knowing that it was right to do so, but not knowing where it would all lead. God told him to go "to the land that I will show you" (Gen 12:1). Yet it was not till some time after he reached Canaan that he was informed that this was the land God would give his descendants (Gen 12:7; later on Abraham himself was included in the same promise, Gen 13:15). To leave the certainties one knows and go out into what is quite unknown—relying on nothing other than the Word of God—is the essence of faith, as the author sees it.

9 Paradoxically, when he got to the land of Canaan that God had promised to him, Abraham lived in it, not as its owner, but as a resident alien. The verb translated "made his home" (*parōkēsen*) is not normally used of permanent residence but, as BAG (s.v.) says, it means to "inhabit . . . as a stranger" (BAG also sees "migrate" as possible here). "The promised land" (more lit. "land of the promise") is an expression found only here in the Bible. As the context plainly shows it means Canaan, but v. 10 indicates that heaven is meant, too. The earthly Canaan is a foretaste of God's heavenly country. Though Canaan was to be his own land in due course, Abraham had to live there as though "in a foreign country." He had no rights. He and his household lived in tents, in temporary dwellings. The whole land had been promised to him. Yet Abraham did not even have a proper house in it.

The verb rendered "lived" (*katoikēsas*) has the notion of settling down. It is normally used of a continuous, permanent dwelling. But Abraham's permanent dwelling place in Canaan was a temporary tent! Right to the end of his life the only piece of the country he owned was the field he purchased as Sarah's burial place (Gen 23). God "gave him no inheritance here, not even a foot of ground" (Acts 7:5). Nor was it any better with Isaac and Jacob. They shared the same promises. They were the descendants through whom God's purpose would be worked out. But all their lifetimes they had no more share in Canaan than Abraham did. Toward the end of Jacob's life the clan went down to Egypt, and when they came back many years later, it was not as sojourners but as a mighty people who made the land their own. The lives of the three patriarchs thus cover the whole time of the temporary dwelling in the land.

10 The reason for Abraham's patient acceptance of his lot was his forward look in faith to "the city with foundations" (actually, "the foundations"). To cultured men in the first century, the city was the highest form of civilized existence. Nothing served so well as the pattern for the ideal community. Buchanan argues that the city in mind was probably Jerusalem, and he cites a good deal of evidence to show the high regard in which Jews held their holy city (in loc.). But it is difficult to see God as the "architect and builder" of the earthly Jerusalem, and we should also bear in mind the author's reference to "the heavenly Jerusalem" (12:22). Buchanan's evidence shows how congenial to Jew as well as Gentile the present reference to the city would have been.

The thought of the heavenly city recurs in v.16; 12:22; 13:14 and it is found elsewhere in the NT; e.g., in Philippians 1:27 (*politeuesthe*, "act as members of a city") and 3:20 and described in Revelation 3:12; 21:10, et al. The description the "city with foundations" raises the question as to what the "foundations" are. We should not look for anything literal; the expression probably means that the city is well based— i.e., a "city with permanent foundations" (TEV). It is eternal, more lasting than earth's ephemeral edifices.

The city owes everything to God, who is its "architect and builder." The first of these words, *technitēs*, means a craftsman or designer. As applied to a city, it may mean an architect or point to what we would call a "city planner." The thought is that the city is entirely designed by God. The second word, *dēmiourgos*, points rather to one who does the actual work. God built the city as well as designed it; it owes nothing to any inferior being. Neither term is applied to God anywhere else in the NT (3:4 uses another word of God's activity in building all things). The thought of this verse shows clearly that more than Canaan was in Abraham's mind when he went out in faith. These words cannot be limited to an earthly place. God is not the "architect and builder" of Canaan any more than he is of any other land.

11 This verse presents us with a problem so difficult that Héring speaks of it as a "cross which is frankly too heavy for expositors to bear" (in loc.). The difficulty is that on the face of it the verse ascribes to Sarah an activity possible only to males: *dynamin eis katabolēn spermatos* ("power for the depositing of semen"). The simplest solution is to delete the words "and [or 'even'] Sarah herself," and this is favored by some commentators. It would give a good connection with the preceding and carry forward the story of Abraham's faith. But there is no MS authority for this reading, and it looks suspiciously like a way of getting rid of the problem, not of solving it. A second suggestion is that we see the words "Sarah herself" as dative and not nominative. The meaning would then be "By faith he, together with Sarah herself, received power. . . ." The whole of the rest of the section is about Abraham's faith, and this would bring this verse into line. It would also agree with "from this one man" in v.12 and with the fact that the promise was made to Abraham, not Sarah. A third possibility is to take the words about Sarah as a parenthesis, as NIV does. For good measure this translation also inserts "Abraham" into the text and makes the rest of the verse refer unambiguously to a male. A fourth approach is to take the word *katabolē* in the sense of "foundation." The word means basically a "throwing down" (LSJ, s.v.), and it is from this that it gets the sense of depositing semen. But it is also used of depositing what it used at the beginning of a building and thus "foundation." It is used in much this sense in 4:3; 9:26 (NIV renders "creation" both times). If it is taken in this sense here, the word for "semen" would be understood in the sense of "descendants," and Sarah would be regarded as having received power for the foundation of a posterity. A decision is not easy, but I incline to the second view (with Bruce [in loc.]; BDF, par. 194 [1]; et al.). Abraham then had faith in connection with the birth of Isaac, and Sarah is linked with him.

There is a further problem in that in Genesis Sarah was anything but an example of faith, for she laughed incredulously at the suggestion that she should bear a son in her old age (Gen 18:9ff.). The author appears to mean that, despite her initial skepticism, Sarah came to share Abraham's faith (otherwise she would not have cooperated with her husband to secure the birth of the boy). The aged couple lacked the physical ability to cause birth, but faith introduced them to the power that brought about the birth of Isaac. "Past age" (which could refer to either of the two but applies to Abraham if the view I am taking is correct) draws attention to the area in which faith had to operate. On the merely human level, there was no hope. But for Abraham there was hope. He knew that God had made a promise and he knew that God is "faithful." As in 10:23, God is described with reference to his promise; and, again as in that passage, he is said to be faithful. Faithfulness to his word is a characteristic of God.

12 "And so" introduces the inevitable result. Because God promised and Abraham believed him, the consequence necessarily followed. The smallness of the beginning is brought out. Abraham was but "one man." Moreover, he was not one from whom a numerous progeny might be anticipated because he was "as good as dead" (an expression referring to his capacity for begetting offspring, not to his general state). By contrast his descendants would be as numerous as the stars in the sky or the sand on the seashore. This part of the verse is not a quotation from a specific OT passage. The words are reminiscent of a number of passages (e.g., Gen 15:5; 22:17; Exod 32:13; Deut 1:10; 10:22; Dan 3:36, LXX). Both the stars and the sand were proverbial for multitude; so the general meaning is that Abraham's descendants would be too many to count. God's blessing is beyond human calculation.

13 The author breaks off his treatment of Abraham for a moment to engage in some general remarks about "all these people," i.e., those he had dealt with thus far. They lived out their lives and died still exercising faith, without having possessed what was promised. "All" allows no exceptions. What is said applies to every one of them. They knew that God had promised certain blessings, but they did not receive them. We must be careful how we understand this, for the author has already said that Abraham "received what was promised" (6:15). Humanly speaking, when there was no hope of having a son, he saw Isaac born. The promise, however, meant far more than that. Actually, it is the fullness of the blessing that is in mind in v.13. The best that happened to the saints of old was that they had glimpses of what God had for them.

Perhaps it will help us to see something of what is meant if we recall Moses' view of the Promised Land. He prayed that God would let him enter the land (Deut 3:23–25), but the most God would permit was for him only to see it (Deut 3:26–28; 34:1–4). The patriarchs did no more than "see" their equivalent of the Promised Land. "See" can be used of various kinds of sight. Here it is plainly an operation of faith that is in mind, and the word points to an inner awareness of what the promises meant. In their attitude, the patriarchs showed that they knew themselves to be no more than "aliens and strangers." The latter term means those living in a country they do not belong to, i.e., resident aliens.

The combination "aliens and strangers" reminds us of Abraham's description of himself as "an alien and a stranger" (Gen 23:4) and Jacob's words to Pharaoh (Gen 47:9). The psalmist could also describe himself as "an alien, a stranger," and add, "as all my fathers were" (Ps 39:12). It is true that Isaac once sowed "crops" (Gen 26:12) and Jacob at one time "built a place for himself" (Gen 33:17). But neither really settled down in the land, and to the end of their lives they were pilgrims rather than residents. The author sees that it was faith that enabled all these great men of old to recognize their true position as citizens of heaven and thus as aliens everywhere on earth.

14–15 To acknowledge the things stated in v.13 has further implications; namely, that the kind of people spoken of are looking for "a country [*patris*] of their own." If they had regarded themselves only as earthlings, they would not have retained the vision of faith with their attention squarely fixed on what is beyond this earth.

There is some difficulty in translating the verb *mnēmoneuō* (NIV, "thinking"). The usual meaning is "remember." Some, however, point out that in v.22 it must mean something like "make mention of," "speak about." So they think that a similar meaning will suit this passage. Others prefer to keep the term in the region of thought. Perhaps NEB's "If their hearts had been in the country they had left" gives the fuller sense. The patriarchs could have gone back had they so chosen, whether we understand this to mean "going back to Mesopotamia" or "going back to the things of this world." There was nothing physical to stop them. But their attitude excluded the possibility.

When Abraham wanted a wife for Isaac, he wanted her to be from his homeland. But he did not go back there himself. Instead, he sent a servant to get the bride and said to him, "Make sure that you do not take my son back there" (Gen 24:6). After Jacob had spent twenty years in Mesopotamia, he still regarded Canaan as "my own homeland" (Gen 30:25); and he heard God say, "Go back to the land of your fathers" (Gen 31:3). Abraham buried Sarah in Canaan, not Mesopotamia, and in due course he was buried there himself (Gen 23:19; 25:9–10), as were Isaac (Gen 35:27–29) and Jacob (Gen 49:29–33; 50:13), Jacob being brought up from Egypt for the purpose. Joseph commanded that the same be done for him (Gen 50:24–26; cf. Exod 13:19; Josh 24:32). All these men wholeheartedly accepted God's word. Had they been earthly minded, they could have gone back to Mesopotamia. But their hearts were set on their heavenly home, and they did not go back. Singlemindedly they walked the path of faith.

16 "Instead" contrasts the actuality with what might have been. The people's longing was for the heavenly country. The adjective "heavenly" connects country with God and with all it means to belong to God. So firm was their commitment to their heavenly calling that God was not ashamed of them. Indeed, he is spoken of again and again as "the God of Abraham, the God of Isaac, and the God of Jacob." Sometimes God uses these very words of himself (Exod 3:6, 15–16). Jesus used the same expression to show the truth that the patriarchs still live (Mark 12:26–27). Not only is God not ashamed of those servants of his, he honored their faith by preparing a city for them (see comments on v.10). The use of the past tense should not be overlooked. It is not that God will one day prepare their city but that he has already done so.

17–18 The writer returns from the patriarchs in general to Abraham in particular. In doing so he brings out something of the significance of the greatest trial that that great man had to endure: God demanded that he sacrifice his son Isaac. We are apt to see this as a conflict between Abraham's love for his son and his duty to God. But for the author the problem was Abraham's difficulty in reconciling the different revelations made to him. God had promised him a numerous posterity through Isaac; yet now he called on him to offer Isaac as a sacrifice. How then could the promise be fulfilled?

Though he did not understand, Abraham knew how to obey. His faith told him that God would work out his purpose, even if he himself could not see how that could be. So he "offered Isaac as a sacrifice." The perfect tense of the Greek verb *prosphero* ("offered") indicates that as far as Abraham was concerned the sacrifice was complete. In will and purpose he did offer his son. He held nothing back. But immediately the same verb is used in the imperfect tense, which means that the action was not in fact completed. Abraham did not fail in his obedience, for God did not require him to slay his son.

Isaac is called *monogenēs* here, which NIV renders "one and only." The term has a meaning like "unique." Abraham had other sons (Gen 25:1–2, 5–6); so *monogenēs* does not mean "only." Yet he had no other born in the way Isaac was and bearing the kind of promises that were made about Isaac. The word for "received" (*anadechomai*) is an unusual one, found again in the NT only in Acts 28:7. MM find many examples of its use in the papyri in the legal sense of "undertake," "assume," and say, "The predominance of this meaning suggests its application in Heb 11^17. The statement that Abraham had 'undertaken,' 'assumed the responsibility of' the promises, would not perhaps be alien to the thought" (s.v.). If we accept this, Abraham's faith is highlighted.

Abraham was not passive; he took the responsibility of being the man through whom God would work out his promise. Yet he was ready to offer the required sacrifice. His dilemma is brought out with the quotation of God's promise from Genesis 21:12. God's promise was to be fulfilled in Isaac, not in another of Abraham's sons. The words "through Isaac" are placed in an emphatic position. The quotation from Genesis underlines the truth that the divine call had singled out the line through Isaac as the line through which God would fulfill his promise.

19 Now comes an explanation of why Abraham, who believed that God was going to fulfill his promises through Isaac, was nevertheless ready to offer up his son. He calculated (*logisamenos*) that God could raise the dead. This would fit in with the Genesis narrative, for as Abraham went off with the boy to sacrifice him—and as we have seen he was fully determined to go through with the program—he said to the servants, "Stay here with the donkey while I and the boy go over there. We will worship and then we will come back to you" (Gen 22:5).

The rest of v.19 probably should be understood as NIV has it: "And figuratively speaking, he did receive Isaac back from death." Abraham had had to reconcile himself to the death of the son in whom he had thought the promises of God would be realized. To have Isaac alive was like getting someone back from the dead. Abraham's unswerving faith in God was vindicated. We should, however, notice that some take "figuratively speaking" (*en parabolē*) to mean "in a way that prefigured the resurrection" (Moffatt, in loc.). Again, some commentators relate "from death" to Isaac's birth, coming from one "as good as dead" (v.12). But neither of these seems likely. We should rather see the words as meaning that Abraham "did not bind the power of God to the life of Isaac but was persuaded that it would be effective in his ashes when he was dead no less than when he was alive and breathing" (Calvin, in loc.).

Notes

8 NIV takes the infinitive ἐξελθεῖν (exelthein, "went") with καλούμενος (kaloumenos, "called"). But it is also possible to see it as epexegetic and take it with ὑπήκουσεν (hypēkousen, "obeyed") to give the meaning "went out obediently."

10 Δημιουργός (dēmiourgos, "builder") is used a good deal by the philosophers to denote the Creator of the universe, but it is unlikely that the author is influenced by such usage. As I. H. Marshall puts it, "The writer here uses a fine, rhetorical phrase to stress the excellence and abiding quality of the heavenly city as one built on firm foundations by God himself; the thought is metaphorical and non-philosophical" (DNTT, 1:387).

11 In uncial MSS there would have been no iota subscript so that ΑΥΤΗ ΣΑΡΡΑ (AUTE SARRA, "Sarah herself") might be either dative or nominative. Most MSS do not read στεῖρα (steira, "barren"), and the word is rejected in the critical editions of Nestlé, Kilpatrick, etc. NIV's "was enabled" translates δύναμιν ἔλαβεν (dynamin elaben, "received power"). The verb will have a passive sense. The power was not something natural to Abraham or within his grasp but something God gave him.

13 The standard πίστει (pistei, "by faith") is here replaced by κατὰ πίστιν (kata pistin, "according to faith"). Some find significance in the change and see a meaning "according to the spirit of faith" or the like. But it is probably a stylistic change with no real difference in meaning.

D. *The Faith of the Patriarchs*

11:20–22

20By faith Isaac blessed Jacob and Esau in regard to their future.
21By faith Jacob, when he was dying, blessed each of Joseph's sons, and worshiped as he leaned on the top of his staff.
22By faith Joseph, when his end was near, spoke about the exodus of the Israelites from Egypt and gave instructions about his bones.

What impresses the author about these patriarchs was that they had a faith that looked beyond death. It was when he thought he was near death that Isaac blessed Jacob and Esau (Gen 27:2, 4). Jacob gave blessings and Joseph gave instructions in the light of the nearness of death. With all three the significant thing was their firm conviction that death cannot frustrate God's purposes. Their faith was such that they were sure God would work his will. So they could speak with confidence of what would happen after they died. Their faith, being stronger than death, in a way overcame death, for their words were fulfilled.

20 Just as Abraham acted in view of things to come, so did Isaac. He blessed his two sons in terms that looked into the distant future (Gen 27:27–29, 39–40). The author says nothing about Jacob's deception of his old father. It might perhaps be objected that the words Isaac spoke with reference to Jacob he thought he was speaking to Esau so that what he said did not really apply and was not an example of soundly based faith. But Isaac quickly recognized that the blessing belonged to Jacob (Gen 27:33), and later he specifically blessed Jacob with full knowledge of what he was doing (Gen 28:1–4). In any case, the author is not interested in such details; it is enough that both blessings concerned "their future." His concern is with the faith that undergirded the patriarch's blessing. On each occasion Isaac spoke out of a firm conviction that a

blessing given in accordance with God's purposes could not possibly fail. Though there were marked differences in the two blessings, these are passed over. They are not relevant. The important thing is Isaac's faith, seen in the fact that the patriarch spoke of blessings that would not be fulfilled until the distant future. Isaac trusted God. Fittingly, the sons are listed in the order in which they received the blessings, not that of their birth.

21 Jacob's claim for inclusion in the list rests on his blessing of his grandsons Ephraim and Manasseh (Gen 48). As with Isaac, the blessing went against the natural order of birth. In fact, when Jacob was dying, Joseph tried to have the major blessing given to Manasseh, the firstborn. But Jacob crossed his hands to pick out Ephraim as the greater. God is not bound by human rules like those that give pride and benefit of place to the firstborn. He fulfills his purposes as he chooses. The incident, like the preceding one, again illustrates the theme of the patriarchal blessing with its fulfillment far distant. At the time the words were spoken, fulfillment could be known only by faith.

To the words about the blessing of the boys, the author adds a reference to a previous incident in which Jacob "worshiped as he leaned on the top of his staff." There is an ambiguity in the text in Genesis 47:31 because the Hebrew was originally written without vowels. The reader supplied them as he went along. Usually this presents no difficulty, but in Genesis 47:31 there is a word that with one set of vowels means "bed" and with another, "staff." The text behind the RSV accepts the former, giving the meaning "Israel bowed himself upon the head of his bed." As he usually does, the author of Hebrews follows the LXX, which takes the word to mean "staff." Some have thought that we should understand the text to mean that Jacob worshiped the top of his staff (there is no "leaning" in the Gr.). But quite apart from the improbability of Jacob's doing any such thing, the linguistics are against it. There is an "on" (*epi*) with the "staff," and we must supply "leaning" or the like to make sense of it. The author, then, speaks of Jacob as adopting a worshipful attitude as he blessed the sons of Joseph.

22 Joseph's faith, like that of the others, looked beyond death, though his words referred to nothing more than his burial arrangements. But the charge to carry his bones to Canaan (Gen 50:24–25; Exod 13:19; Josh 24:32) give evidence of his deep conviction that in due course God would send the people back to that land. Joseph's wish to be buried in Canaan is all the more striking when we remember that, apart from his first seventeen years, he spent all his life in Egypt. But Canaan was the land for the people of God. So despite his short acquaintance with it, Joseph wanted to be buried there. His speaking about the "exodus" of the Israelites from Egypt and his concern about the proper disposal of his bones reflect his high faith that in due course God would act.

E. *The Faith of Moses*

11:23–28

> [23]By faith Moses' parents hid him for three months after he was born, because they saw he was no ordinary child, and they were not afraid of the king's edict. [24]By faith Moses, when he had grown up, refused to be known as the son of Pharaoh's daughter. [25]He chose to be mistreated along with the people of God rather than to enjoy the pleasures of sin for a short time. [26]He regarded disgrace

for the sake of Christ as of greater value than the treasures of Egypt, because he was looking ahead to his reward. [27]By faith he left Egypt, not fearing the king's anger; he persevered because he saw him who is invisible. [28]By faith he kept the Passover and the sprinkling of blood, so that the destroyer of the firstborn would not touch the firstborn of Israel.

No OT character ranked higher in popular Jewish estimation than Moses. He was the great lawgiver, and the law was central to Jewish life. Legend made free with his name, and many astonishing feats were attributed to him. (For example, Josephus says that when Pharaoh's daughter brought the child to the king he put his royal crown on the boy's head, but little Moses flung it to the ground and trod on it [Antiq. II, 233f. (ix. 1)].) Moses is highly honored in the NT, but the references to him there are much more sober (e.g., Acts 7:20–44). The author has a just appreciation for the greatness of Moses but shows none of the extravagances so typical of the Judaism of his time. We may fairly say that both Christians and Jews honored both Abraham and Moses; but whereas the Jews tended to put Moses in the higher place and to see Abraham as one who kept the law before Moses, the Christians, with their emphasis on faith, preferred to put Abraham in the more exalted place and see Moses as one who followed in the steps of Abraham's faith. The author is certainly interested in the way Moses exercised faith, and he gives five instances of faith in connection with the great lawgiver.

23 Moses is mentioned eleven times in Hebrews, which is more than in any other NT epistle (though not so many times as in John and Acts). Like the others in this chapter, he lived by faith. But here the reference to him begins with the faith exercised when he was too young to know what was going on—the faith of his parents. In the account in Exodus the role of Moses' mother receives all the attention, his father not being mentioned. In the LXX, however, the plural verbs in Exodus 2:2–3 show that both parents were involved, and the author follows his customary practice of depending on LXX. In any case, the mother could not have hidden the child without the father's agreement. So both parents were necessarily involved.

NIV says both parents hid Moses "because they saw he was no ordinary child." However, the Greek *asteios* means "beautiful" or perhaps "well-pleasing" rather than "not ordinary." The meaning appears to be that the child was so exceptionally beautiful that his parents believed that God had some special plan for him. The king's edict was for every male Hebrew child to be thrown into the Nile (Exod 1:22). Presumably, anyone who disobeyed would be severely punished. But Moses' parents were people of faith. They hid their beautiful baby for three months, trusting God rather than fearing Pharaoh.

24 The author passes over the putting of the baby in the ark of bulrushes, the finding of the child by Pharaoh's daughter, and the rearing of Moses in Pharaoh's house. He comes at once to Moses' faith as a grown man. "When he had grown up" is probably the best way to understand *megas genomenos* ("having become great"), though the suggestion has been made that there is a reference to the social and political position the man Moses found himself in. Stephen tells us that Moses was about forty years old at the time (Acts 7:23). The author appears to be saying that the decision Moses reached was that of a mature man—not the decision of a child or rebellious adolescent. In full knowledge of what he was doing, Moses "refused to be known as the son of

Pharaoh's daughter," which, as Bruce puts it, "must have seemed an act of folly by all worldly standards" (in loc.). He had open to him a place of great prestige and he could have lived comfortably among the Egyptian aristocracy. But he gave it all up. Some have tried to identify "Pharaoh's daughter," but we lack sufficient information to do this.

25 Moses' decision involved the ready acceptance of oppression as he cast in his lot with God's people instead of the pleasures he could have had at the court. The full expression "the people of God" is not frequent, though it is often implied. Its use here rather than something like "the people of Israel" seems to indicate a religious rather than nationalistic commitment. Moses is seen not as a revolutionary but as a man of faith deliberately classing himself with God's own, even though doing that meant ill treatment. "The pleasures of sin" does not mean Moses saw himself as a dissolute rake while at court. It implies rather that once he saw where God's call lay, it would have been sin for him to turn away from it and align himself with the Egyptians. There would have been pleasures, but they would have been enjoyed only at the expense of disobeying God. Moreover, they would have been purely temporary. Moses had a sense of values. He could estimate at their true worth the suffering and rejection involved in aligning himself with God's people as contrasted with the transitory pleasures of the godless court.

26 Here the point made in v.25 is seen from another angle. While Moses knew what "the treasures of Egypt" were worth, he counted "the disgrace for the sake of Christ" as great riches. This may mean that he received the same kind of reproaches Christ was later to receive. More probably, however, the author thought of Christ as identified in some way with the people of God in OT times. The prophet could say of God, "In all their distress he too was distressed" (Isa 63:9). Similarly, Christ could be said to be involved with the people. Some suggest that we should bear in mind that "the Christ" is equivalent to "the Anointed," and thus this could be a reference to the people of God rather than to an individual. To support this view Psalm 89:51 is sometimes used. But this does not seem to be what the author means. He saw Christ to be the same yesterday as he is today (13:8); so it is much more probable that he thought of him as identified with Israel in OT times (cf. 1 Cor 10:4).

When Moses suffered, he suffered with Christ—the same Christ whom the writer is encouraging his readers to identify with. It no doubt carried great weight with them to realize that they were being called to participate in the same kind of experiences and attitudes the great Moses had. Moses looked forward to the "reward." He bore in mind the just consequences of his actions and was not deceived by the glitter of the Egyptian court. History, of course, has vindicated him. We do not so much as know the name of the Pharaoh of his time; and even if we did, he would be of interest to us chiefly because of his link with Moses. But the choice Moses made resulted in his influence still being felt. It is not "realistic" to opt for the security of worldly safety. Moses did not do this, and he was right. It is faith that finally emerges triumphant, not worldliness.

27 This verse poses a problem because Moses left Egypt on two occasions: he fled to Midian after he had slain the Egyptian oppressor (Exod 2:11–15) and he went out with the rest of the Israelites at the Exodus. There would be little doubt that the former is meant here were it not for the fact that it was fear that led Moses to flee

to Midian after killing the Egyptian (Exod 2:14), whereas here in v.27 he is said not to have feared the king's anger. That this reference to Moses' leaving Egypt is to his flight to Midian is supported by the following:

1. The order of events. The Passover is mentioned in v.28. Therefore, Moses' flight seems to have preceded this event.
2. "He" left Egypt seems a strange way of referring to the Exodus of an entire nation.
3. The Exodus was the result of Pharaoh's request (Exod 12:31–32). Yet it is possible to suppose that Pharaoh's anger was not far away.

Those who see Moses' departure in v.27 as referring to the Exodus draw attention to the following:

1. It is hard to reconcile "not fearing the king's anger" with "Then Moses was afraid" (Exod 2:14). So strong does this appear to some that they call any other view special pleading. Yet we should notice that the flight is not connected with fear in Exodus or anywhere else. Other options were open to Moses, such as leading a slaves' revolt. While his fear was real, his flight appears to have been because he did not think it was God's time for action, or, as the writer of Hebrews puts it, he went out "by faith."
2. The word for "left" (*katelipen*) is best understood of a permanent abandonment. (But would this not also apply to the flight to Midian? After it Moses paid only a short visit to Egypt.)
3. Moses must have expected Pharaoh would get angry at the Exodus, and he apparently did (Exod 14:5).

On the whole it seems best to take the words as referring to the flight to Midian. The author goes on to give the reason for Moses' perseverance in a fine paradox: "He saw him who is invisible." The OT has a good deal to say about Moses' close relationship with God: "The Lord would speak to Moses face to face, as a man speaks with his friend" (Exod 33:11; cf. Num 12:7–8). This close walk with God sustained Moses through all the difficult days.

28 The final example of faith in connection with Moses concerns the Passover. The verb *pepoiēken* may be translated "kept" as in NIV, but some feel that a meaning like "instituted" is required (cf. TEV, "It was faith that made him establish the Passover"). Whichever translation we prefer, the striking thing is Moses' provision for its continuance: "For the generations to come you shall celebrate it as a festival to the Lord—a lasting ordinance" (Exod 12:14). The author's use of the perfect tense agrees with this. He adds a reference to "the sprinkling of blood" (cf. Exod 12:7), which is a further illustration of faith. There was nothing in the previous experience of either Moses or the Israelites to justify this action, but their faith was vindicated when "the destroyer of the firstborn" passed over them. Moses had nothing to go on but the conviction that God had directed him. Clearly, faith was his mainspring.

Notes

27 Ὡς ὁρῶν (*hōs horōn*) might be understood in the sense "as though he saw" (TEV), but better is NIV's "because he saw": ὡς (*hōs*) with the participle "gives the reason for an action" (BAG, s.v.).

F. *The Faith of the Exodus Generation*

11:29–31

²⁹By faith the people passed through the Red Sea as on dry land; but when the Egyptians tried to do so, they were drowned.
³⁰By faith the walls of Jericho fell, after the people had marched around them for seven days.
³¹By faith the prostitute Rahab, because she welcomed the spies, was not killed with those who were disobedient.

The author moves naturally enough from Moses to those associated with him. For some reason he does not mention Joshua, nor does he recount any example of faith during the wanderings in the wilderness. Since the wilderness generation was not noteworthy for faith (though there were some conspicuous exceptions), their omission is understandable. But the omission of Joshua is puzzling. Perhaps we should think of him in connection with the destruction of Jericho.

29 NIV supplies "the people" to bring out the force of the plural verb. Some of those who went out of Egypt with Moses were anything but shining examples of faith. But they must have had some faith to follow Moses through the sea, and it is on this that attention is focused. The crossing of the Red Sea is attributed to God (Exod 14:14) and to the east wind that God sent (Exod 14:21); but the author prefers to concentrate on the faith that enabled the people to respond to what God had done. That their faith and not merely their courage was important is shown by the fate of the Egyptians. The Egyptians were just as courageous as the Israelites, for they attempted to cross in the same way. But they lacked faith, and the result was disaster. Their fate shows that the faith of Moses and his followers was real and not just a formality.

30 That the falling of the walls of Jericho should be ascribed to faith is not surprising (see Josh 6:1–21). What else could account for it? The author does not say whose faith he discerned in the story, though it was probably that of both Joshua and those who followed him. The taking of Jericho is a striking example of the power of faith. Apart from the conviction that God would act, nothing could have been more pointless than the behavior of those warriors. They did not attack. Instead, they simply walked around the city once a day for six days and then seven times on the seventh. But once more faith was vindicated, for the walls tumbled down.

31 "The list of the champions of Faith whose victories are specially noticed is closed by a woman and a gentile and an outcast" (Westcott, in loc.). Rahab the prostitute seems at first sight an unlikely example of faith. But she was highly regarded among both Jews and Christians. According to Jewish tradition, she married Joshua and became the ancestress of eight priests (Tal *Megillah* 14b). She is also listed as one of the four women of surpassing beauty (ibid. 15a; the others were Sarah, Abigail, and Esther).

Rahab is mentioned favorably in James 2:25, and she is listed in the genealogy of the Lord as the wife of Salmon (Matt 1:5). She came from outside Israel and was one who might not be expected to believe in Yahweh, but she acted decisively out of her deep convictions. She put her life at risk, for she would undoubtedly have been destroyed by her countrymen had they known what she was doing. So Rahab did exercise a faith that might have been very costly (Josh 2:1–21). She is contrasted to the "disobedient," which appears to be a general term for those who do not walk in God's ways. No specific act of disobedience is mentioned. Rahab "welcomed" the spies, or, more exactly, "received" them "with peace." She did not act in the spirit of a combatant but looked after Yahweh's men.

Some have tried to soften the description of Rahab and have understood her to be a hostess or an innkeeper. Also certain MSS have inserted the word "called" in another whitewash attempt. But she is designated as "the harlot" (the Heb. word signifies a secular prostitute, not a temple prostitute). It is significant that a woman from such a background could become an example of faith.

G. *The Faith of Other Servants of God*

11:32–38

> [32]And what more shall I say? I do not have time to tell about Gideon, Barak, Samson, Jephthah, David, Samuel and the prophets, [33]who through faith conquered kingdoms, administered justice, and gained what was promised; who shut the mouths of lions, [34]quenched the fury of the flames, and escaped the edge of the sword; whose weakness was turned to strength; and who became powerful in battle and routed foreign armies. [35]Women received back their dead, raised to life again. Others were tortured and refused to be released, so that they might gain a better resurrection. [36]Some faced jeers and flogging, while still others were chained and put in prison. [37]They were stoned; they were sawed in two; they were put to death by the sword. They went about in sheepskins and goatskins, destitute, persecuted and mistreated—[38]the world was not worthy of them. They wandered in deserts and mountains, and in caves and holes in the ground.

From particular cases the author moves to generalities. To continue in such detail would require writing at great length, and the author has no time for that. On the other hand, there are many shining examples of faith, and it would be a pity not to notice them in some way. So the author names a few outstanding men of faith without detailing what their faith led them to do and then goes on to mention certain groups of the faithful. Sometimes men and women of faith did similar things quite independently of one another. It is doubtless some of these whom the author lists.

32 With a neat rhetorical flourish, the author shows that his subject is far from exhausted, even though he does not propose to continue his list. His rhetorical question may be understood as "What more shall I say?" (NIV, Moffatt, in loc.) or "Is there any need to say more?" (JB), depending on whether we take the *ti* to mean "what?" or "why?" Not having time to go through them all, the author lists a half dozen faithful men: Gideon, Barak, Samson, Jephthah, David, and Samuel. The first four of these are mentioned only here in the NT. Samuel is mentioned only twice elsewhere in the NT. David, of course, is mentioned frequently. The reason for the order of these names is not clear. It is neither that of the OT, nor is it chronological. In fact, if we arrange them in pairs, the second of the two in each case is the earlier in time. Samuel might well be placed last as heading up the prophets who came after him, but we can only guess at the reasons for the way the rest are placed.

The writer does not go into detail about what these men did. But if we examine the OT record, we find that each man battled against overwhelming odds so that, humanly speaking, there was little chance of his coming out on top. For men in such positions faith in God was not a formality. It meant real trust when the odds seemed stacked against them. They set worthy examples for the readers in their difficult circumstances. Calvin points out that there were defects in the faith of four of them. Gideon was slow to take up arms; Barak hesitated and went forward only when Deborah encouraged him; Samson was enticed by Delilah; and Jephthah made a foolish vow and stubbornly kept it. Calvin comments, "In every saint there is always to be found something reprehensible. Nevertheless although faith may be imperfect and incomplete it does not cease to be approved by God" (in loc.).

33 Up till now, the writer has characteristically used the dative "by faith" (with an occasional *kata pistin,* "according to faith"). Now there is a change of construction to "through faith" (*dia pisteōs*), though there is probably no great difference in meaning. In the list that follows, there are three groups of three. Westcott (in loc.) points out that we may see them as indicating, first, the broad results of the believers' faith: material victory, moral success in government, spiritual reward; second, forms of personal deliverance: from wild beasts, from physical forces, from human tyranny; third, the attainment of personal gifts: strength, the exercise of strength, and the triumph of strength. In each case it is possible to see OT examples, perhaps the very ones the writer has in mind.

First, the author speaks of those who "conquered kingdoms" (as did Joshua and others), then of men who "administered justice." The Greek word *dikaiosynē* may mean "righteousness" as well as "justice" and some have found the meaning here as "did deeds of righteousness." But NIV is probably correct. The reference seems to be to men like the Judges. The next group may be, as in NIV, those who "gained what was promised," or possibly those who obtained words of promise from God. Either way they were men of faith. In the OT there were a number of men who could be said to have "shut the mouths of lions," notably Daniel (Dan 6:17–22). David also was delivered from a lion (1 Sam 17:34–37), and Benaiah killed one in a pit on a snowy day (1 Chron 11:22; cf. also Samson, Judg 14:5–6).

34 When he speaks of those who "quenched the fury of the flames," the writer probably has in mind the three whom Nebuchadnezzar had cast into the furnace and who then emerged unharmed (Dan 3:23–27). Buchanan takes the words about escaping "the edge of the sword" to refer to people who ran away; "they had successfully escaped when they were forced to flee" (in loc.), but JB translates it as "emerge unscathed from battle." Probably the writer is thinking of people like Elijah, who was not killed by Jezebel (1 Kings 19:2ff.). The OT contains many examples of those "whose weakness was turned to strength," such as Gideon, who also "became powerful in battle and routed foreign armies." It might fairly be said that the typical deliverance of Israel in OT times came about when a small number of Israelites (like Gideon's three hundred [Judg 7:7] or the tiny armies of Israel "like two little flocks of goats" [1 Kings 20:27]) fought at God's direction against vastly superior forces and defeated them. It was God's power that prevailed; he made these puny forces strong enough to defeat mighty enemies.

35 A number of times in Scripture women are said to have received their dead back to life, as Elijah's hostess (1 Kings 17:17–24) and the Shunammite who befriended

Elisha (2 Kings 4:18–37). In the NT there are the son of the widow of Nain (Luke 7:11–14), Lazarus (John 11), and Dorcas, the friend of widows (Acts 9:36–41). Sometimes, however, faith worked in another way. Some accepted torture rather than release in order that "they might gain a better resurrection," i.e., be raised to the life of the age to come with God and not simply be restored to the life of this age (cf. 2 Macc 7:23, 29). A "better" resurrection perhaps implies that all will be raised but that the prospects for apostates are grim. It is better to endure suffering and even torture now in order that the resurrection may be joyous.

36 Others were harshly treated in different fashion. NIV takes *empaigmos* in the sense "mockery" with its translation "jeers." This may well be right, for there is no doubt that other words from this root are used in the NT in such ways. But *empaigmos* itself is found only here in the NT. Outside the NT it may mean something like "derisive torture," as when it is used in 2 Maccabees of the second of the seven brothers who died for their religion. NEB translates, "The second was subjected to the same brutality [*empaigmon*]. The skin and hair of his head were torn off—"(2 Macc 7:7). "Jeers" may well be the way we should translate the word here, but it is not gentle mockery that is meant. Other forms of ill-treatment are added: floggings, chains, and imprisonment.

37 Stoning was a characteristic Jewish form of execution. Some of the men of faith had suffered at the hands of their fellow-countrymen. To be "sawed in two" was a most unusual form of killing. According to tradition this was the way the prophet Isaiah was killed (*The Martyrdom of Isaiah* 5:1ff.). The statement that some were put to death "by the sword" is important, lest it be deduced from v.34 that men of faith were safe from this fate. While God could deliver them from it, his purpose might be for some believers to be slain in this way. It is not for men of faith to dictate. They trust God and know that, whether in life or death, all will ultimately be well. From the various ways men of faith died, the writer turns to consider the hardships they had to endure in their lives. Their clothing had been the simplest. Apparently the prophets sometimes wore sheepskins (cf. the reference to Elijah's "garment of hair," 2 Kings 1:8). The reference here is not, however, so much to a definite class (like the prophets) as it is to men of faith in general who were roughly clad. That they were "destitute" is in accord with this, for the author is speaking of men without earthly resources. Misery pressed on them as they were "persecuted and mistreated."

38 To all outward appearance, these people of faith were insignificant and unimportant. But the true situation was very different. They were worth more than the whole world, though they lacked everything. The author appeals to deep realities, not apparent on the surface of things. The despised and ill-treated group of servants of God was of greater real worth than all the rest of humanity put together. Their description is rounded off with the reminder that they had no settled homes. They wandered in lonely places, and their shelters were "caves and holes in the ground" (i.e., underground caves). The heroes of the faith had no mansions; they cared for other things than their own comfort.

Notes

34 The plural στόματα (stomata, "mouths") is linked with the singular μαχαίρης (machairēs, "sword"). From this some have deduced that the writer had a two-edged sword in mind. This, however, seems not to be the thought. It is rather that there were many examples of sword-type violence.

35 "Tortured" renders ἐτυμπανίσθησαν (etympanisthēsan). The τύμπανον (tympanon) was a drum; the meaning appears to be that the victims of this kind of torture were stretched (on a rack or a wheel?) tight as the skin on a drum and then beaten to death.

"Refused to be released" renders οὐ προσδεξάμενοι τὴν ἀπολύτρωσιν (ou prosdex-amenoi tēn apolytrōsin, "not having accepted the redemption"). It is important that "re-demption" be given its full force. These people were not offered unconditional freedom. The writer had more than release in mind—viz., release on payment of a price and that price apostasy.

37 A number of MSS read ἐπειράσθησαν (epeirasthēsan, "they were put to the test") either before or after ἐπρίσθησαν (epristhēsan, "they were sawed in two"). But this appears to be an error due to dittography.

H. *The Promise*

11:39–40

39These were all commended for their faith, yet none of them received what had been promised. 40God had planned something better for us so that only together with us would they be made perfect.

The author rounds off this section with a reminder of the great privilege Christians have. The giants of the faith had done great things for God in their times, and there is no question regarding God's approval of them. Nevertheless, they would not be "made perfect" apart from the humble followers of Jesus.

39 "These" refers to the preceding heroes of the faith; "all" omits none of them. God never forgets any of his faithful servants. The characteristic now singled out is that they had "witness" borne to them (martyrēthentes; NIV, "were commended") on account of their faith. The importance of faith, which has been stressed throughout the chapter, continues to the end. But for all their greatness and for all the blessing God gave them, these heroes of the faith did not receive "the promise" (tēn epangeli-an). Verse 33 tells us that they "gained what was promised." Indeed, Abraham was cited as an example of that as far back as Hebrews 6:15. But here it is not a question of "the promises" but of "the promise." God made many promises to his people and kept them. So there were many blessings that they received along the way. But the ultimate blessing (which the author characteristically sees in terms of promise) was not given under the old dispensation. God kept that until Jesus came.

40 God's plan provided for "something better for us." The indefinite pronoun leaves the precise nature of the blessing undefined. The important thing is not exactly what it is but that God has not imparted it prematurely. "Us" means "us Christians"; we who are Christ's have our place in God's plan. And that plan provides that the heroes of the faith throughout the ages should not "be made perfect" apart from Christians.

Salvation is social. It concerns the whole people of God. We can experience it only as part of the whole people of God. As long as the believers in OT times were without those who are in Christ, it was impossible for them to experience the fullness of salvation. Furthermore, it is what Christ has done that opens the way into the very presence of God for them as for us. Only the work of Christ brings those of OT times and those of the new and living way alike into the presence of God.

IX. Christian Living

The last main section of the epistle is largely devoted to the practical business of living out the Christian faith. In it there are exhortations to a variety of Christian duties.

A. Christ Our Example

12:1-3

> Therefore, since we are surrounded by such a great cloud of witnesses, let us throw off everything that hinders and the sin that so easily entangles, and let us run with perseverance the race marked out for us. 2Let us fix our eyes on Jesus, the author and perfecter of our faith, who for the joy set before him endured the cross, scorning its shame, and sat down at the right hand of the throne of God. 3Consider him who endured such opposition from sinful men, so that you will not grow weary and lose heart.

The writer begins by pointing to what Christ has done for us. In one of the great, moving passages of the NT, he points to the Cross as the stimulus that nerves Christ's people to serious and concentrated endeavor as they face the difficulties involved in living out their faith.

1 "We" links the writer to his readers. He is a competitor in the race as well as they and writes as one who is as much caught up in the contest as they are. The word "cloud" (*nephos*, only here in the NT) may be used of a mass of clouds in the sky (the more common *nephelē* means a single cloud). But it is also used from time to time of a throng of people, when it emphasizes the number. The witnesses are a vast host.

There is a question whether we should understand "witnesses" as those who have witnessed to the faith or as spectators witnessing the present generation of Christians. Normally the word is used in the former sense, and it is doubtful whether it ever means simply "a spectator." Still it is difficult to rid the word of this idea in 1 Timothy 6:12 (perhaps also in Heb 10:28), and the imagery of the present passage favors it. The writer is picturing athletes in a footrace, running for the winning post and urged on by the crowd. He speaks of the runners as "surrounded," which makes it hard to think of them as looking to the "witnesses" and all the more so since they are exhorted to keep their eyes on Jesus (v.2). Both ideas may be present. Perhaps we should think of something like a relay race where those who have finished their course and handed in their baton are watching and encouraging their successors.

With the great gallery of witnesses about us, it is important for us to run well. So we are exhorted, "Let us throw off everything that hinders." "Everything that hinders" translates *onkos* (only here in the NT), a word that may mean any kind of weight.

It is sometimes used of superfluous bodily weight that the athlete sheds during training. Here, however, it seems to be the race rather than the training that is in view. Athletes carried nothing with them in a race (they even ran naked), and the writer is suggesting that the Christian should "travel light." He is not referring to sin, for that follows in the next clause. Some things that are not wrong in themselves hinder us in putting forward our best effort. So the writer tells us to get rid of them.

Christians must also put off every sin. There is a problem relating to the adjective rendered "that so easily entangles" (*euperistatos*), for it is found nowhere else. The word is made up of three parts that mean respectively "well," "around," and "standing." Most scholars accept some such meaning as "easily surrounding" or "easily entangling." Sin forms a crippling hindrance to good running. Christians then, are to lay aside all that could hinder them in their race and are to "run with perseverance." The author is not thinking of a short, sharp sprint but of a distance race that requires endurance and persistence. Everyone has from time to time a mild inclination to do good. The author is not talking about this but about the kind of sustained effort required of the long-distance runner who keeps on with great determination over the long course. That is what the heroes of faith did in their day, and it is that to which we are called.

2 We are to run this race "with no eyes for any one or anything except Jesus" (Moffatt, in loc.). It is he toward whom we run. There must be no divided attention. The "author and perfecter of faith" (there is no "our" in the Gr.) may mean that Jesus trod the way of faith first and brought it to completion. Or it may mean that he originated his people's faith and will bring it to its perfection. Since it is not easy to think that the author sees the faith by which Jesus lived as essentially the same as our own, perhaps it is better to see the emphasis on what he does in his followers. (Yet the thought of example will not be entirely absent, for we should bear in mind that Jesus' kinship with men has been stressed in this epistle.) As the heroes of faith in chapter 11 are OT characters, there is the thought that Jesus led all the people of faith, even from the earliest days.

The expression rendered "for the joy set before him" is problematic. The preposition *anti* strictly means "in the stead of," "in the place of." Accordingly the meaning may be that in place of the joy he might have had Jesus accepted the cross. The "joy" is then the heavenly bliss the preincarnate Christ surrendered in order to take the way of the Cross. He replaced joy with the Cross. But *anti* sometimes has a meaning like "for the sake of" (F. Büchsel sees this in Eph 5:31 etc.; TDNT, 1:372). So with this understanding of the term the meaning is that Jesus went to the Cross because of the joy it would bring. He looked right through the Cross to the coming joy, the joy of bringing salvation to those he loves. The latter meaning is preferable. For this joy, then, Jesus "endured the cross" (or, perhaps, "endured a cross").

The "cross" is not as common a way of referring to the death of Jesus as we might have expected. Actually, this is the one occurrence of the word outside the Gospels and Pauline Epistles. If one "scorns" a thing, one normally has nothing to do with it; but "scorning its shame" means rather that Jesus thought so little of the pain and shame involved that he did not bother to avoid it. He endured it. Then, having completed his work of redemption, he "sat down at the right hand of the throne of God" (see comments on 1:3). The perfect tense in the verb "sat down" points to a permanent result. The work of atonement ended, Christ is at God's right hand forevermore.

3 "Consider" (*analogisasthe*, used only here in the NT) is a word used in calculations. The readers are invited to "take account of" Jesus. He is described as one who "endured" (the perfect tense points to the abiding result). The example he set remained before the readers. He endured "opposition from sinful men" and thus was in the same kind of position the readers found themselves in. They must not think their situation unique. They were not called upon to put up with something their Master had not first endured. Several commentators point out that the two verbs used at the end of this verse, "grow weary and lose heart," are both used by Aristotle of runners who relax and collapse after they have passed the finishing post. The readers were still in the race. They must not give way prematurely. They must not allow themselves to faint and collapse through weariness. Once again there is the call to perseverance in the face of hardship.

Notes

1 "Therefore" translates τοιγαροῦν (*toigaroun*), found again in the NT only in 1 Thess 4:8. It is an inferential particle meaning "wherefore then, so therefore" (A-S, s.v.).

Notice that in this verse the words τοσοῦτον (*tosouton*) and ὄγκον (*onkon*) are thrust forward for emphasis.

A number of commentators accept the reading of P[46], εὐπερίσπαστον (*euperispaston*, "easily distracting"). This is attractive, but it is not easy to see why, if it was original, it has left so little mark on the textual tradition. "Race" translates ἀγῶνα (*agōna*), the technical expression for a contest in the games.

2 Ἀφοράω (*aphoraō*) means "to look away from all else at, fix one's gaze upon" (A-S, s.v.). It is no casual glance but a firmly fixed gaze that is meant.

3 There is a difficult textual problem posed by the fact that most of the oldest authorities read the plural εἰς ἑαυτούς (*eis heautous*, "against themselves"). The singular "against him" is obviously superior; in fact, a number of commentators maintain that it alone makes sense. But precisely because it makes so much better sense many argue that the plural—the more difficult reading—must be accepted. If it is, then the meaning is that Jesus received opposition "from sinners against themselves"; i.e., sinners doing hurt to themselves (cf. Num 16:38; Prov 8:36; Jude 11).

B. *Discipline*

12:4–11

⁴In your struggle against sin, you have not yet resisted to the point of shedding your blood. ⁵And you have forgotten that word of encouragement that addresses you as sons:

"My son, do not make light of the Lord's discipline,
  and do not lose heart when he rebukes you,
⁶because the Lord disciplines those he loves,
  and he punishes everyone he accepts as a son."

⁷Endure hardship as discipline; God is treating you as sons. For what son is not disciplined by his father? ⁸If you are not disciplined (and everyone undergoes discipline), then you are illegitimate children and not true sons. ⁹Moreover, we have all had human fathers who disciplined us and we respected them for it. How much

more should we submit to the Father of our spirits and live! [10]Our fathers disciplined us for a little while as they thought best; but God disciplines us for our good, that we may share in his holiness. [11]No discipline seems pleasant at the time, but painful. Later on, however, it produces a harvest of righteousness and peace for those who have been trained by it.

Suffering comes to all; it is part of life, but it is not easy to bear. Yet it is not quite so bad when it can be seen as meaningful. The author has just pointed out that Christ endured his suffering on the cross on account of the joy set before him. His suffering had meaning. So for Christians all suffering is transformed because of the Cross. We serve a Savior who suffered, and we know he will not lead us into meaningless suffering. The writer points to the importance of discipline and proceeds to show that for Christians suffering is rightly understood only when seen as God's fatherly discipline, correcting and directing us. Suffering is evidence, not that God does not love us, but that he does. Believers are sons and are treated as sons.

4 The "struggle [*antagōnizomai* retains the imagery of athletic games] against sin" seems to refer not to sin the readers might be tempted to commit (though some think apostasy is in mind) but to the sin of oppressors who tried to terrorize them into abandoning their faith. Shedding blood would not accompany the normal course of temptation, but it was a very real possibility for those facing persecution. Jesus had been killed, and many of those honored in chapter 11 had likewise been killed for their faithfulness to God. The words "not yet" show that there was real danger and that the readers must be ready for difficult days. But they had not had to die for their faith. The comparative mildness of their sufferings must not be overlooked, the writer is saying. They were evidently concerned at the prospect facing them, and he points out that their experience is not nearly so difficult as that of others.

5–6 They had forgotten an important point: Scripture links suffering and sonship, as Proverbs 3:11–12 shows. The address "My son" is normal for a maker of proverbs who assumes a superior but caring position. The author, however, sees a fuller meaning in these words than that, for they are words from God to his people. When God speaks of discipline and rebuke, it is sons that he addresses. It is interesting that this warning is called "that word of encouragement." The certainty of suffering encourages the believer rather than dismays him because he knows that it is God's discipline for him. Incidentally, it seems not improbable that the words might perhaps be taken as a question: "Have you forgotten?"

The word for discipline combines the thoughts of chastening and education. It points to sufferings that teach us something. In v.4 the striving was against sin, but somehow the hand of God was in it, too. No circumstances are beyond God's control, and there are none he cannot use to carry out his purpose. So the believer is not to belittle the significance of his sufferings nor lose heart in the face of God's correction. "Those he loves" comes first in the Greek, which gives it a certain emphasis. God disciplines people he loves, not those he is indifferent to. The readers should see the sufferings they were experiencing as a sign of God's love, as Scripture already assured them. It is the son that is punished and "every son" (*panta huion*) at that.

In the ancient world it was universally accepted that the bringing up of sons involved disciplining them. Therefore, we should not read back modern permissive attitudes into our understanding of this passage. The Roman father possessed absolute authority. When a child was born, he decided whether to keep or discard it. Throughout its life he could punish it as he chose. He could even execute his son and, while this was rarely done, the right to do it was there. Discipline was only to be expected.

7 NIV takes the verb "endure" as imperative. This may well be correct, though it could be an indicative. The important thing here is the emphatic position of the words "as discipline" in the Greek sentence. It is not as misery, accident, or the like that Christians should understand suffering but as discipline. God uses it to teach important lessons. It shows that "God is treating you as sons." The rhetorical question appeals to the universality of fatherly discipline. It was unthinkable to the writer and his readers that a father would not discipline his sons. Perhaps we should notice in passing that while the author clearly sees believers as children of God, he does not specifically call God father (except in a quotation in 1:5; cf. also "the Father of spirits," v.9).

8 The hypothetical possibility of being without chastisement is looked at and a devastating conclusion drawn. "Everyone," he says, "undergoes discipline" (*hēs metochoi gegonasin pantes;* lit., "of which all are sharers"), which recalls the "everyone" of v.6. It is the universal experience of children that life means discipline. If anyone does not receive discipline, then, the author says, he is "illegitimate." The word *nothos* is used of one born of a slave or a concubine, or of the illegitimate in general (see LSJ, s.v.). The point is that they are not heirs, not members of the family. For them the father feels no responsibility. Their freedom from discipline is not evidence of a privileged position. Rather the reverse is true. They are bastards—"not-sons" (*ouch huioi*).

9 The writer appeals to the practice and result of discipline exercised in the human family. He and his readers have had experience of discipline; they have had fathers who were *paideutai,* "correctors," "discipliners." Fathers are seen in their capacity as chastisers, trainers of their children by punishing them when they go wrong. The effect of such paternal chastisement is to arouse respect, not resentment. How much more, then, should believers submit to God's discipline! "The Father of spirits" (there is no "our" in the Gr.) is a most unusual expression found only here in Scripture, though a similar expression occurs in Numbers 16:22; 27:16. The spirits might be those of "righteous men made perfect" (v.23), but there seems no reason for limiting it in this way. But likewise there is no reason why we should press the expression to mean a universal fatherhood. A number of translations render this phrase "our spiritual Father" (TEV, NEB, JB), and something like this seems meant. The verb "live" (*zaō*) is used here of "the glory of the life to come" (BAG, s.v.). When people subject themselves to God, accepting life's sufferings as discipline from his fatherly hand, they enter the life that is alone worthy of the name.

10 There is a difference in the quality of the discipline we have received from our earthly fathers and that which comes from God. They disciplined us "for a little while," i.e., the comparatively brief days of childhood; and they did it "according to their lights" (NEB). They did their best, but the phrase seems to imply that they made mistakes. But God's discipline is always "for our good." There is nothing of the "hit or miss" about it. It is aimed at our good and the aim is "that we may share in his holiness." The word "holiness" (*hagiotēs*) is not common (elsewhere in the NT it occurs only in a variant reading in 2 Cor 1:12). It points to God's holy character. The aim of God's chastisement of his people is to produce in them a character like his own.

11 At the time it takes place, chastisement is never a happy, joyous affair. On the contrary, sorrow (*lypē*) goes with it. But while it does not "seem pleasant," it does produce a result the writer calls a "harvest of righteousness and peace." The adjective *eirēnikos* (tr. "peace" in NIV) is interesting. Moffatt comments, "The writer might be throwing out a hint to his readers, that suffering was apt to render people irritable, impatient with one another's faults. The later record even of the martyrs, for example, shows that the very prospect of death did not always prevent Christians from quarreling in prison" (Moffatt, in loc.). It is important that suffering be accepted in the right spirit; otherwise it does not produce the right result. So the author goes on to speak of those who have been "trained" by it, where the word *gegymnasmenois* (once more the metaphor from athletics) points to those who have continued to exercise themselves in godly discipline. It is not a matter of accepting a minor chastisement or two with good grace; it is the habit of life that is meant. When that is present, the "peaceable fruit" follows.

Notes

5 Ὀλίγος (*oligos*, "little") connects with ὥρα (*ōra*, "care") to give ὀλιγωρέω (*oligōreō*, "think little of").

10 The construction εἰς τό (*eis to*) plus an infinitive expresses purpose. It is found eight times in Hebrews. Here it indicates that God does not discipline his people aimlessly but with a definite end in view.

C. *Exhortation to the Christian Life*

12:12–17

> [12]Therefore, strengthen your feeble arms and weak knees. [13]"Make level paths for your feet," so that the lame may not be disabled, but rather healed.
> [14]Make every effort to live in peace with all men and to be holy; without holiness no one will see the Lord. [15]See to it that no one misses the grace of God and that no bitter root grows up to cause trouble and defile many. [16]See that no one is sexually immoral, or is godless like Esau, who for a single meal sold his inheritance rights as the oldest son. [17]Afterward, as you know, when he wanted to inherit this blessing, he was rejected. He could bring about no change of mind, though he sought the blessing with tears.

From the acceptance of life's discipline in general, the writer turns to the way this discipline is applied in Christian experience. It is important that God's people live as God's people. They are not to take their standards from the ungodly.

12 "Therefore" links this exhortation to what has gone before. Because of what they now know of God's loving discipline, they must put forward their best effort. The "hands" (not "arms" as NIV) are pictured as "limp" (JB) and thus useless. They accomplish nothing. The knees are "weak." There is a reference to similar hands and knees in Isaiah 35:3 (cf. Ecclus 25:23), and the writer may have taken his imagery from there. "Strengthen" is NIV's translation of *anorthōsate* ("make upright" or "straight"). The picture is of someone whose hands and legs are for some reason out of action but are put right. The exhortation implies that the readers are acting as though spiritually paralyzed. They are urged to put things right and get moving.

13 A quotation from Proverbs 4:26 is added. NIV takes the words *orthas poieite* to mean "make level," though they are usually understood as "make straight." Clearly the idea is to put the paths into better order in order to facilitate travel, specifically for the lame. The writer is mindful of the fact that Christians belong together. They must have consideration for the weak among their members, i.e., the "lame." There is a problem relating to the verb rendered "be disabled" (*ektrapē*, more lit., "turned away"). It might mean that the lame are not to be turned from the right way (so Snell, for example, in loc.). BAG (s.v.) note that linguistically there is another possibility— "that what is lame might not be avoided"—but this meaning is obviously unsuitable to the context. The following reference to healing makes it certain that it is something like dislocation that is meant (as in RSV, NEB, etc.). By taking care for the defective members of the congregation, the stronger members can help them along the way. Where the Christian life is in any way "out of joint," steps should be taken to revitalize it.

14 The NT contains a number of exhortations to believers to be at peace, either with one another or with people in general (cf. Matt 5:9; Mark 9:50; Rom 12:18). People are often selfish and abrasive, but this is not the way Christians should be. For them peace is imperative, and they must "make every effort" to attain it. Commentators differ as to whether "all men" is to be taken in its widest sense or whether the writer means "all fellow believers." Granted that it is especially important for Christians to live in harmony with one another, there seems to be no reason for taking "all" in anything other than its normal meaning. The readers are to make every effort to live at peace with all people. We need not doubt that the writer is especially interested in harmony in the Christian community, but he has so worded his exhortation that it covers all relations and not only those among believers.

Coupled with peace is "holiness." The rendering "to be holy" (NIV, TEV) misses the point that "holiness" is a noun set alongside "peace" as the object of the verb. Holiness means being set apart for God. It is characteristic of the believer. As Barclay puts it, "Although he lives in the world, the man who is *hagios* must always in one sense be different from the world and separate from the world. His standards are not the world's standards" (in loc.). Without this readiness to belong to God, this being separated to God, no one will see God. Jesus said that the pure in heart see God (Matt 5:8), and no one has a right to expect that vision without that qualification.

15 The verb rendered "see to it" (*episkopountes*) is an unusual one. It conveys the idea of oversight (the verb is connected with the noun we translate as "bishop"). In this context the thought is that believers must have care for one another. The writer speaks of three things in particular the readers must avoid. The first is coming short of God's grace. Paul could speak of receiving God's grace in vain (2 Cor 6:1) and of falling from grace (Gal 5:4). It is something like this that is in mind here. God is not niggardly in offering grace. He gives his people all they will take. Accordingly, it is important for them not to fail to make use of their opportunities.

The second contingency to guard against is the springing up of a "bitter root." The expression is reminiscent of Deuteronomy 29:17. But if it is a quotation from the LXX, it is fairly free. A "bitter root" is a root that bears bitter fruit. The metaphor is taken from the growth of plants. Such growth is slow, but what is in the plant will surely come out in time. So it is possible for a seed of bitterness to be sown in a community and, though nothing is immediately apparent, in due time the inevitable fruit appears. It will certainly "cause trouble." The effects of bitterness cannot be localized: it "can poison a whole community" (JB). "Defile" in the first instance refers to ceremonial defilement (John 18:28), but it is also used of moral defilement. Bitterness defiles people and makes them unfit to stand before God. When bitterness is allowed to grow, it has wide-ranging effects. It defiles "many."

16 The third warning begins with a reference to the "sexually immoral" (*pornos,* "fornicator"). The OT has passages that use sexual sin as a metaphor for idolatry and the like. Some have felt that this is the way the word should be taken here. But there seems nothing in the context to demand it, so it is better to take the word literally. A further question is whether *pornos* is meant to apply to Esau. There is no evidence in the OT that Esau was a fornicator, though some have taken the fact that he married Hittite wives (Gen 26:34) to be the object of the allusion. In Jewish legend Esau was accused of many sins including this one. But there seems no reason for thinking that the writer of the epistle has this in mind. He seems to be warning his readers against two things: fornication and being "godless" like Esau.

The word rendered "godless" (*bebēlos*) means "unhallowed," "profane." The author is saying that Esau was not spiritually minded but rather a man taken up with the things of the here and now. This is apparent in the incident referred to, when Esau for just one meal bargained away "his inheritance rights as the oldest son" (cf. Gen 25:29–34). He could not recognize its true value. His insistence on the gratification of his immediate needs led him to overlook the importance of his rights as the firstborn. For a small immediate gain, he bartered away what was of infinitely greater worth. So with the apostates.

17 The opening word (*iste*) may be imperative "know" or indicative "as you know," as NIV takes it. The writer appeals to knowledge common to his readers and himself. Nothing is known about Esau's change of mind other than what we read here. It appears that in due course Esau came to realize he had made a mistake. He wanted to go back but found he could not. Some take the second part of the verse to mean that he could not change Isaac's mind, but this has to be read into the text. Isaac is not mentioned. The meaning is, rather, "he could not find a way to change what he had done" (TEV). There is a finality about what we do. Barclay points out that "if a young man loses his purity or a girl her virginity, nothing can ever bring it back. The choice was made and the choice stands" (in loc.). Notice that it is not a question of forgiveness. God's forgiveness is always open to the penitent. Esau could have come back to God. But he could not undo his act.

D. *Mount Sinai and Mount Zion*

12:18–24

18You have not come to a mountain that can be touched and that is burning with fire; to darkness, gloom and storm; **19**to a trumpet blast or to such a voice speaking words, so that those who heard it begged that no further word be spoken to them, **20**because they could not bear what was commanded: "If even an animal touches the mountain, it must be stoned." [21]The sight was so terrifying that Moses said, "I am trembling with fear."

[22]But you have come to Mount Zion, to the heavenly Jerusalem, the city of the living God. You have come to thousands upon thousands of angels in joyful assembly, [23]to the church of the firstborn, whose names are written in heaven. You have come to God, the judge of all men, to the spirits of righteous men made perfect, [24]to Jesus the mediator of a new covenant, and to the sprinkled blood that speaks a better word than the blood of Abel.

The writer proceeds to contrast the Jewish and Christian ways by contrasting the terrors associated with the giving of the law on Mount Sinai with the joys and the glory associated with Mount Zion. He sounds the note of warning that great privilege means great responsibility.

18 The older MSS omit "mountain." The meaning might then be thus: "You have not come to a fire that can be touched." It is better, however, to see it as quite general: "You have not come to anything that can be touched." There can be no doubt that the events on Sinai are in mind, though the writer chooses not to refer to the mountain specifically but to what it represented—the outward, the physical, and the material (cf. JB, "What you have come to is nothing known to the senses"). The phenomena listed are all associated with the Sinai event (see Deut 4:11). Elsewhere they are all linked with the presence of God: fire (Judg 13:20; 1 Kings 18:38), darkness (1 Kings 8:12), and tempest (Nah 1:3); the trumpet (v.19) being associated with the end time when God will manifest himself (Matt 24:31; 1 Cor 15:52; 1 Thess 4:16). The picture is one that strikes terror into the heart.

19 The trumpet is spoken of repeatedly in connection with Sinai (Exod 19:16, 19; 20:18). And on that occasion the people heard the voice of God (Deut 5:24). But the effect of it all was to terrify them, and they asked that they should hear God's voice no more (Exod 20:19; Deut 5:25–27). They were overcome with awe and wanted no further part in the wonderful events.

20 The fearfulness of the giving of the law on Sinai is brought out with reference to one of the commands laid on the people, namely, that neither man nor beast should even touch the mountain under penalty of death. The writer uses a present participle in saying "what was commanded," which makes it all terrifyingly present. The command that nothing touch it indicates the holiness and separateness of the mountain. The quotation is from Exodus 19:13. Killing by stoning (Exod 19:13 also permitted shooting, i.e., with darts or arrows) was prescribed so that those taking part in it would not need to touch the mountain themselves.

21 There is a further indication of the awesomeness of it all. At the time of the giving of the law, Moses was the leader of the people. He was known as one who had an especially close relationship with God (Exod 33:11). Yet even he was terrified. The words quoted are not found in the Sinai narrative but do occur at the time of the golden calf (Deut 9:19). The author may have had access to a tradition that recorded these words on this occasion. Or he may be including Moses in the general fear spoken of in Exodus 20:18. Or possibly he is taking words spoken on one occasion and applying them to another to which they also refer. At any rate, he is picturing an awe-inspiring occasion, one that affected all the people and terrified even Moses, the man of God.

22 "But" is the strong adversative (*alla*) and introduces a marked contrast. It is not a Sinai type experience that has befallen Christians. They "have come" (the perfect tense points to an accomplished and continuing state) to Mount Zion. This is one of the hills on which the city of Jerusalem was built. It sometimes stands for that city (Matt 21:5), and stands here, of course, for that city as the home of God's people. It is also called "the heavenly Jerusalem" and "the city of the living God." Elsewhere in the NT there is the thought of the Jerusalem above (Gal 4:26, where again there is a contrast with Mount Sinai; cf. also Rev 3:12; 21:2, 10).

The author has already spoken of "the city with foundations, whose architect and builder is God" (11:10). He is bringing out the thought of the ideal, heavenly city. His mention of "the living God" (see comments on 3:12) emphasizes the thought that this city is no static affair; it is the city of a vital, dynamic, living Being, one who is doing things. Its inhabitants include large numbers of angels. NIV says that there are "thousands upon thousands" of them, which is the translation of the one word *myriasin*. Originally this meant ten thousand, but it came to be used for a very large number. (For angels at Sinai, see Deut 33:2. The heavenly city is not deficient on this score.)

Scholars differ as to whether we should take the expression "joyful assembly" with angels (as NIV) or with the following verse (as TEV, "you have come to the joyful gathering of God's oldest sons"). While it cannot be proved to be the only way, NIV's understanding of it fits the Greek better and should probably be accepted. The word meant originally a national festive assembly to honor a god, then more generally any festal assembly.

23 "The church of the firstborn" is another difficult expression. Does it mean the angels just spoken of? They are not usually called a "church," but the word basically means an assembly and so could be applied to angels. If it refers to people, it is not easy to see it as the church triumphant because that is the same as "the spirits of righteous men made perfect" at the end of the verse. Nor is it easier to see it of the church here and now, for (1) the readers would be included and would be "coming" to themselves, and (2) it would give a strange sequence—angels, the church on earth, God, the departed. Angels are not normally described as having their "names . . . written in heaven," whereas there are references to the recording of the names of the saved (e.g., Luke 10:20; Rev 21:27). Perhaps the best solution is to see a reference to the whole communion of saints, the church on earth and in heaven. Believers not only come *to* it but *into* it. This would follow naturally on the reference to angels, after which there is the thought of God as Judge and those who have been vindicated by his judgment.

Montefiore (in loc.) objects to the usual translations like "God, the Judge of all" partly because they do not take account of the Greek word order and partly because they miss the force of the argument. God is not third on the list of the inhabitants of heaven; rather, the author's concern is "with the Judge (who is God) who has rewarded the spirits of righteous men." It is unusual to have the departed referred to as "spirits." The expression is probably used to give emphasis to the spiritual nature of the new order the "righteous men" find themselves in. There is a sense in which they are not made perfect without Christians (11:40). But there is also a sense in which they have been brought to the end for which they were made.

24 The climax is reached with the reference to Jesus, seen here as "the mediator of a new covenant." The word for "new" (*neas*) is applied to the covenant only here. It refers to what is recent. The covenant involves "sprinkled blood" (cf. 9:19–22), which reminds us of the cost of the covenant. The idea of blood speaking is not common, and there is undoubtedly a reference to Genesis 4:10 where Abel's blood cried from the ground for vengeance on his killer. Jesus' blood speaks "a better word" than that. His blood opens up a way into the holiest for people (10:19): Abel's blood sought to shut out the wicked man.

Notes

18 The use of the perfect tense προσεληλύθατε (*proselēlythate*, "you have come") should be noted. It may mean that the position once taken up by the Jews is retained. For them there is still nothing but the equivalent of Sinai. Ὄρει (*orei*, "mountain") is read by many MSS but omitted by the oldest authorities. There would be every tendency for a scribe to insert it but none to omit it. It can scarcely be original.
22 It is striking that in vv.22–24 there is no article until we come to τὸν Ἄβελ (*ton Abel*). "The thoughts are presented in their most abstract form" (Westcott, in loc.).

E. *A Kingdom That Cannot Be Shaken*

12:25–29

25See to it that you do not refuse him who speaks. If they did not escape when they refused him who warned them on earth, how much less will we, if we turn away from him who warns us from heaven? 26At that time his voice shook the earth, but now he has promised, "Once more I will shake not only the earth but also the heavens." 27The words "once more" indicate the removing of what can be shaken —that is, created things—so that what cannot be shaken may remain.

28Therefore, since we are receiving a kingdom that cannot be shaken, let us be thankful, and so worship God acceptably with reverence and awe, 29for our God is a consuming fire.

Earthly, material things (things that can be "shaken") will not last forever. By contrast, God's kingdom is unshakable, and the author uses the contrast as an exhortation to right conduct. He has made it plain that God will not trifle with wrongdoing. The persistent sinner can reckon only on severe judgment. God will bring all things present to an end. Accordingly, the readers should serve him faithfully.

25 Several times in this epistle Judaism and Christianity have been contrasted, and here the contrast concerns the way God speaks. Some feel there is a contrast between Moses and Christ. This may be so, but the basic contrast is between the way God spoke of old and the way he now speaks. Israel of old "refused" him, which means that in their manner of life they rejected what God said and failed to live up to what he commanded (cf. Deut 5:29; the writer cannot be referring to Israel's refusal to hear God's voice because they were praised for this, Deut 5:24–28). What God said was a warning "on earth" because it was connected with the revelation made at Sinai. If, then, the Israelites of old did not escape the consequences of their refusal of a voice on earth, the readers ought not to expect that they will escape far worse consequences if they "turn away from him who warns us from heaven."

26 Here the solemnity of Sinai is recalled. Repeatedly we are told that then the earth shook (Exod 19:18; Judg 5:4–5; Ps 68:8; 77:18; 114:4, 7). The writer has already spoken of the awe-inspiring nature of what happened when the law was given. Now the reference to the shaking of the earth brings it all back. At the same time it enables him to go on to speak of a promise that involved a further shaking, that recorded in Haggai 2:6. The prophet looked forward to something much grander than Sinai. Then God shook the earth, but Haggai foresaw a day when God would shake "not only the earth but also the heavens." This will be no small event but one of cosmic grandeur. The reference to heaven and earth may be meant to hint at the concept of the new heaven and the new earth (Isa 66:22). At any rate, it points to the decisive intervention that God will make at the last time.

27 The writer picks out the expression "once more" (*eti hapax;* lit., "yet once more") to point out the decisive significance of the things of which he is writing. There is an air of finality about it all. This is the decisive time. The word rendered "the removing" (*metathesin*) can mean a "change" (as in 7:12 of a change of law). But "removal" is also possible and seems better in this context. What can be shaken will be removed in that day. NIV renders *hōs pepoiēmenōn* as "that is, created things" (RSV, "as of what has been made"), and this is the sense of it (*poieō* is often used of God's creative activity). This physical creation can be shaken, and it is set in contrast to what cannot be shaken. These are the things that really matter, the things that have the character of permanence. The author does not go into detail about the precise nature of the ultimate rest. But whatever it may be, it will separate the things that last forever from those that do not. "So that" introduces a clause of purpose. It is God's will for this final differentiation to be made so that only what cannot be shaken will remain.

28 The "kingdom" is not a frequent subject in this epistle (the word occurs in a quotation in 1:8 and in the plural in 11:33). This is in contrast to the synoptic Gospels, where the "kingdom" is the most frequent subject in the teaching of Jesus. But this passage shows that the author understood ultimate reality in terms of God's sovereignty. This reality contrasts with earthly systems. They can be shaken and in due course will be shaken. Not so God's kingdom! The author does not simply say that it will not be shaken but that it cannot be shaken. It has a quality found in nothing earthly. The kingdom is something we "receive." It is not earned or created by believers; it is God's gift.

It is not quite certain how we should understand the expression "let us be thankful" (*echōmen charin*). A strong argument for this rendering is that it is the usual meaning of the expression. But *charis* means "grace"; and, as Montefiore (in loc.) points out, elsewhere in this epistle it signifies "grace" rather than "gratitude." He thinks that the duty of thanksgiving is not inculcated elsewhere in Hebrews nor is it particularly appropriate here. So he prefers to translate it, "Let us hold on to God's grace" (JB is similar). Montefiore's position is favored by the following "through which" (*di' hēs*), which NIV renders "and so." The writer appears to be saying that we must appropriate the grace God offers and not let it go, because it is only by grace that we serve as we should. "Worship" may be too narrow for *latreuōmen*, for the word can be used of service of various kinds. KJV renders it "serve." Whether the meaning is service in general or worship in particular, it must be done "with reverence and awe." The combination stresses the greatness of God and the lowly place his people should take in relation to him.

29 In an expression apparently taken from Deuteronomy 4:24, the writer emphasizes that God is not to be trifled with. It is easy to be so taken up with the love and compassion of God that we overlook his implacable opposition to all evil. The wrath of God is not a popular subject today but it looms large in biblical teaching. The writer is stressing that his readers overlook this wrath at their peril. Baillie speaks of the wrath of God "as being identical with the consuming fire of inexorable divine love in relation to our sins" (D.M. Baillie, *God Was in Christ* [London: Faber & Faber, 1955], p. 189). It is something like this to which the writer directs his readers' attention.

Notes

26 There are several rabbinic passages that show that Hag 2:6 was frequently considered in discussing messianic questions, notably the date of the coming of the Messiah (Tal *Sanhedrin* 97b; Exod R, 18.12; Deut R, 1.23; etc.)

27 The writer uses participles that strictly mean "the things being shaken . . . the things not being shaken." But verbal adjectives were not a prominent feature of Gr. during the NT period, and this use of passive participles in the sense of verbal adjectives was not uncommon (see BDF, par. 65 [3]).

28 Some MSS read the indicative ἔχομεν (*echomen*, "we have") instead of the subjunctive ἔχωμεν (*echōmen*, "let us have"). But most scholars hold that support for the latter and its suitability to the context demand that it be preferred. There would have been little difference in pronunciation, and it would have been easy for a scribe to confuse them.

The first twelve chapters of Hebrews form a closely knit argument. Chapter 13 is something of an appendix dealing with a number of practical points. Some commentators find the difference so striking that they think it an addition by someone other than the author of the first twelve chapters. This is going too far. There is no linguistic difference, and, while the argument is not so tight, it is in the manner of the author, especially the section on the cross (vv. 9-14).

F. *Love*

13:1-6

¹Keep on loving each other as brothers. ²Do not forget to entertain strangers, for by so doing some people have entertained angels without knowing it. ³Remember those in prison as if you were their fellow prisoners, and those who are mistreated as if you yourselves were suffering.

⁴Marriage should be honored by all, and the marriage bed kept pure, for God will judge the adulterer and all the sexually immoral. ⁵Keep your lives free from the love of money and be content with what you have, because God has said,

"Never will I leave you;
    never will I forsake you."

[6]So we say with confidence,

"The Lord is my helper; I will not be afraid.
    What can man do to me?"

Christians are to be concerned for the needs of others. Those Christ has died for cannot live for themselves. Christianity is faith in action and that means love at work. So the writer draws attention to something of what it means to live in love.

1 "Brotherly love" (*philadelphia*) is a most important virtue in the NT. Those who are linked in the common bond of having been saved by the death of Jesus cannot but have warm feelings toward one another (cf. Rom 12:10; 1 Thess 4:9; 1 Peter 1:22; 2 Peter 1:7; in the OT see Ps 133:1). Calvin comments, "We can only be Christians if we are brethren" (in loc.).

2 To "brotherly love" the author adds "hospitality" (*philoxenia*, "love of strangers"). Entertaining angels unawares reminds us of Abraham (Gen 18:1ff.) and Lot (Gen 19:1ff.). The writer is not advocating hospitality on the off chance that one might happen to receive an angel as guest but rather because God is pleased when believers are hospitable. Sometimes unexpectedly happy results follow acts of hospitality. It was highly esteemed in the ancient world and was certainly very important for Christians. Accommodation at inns was expensive, and in any case inns had a bad reputation. But as Christian preachers traveled around, believers gave them lodging and so facilitated their mission. Without hospitality in Christian homes, the spread of the faith would have been much more difficult.

3 The writer takes a further step in turning his attention to prisoners. Guests may come unbidden, but prisoners must be actively sought out. In the first century prisoners were not well treated, and they depended—often even for necessities like food—on sympathizers. Sometimes people withheld help for fear of identifying themselves with the prisoners and suffering similar punishment. But Christians should have compassion on those in prison "as if you were their fellow prisoners." "If one part suffers, every part suffers with it," wrote Paul (1 Cor 12:26); and there is something of the same thought here. Believers should feel so much for their friends in prison and for "those who are mistreated" that they become one with them. Compassion is an essential part of Christian living.

4 From love for the badly treated the author turns to love within the marriage bond. We should probably understand the opening expression as an imperative: "Let marriage be held in honor" (RSV). "By all" (*en pasin*) might be masculine, "among all men," or neuter, "in all circumstances," probably the latter. Some ascetics held marriage in low esteem, but the author repudiates this position. "The marriage bed" is a euphemism for sexual intercourse. He considers the physical side of marriage important and "pure." Contrary to the views of some thinkers in the ancient world, there is nothing defiling about it. Over against honorable marriage he sets "sexual immorality" (*pornous;* the word is usually rendered "fornicators") and "adulterers" (*moichous*, used where violation of the marriage bond is involved).

146

All forms of sexual sin come under the judgment of God. This was a novel view to many in the first century. For them chastity was an unreasonable demand to make. It is one of the unrecognized miracles that Christians were able not only to make this demand but to make it stick. The word "God" comes last in the Greek and is emphatic. Sexual sinners are likely to go their way, careless of all others. But in the end they will be judged by none less than God.

5 Sins of impurity and covetousness are also linked elsewhere in the NT (e.g., 1 Cor 5:10-11; Eph 4:19; 5:3-5; 1 Thess 4:3-6). The covetous man pursues his selfish aims, whether sexual or financial, without regard to the rights of others. So the writer warns against the love of money and urges contentment with what one has. In any case covetousness is needless, for the believer has the promise that God will never leave him nor forsake him. The origin of this quotation is not clear; the words do not correspond exactly to any OT passage, though there are several statements that are rather like it (e.g., Gen 28:15; Deut 31:6, 8; Josh 1:5; 1 Chron 28:20; Isa 41:17; perhaps closest is Josh 1:5). It is interesting that Philo has the same quotation in the same words (*On the Confusion of Tongues* 166). Accordingly, it seems that both Philo and the writer of Hebrews are quoting from a version of the LXX that has not survived. Be that as it may, the words point to the complete reliability of God. Since he has promised to help his own, covetousness in all its forms is useless. God's people are secure no matter what comes, because he is with them. Beside this great fact, the petty securities of worldly possessions, position, and the like do not matter at all.

6 Despondency is foreign to Christians. They can speak "with confidence" (*tharroun-tas*, a participle that indicates an attitude of courage and trust). "We" once more links the writer with his readers. He sees his lot as bound up with theirs. The quotation from Psalm 118:6 is exact, agreeing with the LXX (117:6). There are three points in this confidence. First, the Lord is the psalmist's (and our) helper. This carries on the argument of the previous verse, sharpening a little the thought of the assistance that the believer may count on. Second, there is the ringing declaration of confidence as the psalmist renounces fear. With the Helper he has at his side, there is no reason for fear, and he has none. Third, there is the rhetorical question that underlies man's insignificance. The question is "What will man do to me?" rather than "What can man do to me?" as in NIV, JB, NEB, RSV, and TEV. It is performance rather than capacity the psalmist is speaking of. He is not thinking theoretically but of what will happen. Man will not succeed in anything he attempts to do against one who trusts in God.

Notes

2 The present imperative μὴ ἐπιλανθάνεσθε (*mē epilanthanesthe*, "do not forget") may indicate that the readers of this epistle were in fact forgetting this duty. The most natural way of taking it is of an action already in progress.

3 NIV is a trifle free at the end of this verse where the Gr. means rather "as being yourselves in [the] body" and the question is "What does 'in body' [*en sōmati*] mean?" Some have taken it to mean "in the body of Christ" (e.g., Calvin). But it seems rather to be an unusual way of referring to life here and now, in bodies like ours. With such bodies imprisonment like that suffered by the friends was always possible and the thought should promote compassion.

147

6 Of the construction introduced by ὥστε (*hōste,* "so"), E.A. Abbott says that it "rather suggests what we *may* say than states what we *do* say" (*Johannine Grammar* [A. & C. Black, London, 1906], 2203*b*).

G. *Christian Leadership*

13:7–8

> [7]Remember your leaders, who spoke the word of God to you. Consider the outcome of their way of life and imitate their faith. [8]Jesus Christ is the same yesterday and today and forever.

The concluding section of the epistle contains a number of small, disconnected units. From love the writer passes to a few thoughts about Christian leaders. This is important, for there is not much in the NT about the way Christians should treat their leaders. There is, however, more about how leaders themselves should behave.

7 Three times in this chapter the present participle of the verb *hēgeomai* occurs in the sense of "leader" (here, vv. 17, 24). The term is a general one and is used of leaders of religious bodies as well as of princes, military commanders, etc. This makes it difficult to say precisely who these leaders were or what they did. They may have been "elders," but that word is not used of them and so we cannot be sure that they were elders. They "spoke the word of God" so that one of their principal functions was preaching or teaching. But again the word is a general one. The aorist tense may well point to a specific time—that of the original proclamation of the gospel to these readers (cf. 2:3). "The word of God" is the totality of the Christian message, and the expression reminds the readers that this is no human invention but of divine origin.

The word translated "outcome" (*ekbasis,* again in the NT only in 1 Cor 10:13) is understood by many as a euphemism for death, often as a martyr's death (so Héring, Westcott, Moffatt). "Martyr's death" does seem to be stretching the word a bit. On the whole, however, it seems as though past leaders were in mind (though TEV is much too definite with "Remember your former leaders . . . . Think back on how they lived and died"). The past tenses and the word *ekbasis* support this, though it is not impossible to see the meaning as "consider the result of their manner of life." They are held up as examples to be imitated and, specifically, their faith is singled out. Faith is the important thing, and the readers were being tempted to unbelief in falling back from the Christian way. They should instead follow these good examples of faith.

8 In this profound and wonderfully succinct verse, the writer's thoughts turn again to Christ. Earthly leaders come and go, but he is always there. The full name "Jesus Christ" (again in Hebrews only in 10:10; 13:21) adds solemnity to this pronouncement. *Echthes* ("yesterday") should probably not be taken to refer to Christ's preexistence or the Incarnation. It stands for the past as a whole and is part of an expression taking up past, present, and future into an impressive statement of Christ's unchanging nature. The readers need not fear that Christ is different now or will be different in the future from what he has been in the past. Past or present makes no difference to the eternal Savior. "Forever" (*eis tous aiōnas,* "into the ages," "to eternity") takes the continuity as far into the future as it will go. No matter what ages lie ahead, Christ will be unchanged through them. Christian conduct is based on this certainty. Christ will never be superseded.

H. *Christian Sacrifice*

13:9–16

⁹Do not be carried away by all kinds of strange teachings. It is good for our hearts to be strengthened by grace, not by ceremonial foods, which are of no value to those who eat them. ¹⁰We have an altar from which those who minister at the tabernacle have no right to eat.

¹¹The high priest carries the blood of animals into the Most Holy Place as a sin offering, but the bodies are burned outside the camp. ¹²And so Jesus also suffered outside the city gate to make the people holy through his own blood. ¹³Let us, then, go to him outside the camp, bearing the disgrace he bore. ¹⁴For here we do not have an enduring city, but we are looking for the city that is to come.

¹⁵Through Jesus, therefore, let us continually offer to God a sacrifice of praise— the fruit of lips that confess his name. ¹⁶And do not forget to do good and to share with others, for with such sacrifices God is pleased.

The writer has put strong emphasis on the centrality of Christ's sacrifice and keeps this steadily in view as he approaches the end of his letter. He has some erroneous teaching in mind, but we cannot define it with precision. He and his readers both knew what it was; so there was no need for him to be specific. Whatever it was, the unchangeability of Christ should inspire them to refuse its curious diversities and novel teaching.

Once more the writer draws attention to Christ's sacrifice, using the ceremonies of the Day of Atonement as the basis. Some may have thought the Christian way an impoverished one, lacking the sacrifices that were central to religion in the ancient world. But Christians do have sacrifices, none the less real for being spiritual and not material.

9 The writer warns against being carried away by "all kinds of strange teachings." "All kinds of" renders *poikilais*; literally, "many-colored." Since it points to a great variety of teaching, it is difficult to identify specifically what is in mind. There was not one straightforward piece of wrong teaching but a variety of wrong teachings. "Strange" renders *xenais* ("foreign," i.e., foreign to the gospel). The readers should know better than to go after such teachings, for they have known the grace of God. The heart, as often, stands for the whole of the inner life; and this is sustained, not by anything material, such as food, but by grace. God is the source of the believer's strength as he lives out the Christian life.

Though there is nothing in the Greek to correspond to the adjective "ceremonial," which NIV prefixes to "foods," this is probably a correct gloss. Most religions of the day had food regulations, as did the Jews; but usually this meant that some foods were regarded as "unclean." The foods were not regarded as "good for our hearts." So it seems likely that what the worshipers took to be the beneficial effects of some sacrificial meal are in mind. The author denies it. The real life of man is not sustained on the level of things to eat. It requires the grace of God. The end of the verse means something like "in which those who walk are not profited" (NIV has paraphrased). This points to a way of life in which "foods" are a dominant element.

10 Some see the "altar" as the communion table (from which Christians, but not others, eat). But this is a curious way of interpreting the passage in the light of the point just made. This would simply be substituting one material thing for another, and the whole argument would fall to the ground. Instead, the writer is saying that the cross is distinctive to the Christian way. It was on a cross that the Christian sacrifice was offered. Thus it may not improperly be spoken of as an "altar." In a Christian context the sacrifice must be on the cross as the author has made abundantly clear in a number of places. "Those who minister at the tabernacle" are often understood to be the Jewish priests. But the word *latreuontes* ("those who minister") may be used of the service of others than priests, and the participle is used of worshipers in 9:9; 10:2. The writer seems to be speaking of Jewish worshipers in general. Those who worship at the tent have, as such, no rights in the altar of the cross. The crucified Savior means nothing to them. The writer is pointing his readers to the privilege Christians have and warning them against losing it.

11 "For" (*gar,* which NIV omits) leads from the general idea of serving the altar to a specific example, one taken from the Day of Atonement ceremonies in all probability. The doubt is caused by the fact that the expression that NIV renders "the Most Holy Place" (*ta hagia*) may be used of the "Holy Place" (as in 9:2); and there were sin offerings other than those of the Day of Atonement when the bodies were burned outside the camp (Lev 4:12, 21). But there have been references to the Day of Atonement earlier in the epistle, which also seems to fit the present passage better than the other sin offerings. On that Day the high priest brought the blood of the victims into the Most Holy Place (Lev 16:14–15), but the bodies of the animals were burned outside the camp (Lev 16:27). The word used here for "animals" (*zōon*) is not common in the Bible and does not appear to be used elsewhere of sacrificial victims. The bodies of the animals used on the Day of Atonement were burnt up—totally consumed—in the fire. This was "outside the camp," the word drawing attention to the wilderness situation ("camp," *parembolē,* basically a military term, was readily applied to such situations as that of Israel in the wilderness).

12 "And so" (*dio*) introduces an inference. The Day of Atonement typologically foreshadowed the atoning work of Jesus. The author apparently is reasoning that because the type involved an activity "outside the camp," there will be an equivalent with the antitype. The parallel is not complete because in the case of the sin offerings the animal was actually killed inside the camp and only the carcass disposed of outside the camp (though the red heifer, "which was a kind of sin-offering, was slaughtered outside the camp," Bruce, in loc.). The type was clear enough. The human name Jesus brings before us the picture of the Man, suffering for us. The conjunction *hina* introduces a clause of purpose. His suffering was not aimless but was designed with a specific object in mind, "to make his people holy."

The verb *hagiazō* means "to set aside for God"; and it is applied both to things used for ritual purposes and to people who are thus taken out of the circle of the merely worldly and brought into the number of the people of God. This process was effected "through his own blood." The expression puts some emphasis on the fact that Christ did not need an external victim (as did the high priests) but brought about the sanctification in question by the sacrifice of himself. "Blood" clearly signifies "death," as is commonly the case in the NT—and, for that matter, in the OT. There are some scholars who think the meaning is "life," but this seems untenable (cf. my discussion in ch. 3 of my *Apostolic Preaching of the Cross,* 3rd ed. [Grand Rapids: Eerdmans, 1965]).

"People" can mean people in general; but more characteristically it means "the people of God," a meaning that suits this passage. To effect this purpose, then, Jesus suffered "outside the gate." Though not stated elsewhere in the NT, this is implied in John 19:17; and, anyway, crucifixions took place outside cities. Snell argues from Leviticus 10:1–5; 24:14, 23 that "*people* were taken 'outside the camp' when they were accursed under the Law and rejected, as much as the ritually useless bodies were after the sacrifice was finished" (in loc.). He goes on to argue that "our Lord's offering has been first compared with that on the Day of Atonement . . . and is next said to have involved formal rejection by the authorities of the old Judaism" (ibid.). That does seem to be the point of the reference. Jesus was rejected by Jewish authorities, and his death outside Jerusalem symbolized this.

13 This leads to an appeal to the readers to "go to him outside the camp" (the compound verb *exerchomai,* "to go out," and the adverb *exō,* "outside," emphasize the thought of "out," "outside"). Christ is outside the camp of Judaism, and the readers are encouraged to go to him where he is. To remain within the camp of Judaism would be to be separated from him. Here there may be an allusion to Moses' pitching "the tent of meeting" outside the camp and to the people's going out to it (Exod 33:7). But in the case of Christ, there was a price to pay—that of sharing in the rejection he had undergone, "bearing the disgrace he bore." In 11:26 Moses was said to have accepted "disgrace for the sake of Christ" (the same expression as here). To align oneself with Christ is to subject oneself to scorn, reproach, and perhaps more. But consistently throughout this epistle the writer has argued, as he does here, that it is well worth it. Furthermore, his readers must have a different outlook from that of contemporary Judaism. The Jews held that the way Christ died proved him to be accursed (Deut 21:23; Gal 3:13). The readers must be ready to stand outside Judaism with the Christ who bore the curse for them "outside the camp."

14 The writer reinforces his appeal to go to Jesus by reminding Christians that they have no stake in any earthly city, Jewish or otherwise. For people with such an outlook it is no great matter to be "outside the camp." As in 11:10 (where see the comments) the "city" will stand for the highest and best in community life, the heavenly city. That is not to be found "here," i.e., "here on earth." In this sense no earthly city is "enduring." All earthly cities are transient, temporary. But Christians are looking for a city to come. People love to look for earthly security. But the best earthly security is insecure. The readers should pursue that which is really lasting. They should put earnest endeavor (*epizēteō;* NIV, "we are looking") into striving for the abiding city, not into maintaining their grip on any fleeting earthly one.

15 The verse begins with an emphatic "through him" (NIV apparently tries to add force by substituting "Jesus" for "him"). It is through Jesus and not the Jewish priests (or any other priests) that men offer to God acceptable sacrifice. The verb *anapherō* is the technical one for the offering of sacrifices of animals and the like. The author uses it of the only sacrifices Christians offer, spiritual sacrifices. So he urges them to offer "a sacrifice of praise" (the expression occurs in LXX in Lev 7:13, 15 and with the definite articles in Lev 7:12), i.e., a sacrifice consisting of praise. The thought that the sacrifice Christians offer is spiritual occurs elsewhere, as in Romans 12:1 (cf. the similar thought that the essence of religion is ethical and spiritual, James 1:27). This sacrifice is to be offered "continually." In systems like Judaism sacrifices were offered at set times, but for Christians praise goes up all the time. Since a loving God is working out his purposes all the time, there are no circumstances in which praise should not be offered (cf. 1 Thess 5:18). The sacrifice is further explained in an expression from Hosea 14:2 (LXX 14:3; cf. Prov 18:20), "the fruit of lips that confess his name." In the light of the Cross, there is no room for sacrifices such as those the Jews offered. Now believers offer the sacrifice of praise and acknowledge Christ.

16 The writer gives two more examples of the sacrifices Christians offer. "To do good" (*eupoiia*, only here in the NT and not in the LXX) is a general term, while "fellowship" or "sharing" (*koinōnia*) is more specific. It signifies sharing with others such things as we have: money, goods, and, of course, those intangibles that make up "fellowship." Animal sacrifices were the almost universal religious practice. Christians had nothing of the sort, but the writer is making the point that this did not mean they had nothing to offer. They had their sacrifices, some of which he has listed, and it is "with such sacrifices" that God is well pleased. Christ's suffering "outside the camp" has altered everything. Now God looks to people to take Christ's way. And that means they offer no animals but make their response to what Christ has done for them in praise, good deeds, and works of love and charity.

Notes

---

10 Some understand "we have an altar" to mean "we Jews have an altar." The Jews did have an altar, and even so there were some sacrifices of which the priests did not eat, such as those on the Day of Atonement. But this is not a very natural way of reading the passage. In any case, the author writes as a Christian to people who have made a Christian profession. (Whether he or they were in fact Jews we do not know for certain.)
14 There is a play on words with the participles μένουσαν (*menousan*, "enduring"), and μέλλουσαν (*mellousan*, "is to come").

I. *Christian Obedience*

13:17

> [17]Obey your leaders and submit to their authority. They keep watch over you as men who must give an account. Obey them so that their work will be a joy, not a burden, for that would be of no advantage to you.

The author is mindful of the responsibility of Christian leaders to whom he has already referred (v. 7). In due course they must give account to God for their flock. So he urges his readers to keep this in mind and not make things hard for their leaders.

17 The readers are to be obedient to their leaders. In v. 7 the leaders were men who had died. Here, however, those alive and currently in places of authority are meant. (At the same time we should perhaps notice that there is nothing in the Gr. to correspond to NIV's "their authority"; *hypeikete* means simply "yield" or "submit," i.e., to them.) NIV omits "for" (*gar*), which introduces the reason for the submission. The pronoun *autoi* puts some emphasis on the subject: "They and no one else." The verb "keep watch" (*agrypneō*) means literally "keep oneself awake, be awake" (BAG, s.v.). There is the imagery of the leaders keeping awake nights in their concern for their people.

"They keep watch over you" is more literally "they keep watch for your souls," where it is a question whether NIV (also NEB) is right and "souls" (*psychōn*) is simply a periphrasis for "you," or whether, as a number of commentators think, the thought is of the spiritual life. In view of the similar use of *psychē* in 10:39 (lit., "of faith, to the saving of the soul"), it may well be that we are to see here a reference to spiritual well-being. The leaders are concerned for the deep needs of their people, not simply for what lies on the surface. They are concerned, because they must render account. Leaders are responsible, and God will call them to account one day. The writer pleads that the readers will so act that keeping watch will be a thing of joy for the leaders (Paul could speak of the Thessalonians as his "glory and joy": 1 Thess 2:20; cf. Phil 2:16; 3 John 4). The alternative is for them to do it with "groaning" (*stenazontes;* NIV, "a burden"), which, he says, would be "of no advantage" for the readers.

J. *Prayer*

13:18-19

> 18Pray for us. We are sure that we have a clear conscience and desire to live honorably in every way. 19I particularly urge you to pray so that I may be restored to you soon.

A short appeal for prayer reveals both the writer's conviction that prayer is a powerful force and his hope that he will soon see his correspondents again. Following immediately on the reference to the leaders, this leads a number of commentators to see the writer as one who had once been a leader in the group. His desire to "be restored to you" (v.19) shows clearly that he had once worked among them in some capacity.

18 The present imperative "Pray" (*proseuchesthe*) looks for a continuous activity and implies that they had already been doing this. "Keep praying for us" is its force. There is a question whether we should take the plural "us" as a genuine plural or as epistolary, meaning "I" (as in 5:11; 6:9, 11). The plural in this verse is followed by a singular in v.19, and exactly opposite conclusions have been drawn from this. Westcott and Kent (in loc.), for example, think the plural genuine and that the writer associates others with him (for a similar transition from plural to singular, cf. Gal 1:8-9; Col 4:3). But Bruce and Hewitt (in loc.) think that the singular shows the plural to be no more than literary. I see no reason for thinking that others are associated with the writer; so I incline to this latter view.

The writer has rebuked his readers from time to time; he has warned them of the dangers in their conduct and exhorted them. But he depends on them, too, and looks to them now to support him with their prayers. At the same time there is a problem arising from the way he puts his request. He says, "Pray for us, for we are persuaded that we have a good conscience" (NIV omits the "for" [*gar*]; this makes it a separate statement and thus eliminates the problem). Having a good conscience is a most unusual reason for requesting prayer. We could understand it if the writer spoke of his difficulties or the like. Lacking knowledge of the circumstances, we cannot be sure. Yet it seems that the readers have been accusing the writer of some fault. Moffatt suggests that they may have attributed his absence from them to unworthy motives (in loc.). Something had gone wrong. The writer protests that he has a clear conscience and that this is a reason for asking for their fellowship in prayer.

The adjective "good" (*kalēn*) is applied to conscience only here in the NT (elsewhere we find *agathē*). The writer is not aware of having committed any sin. He goes on to affirm his determination "to live honorably" (the adverb is *kalōs*) and that "in every way." He allows no exceptions but expresses wholeheartedness. "Desire" is perhaps a little weak for *thelontes,* for the verb expresses the set of the will, not merely a wish. The writer professes a firm determination to live in the way indicated.

19 The author underlines the importance of the readers' doing as he asks. He appeals (*parakalō,* NIV, "urge") strongly, where the adverb *perissoterōs* (which NIV renders "particularly") means something like "more abundantly," "beyond measure." What it was that prevented him from being "restored" to them is not said, but evidently the obstacle was considerable. Some have suggested that he had been imprisoned for his faith. We know too little of the circumstances to rule this out, but there is nothing to indicate it. Others think it was sickness. We simply do not know. The language seems to show that it was something outside the writer's control and that it needed a good deal of prayer. The problem was with the writer, not the readers, because he specifically asks for prayer for himself.

Notes

19 The adverb τάχιον (*tachion*) is comparative in form and may be used in the sense "more quickly." But the comparative had lost some of its force and the word may mean no more than "soon."

X. Conclusion

The writer has finished what he has to say. It remains for him only to round off his letter, and he does so with a magnificent doxology and a few greetings.

A. *Doxology*

13:20–21

> [20]May the God of peace, who through the blood of the eternal covenant brought back from the dead our Lord Jesus, that great Shepherd of the sheep, [21]equip you with everything good for doing his will, and may he work in us what is pleasing to him, through Jesus Christ, to whom be glory for ever and ever. Amen.

This doxology gathers up a number of the themes that have meant so much as the argument of the epistle has unfolded: the blood, the eternal covenant, the lordship of Jesus, the importance of doing his will. It also introduces some things not yet dealt with. This is the only place in the epistle, for example, where Jesus is seen as our Shepherd or where the Resurrection is specifically referred to. The whole forms a superb doxology that has meant much to Christians throughout the centuries.

20 God is called "the God of peace" a number of times in the Pauline writings (Rom 15:33; 16:20; 2 Cor 13:11; Phil 4:9; 1 Thess 5:23). "Peace" connotes the fullest prosperity of the whole man, taking up as it does the OT concept of the Hebrew *šālôm* (see comments on 7:2). Here it reminds us that it is God in whom all our prosperity is centered. There is no well-rounded life that does not depend on him. The expression is especially suitable in view of what the epistle discloses of the condition of the readers. They have had to cope with some form of persecution and were still not free from opposition. They were tempted to go back from Christianity and have had to be warned of the dangers of apostasy. They may have had doubts about who their true leaders were. It is well for them to be reminded that real peace is in God.

The doxology goes on to characterize God in terms of the Resurrection. In the NT, Jesus is occasionally said to have risen. It is, however, much more common in the NT for the Resurrection to be ascribed to God, as here (though the verb *anagō* is not common in this connection). The one whom God brought up from the dead is now described as "the great Shepherd of the sheep." The language seems to be derived from Isaiah 63:11. "Where is he who brought them through the sea, with the shepherd of his flock?"—though the thought here is, of course, quite different. Christ is called a shepherd in the great treatment of the shepherd theme in John 10 and again in 1 Peter 2:25 (cf. also Matt 26:31; Mark 14:27). It is a piece of imagery that stresses the care of our Lord for his own, for sheep are helpless without their shepherd. But an aspect we in modern times sometimes miss is that the shepherd has absolute sovereignty over his flock (cf. Rev 2:27; 12:5; 19:15; in each case the verb rendered "rule" in NIV means "to shepherd"). The adjective "great" is used because Christ is not to be ranked with other shepherds. He stands out.

The Resurrection is linked with "the blood of the eternal covenant" (cf. Isa 55:3; Zech 9:11). It is interesting to see how the thought of covenant persists to the end. It has been one of the major themes of this epistle. The adjective again brings out the point that this covenant will never be replaced by another as it replaced the old covenant. It is perpetual in its validity. And it was established by blood. The author never forgets that. For him the death of Jesus is central. At the same time, his linking it with the Resurrection shows that he did not have in mind a dead Christ but one who, though he shed his blood to establish the covenant, lives for ever. Last in this verse in the Greek (and with some emphasis) come the words "our Lord Jesus." The expression is unusual outside of Acts, where it occurs a number of times. It combines the lordship of Christ and his real humanity, two themes of continuing importance.

21 The prayer is that God will "equip" the readers "with everything good for doing his will." The verb "equip" (*katartizō*) is often used of mending what is broken and torn, and some see a reference to putting right what was amiss in the spiritual life of the readers. A prayer that God would put things right would be quite in place. But in this context perhaps the meaning is "supply you with what you need to live the Christian life"; so NIV gives the right meaning. "Everything good" is comprehensive. The writer wants nothing to be lacking. Notice the emphasis on doing the will of God, a thought we have had before in this epistle.

It is also interesting to notice the juxtaposition of "doing his will" and "may he work in us." From one point of view a deed is the deed of man, but from another it is God working in and through his servant. We should not overlook the significance of the word "us." As he has done so often, the writer links himself with his readers. He looks for God to do his perfect work in them and in him alike. He is not aloof and a special case; he needs the grace of God as much as they do. He wants God to do in us "what is pleasing to him," where "pleasing" (*euarestos*) renders a word used only here in

Hebrews but eight times elsewhere in the NT. In Titus 2:9 it refers to slaves being pleasing to their masters; elsewhere it always refers to people being acceptable to God. But men can do what is acceptable to God only through Jesus Christ. Therefore, the prayer includes this point.

Whether "to whom" refers to the Father or to Christ poses a problem. Grammatically it could be either. A number of commentators take it to refer to God on the ground that *ho theos* is the subject of the main verb and that in any case doxologies mostly refer to him. Others point out that "Jesus Christ" immediately precedes the word in question and that in any case this epistle puts emphasis on Christ and his work for men. So it seems that a good case can be made for either. I do not see how the question can be resolved. Perhaps the writer was not making a sharp distinction.

The doxology concludes with "for ever and ever. Amen." A number of important MSS omit the words "and ever." It is the kind of addition scribes would naturally insert if it was lacking in the text before them. There seems, however, to be no reason for anyone to omit it if it were original; so the shorter reading should probably be preferred. It is curious that doxologies should include "Amen," as this one does, for the word was normally the response of a congregation. Perhaps initially a doxology was spoken by the leader of a congregation and the people responded with their "Amen." In time the response was added to the doxology, as being the normal thing. Be that as it may, the "Amen" makes a satisfying close.

B. *Final Exhortations*

13:22–25

> [22]Brothers, I urge you to bear with my word of exhortation, for I have written you only a short letter.
> [23]I want you to know that our brother Timothy has been released. If he arrives soon, I will come with him to see you.
> [24]Greet all your leaders and all God's people. Those from Italy send you their greetings.
> [25]Grace be with you all.

The author now rounds off the whole epistle with a final appeal and a brief section of greetings. The greetings show that the epistle was being sent to a definite, known group of Christians with whom the author had ties.

22 "I urge" (NIV, NASB) may be the right way to translate *parakalō;* but it seems to mean something more like "I beg you" (TEV, NEB; cf. "I do ask you, brothers, to take these words of advice kindly" [JB]). There is appeal in it, but also encouragement. The letter has had its share of rebukes and stern warnings, and the writer now softens the impact a little with this appeal and with the affectionate address "Brothers." He calls his epistle the "word of exhortation" ("my" is inserted by NIV, RSV). A similar expression is found in Acts 13:15, where it clearly means a homily. So the point of it here may be that this letter is rather like a written sermon. "Exhortation" (*paraklēseōs*) includes the note of encouragement as elsewhere in the letter. It contains a good deal of exhortation here; but the writer means it as encouragement, not as rebuke.

The author goes on to say that he has written only briefly. Some commentators think that such a description can scarcely apply to an epistle as long as this one and so suggest that perhaps chapter 13 (or part of it) was added to some previously existing writing and that this expression refers only to the "addition." Against that it is hard to see why anyone would bother to apologize for writing anything as short as this chapter. It is better to see it as applying to the whole. For the letter *is* short, considering the subject matter. Some of the subjects could have been dealt with at much greater length. There has been some straight speaking. So before he finishes, the writer adds this brief section inviting the readers to take it in the right spirit. It would all be much worse if they did not.

23 "I want you to know" renders the word *ginōskete,* which could be either indicative, "you know," or imperative, "Know!" On the whole it seems more likely to be the latter (as implied by "I want you to know"), for the writer is evidently giving some new information, whereas the indicative would mean that he was repeating something they already knew (why would he do so?). Timothy is no doubt the companion of Paul (no other Timothy is known to us from those times) and he seems to have had some ties with both the readers and the writer. Otherwise we would expect a general expression instead of "our brother Timothy."

It is not clear what "released" means, for the word can refer to starting off on a journey (as in Acts 13:3; 28:25) or making other beginnings. Timothy may have started on a journey or he may have been released from some obligation. But on the whole it seems most likely that the term, used absolutely as it is, means that he had been released from imprisonment. All that we can say for certain is that Timothy had left the place where he was. The writer now expected that he would come to the place where Timothy was and hoped that then the two of them might go on to visit the readers. But evidently he intended moving fairly soon, whether or not Timothy came.

24 For the third time in the chapter, the leaders come to our attention. That they are to be greeted by the recipients of the letter makes it clear that the "leaders" were not the recipients and, furthermore, that the letter was not sent to the whole church. That greetings were to be sent shows that the recipients were on good terms with the leaders. The words "and all" may be significant—viz., there are no exceptions. "The saints" (*hoi hagioi;* NIV, "God's people") is a common NT description of the p.ople of God, but it is found in this epistle again only in 6:10. It means God's people as those consecrated to him, set apart to do him service. The greeting from "those from Italy" raises the question whether they were Italians living abroad or in their own country. The words could mean either. (Acts 10:23 has a similar expression for those still living in their homeland and Acts 21:27 for those living away from their homeland.) There seems no way of determining the point.

25 The NT letters normally end with a prayer for grace for the recipients. Grace is a fitting note on which to end a letter like this one, so full of what God has done for people in Christ. There are some variant readings, but NIV has the text that most agree is correct. The author then closes by praying for God's grace for all his friends. He omits none from his concern or from God's.

Notes

21 Καταρτίσαι (*katartisai*) is apparently the only example of the optative in the epistle (BDF, par. 384). It expresses a wish: "May he equip. . . ."

A number of MSS read ὑμῖν (*hymin*, "in you") instead of ἡμῖν (*hēmin*, "in us"), and a few scholars favor it because of the sense and the preceding ὑμᾶς (*hymas*, "you"). But these are precisely the reasons that would induce scribes to change from ἡμῖν (*hēmin*), which has better support. There seems little doubt that we should accept it.

JAMES

Donald W. Burdick

JAMES

Introduction

1. Authorship
2. Date
3. Destination
4. Occasion and Purpose
5. Canonicity
6. Relation to Other Writings
7. Theological Values
8. Bibliography
9. Outline

1. Authorship

Even though this epistle names its author, it does not specify his actual identity. James was a common name in the first century. Indeed, there are in the NT four men called James. Of these, only two have ever been seriously suggested as possible authors of this epistle. A very few scholars have understood the writer to be James the son of Zebedee, one of the twelve apostles. Most scholars, however, have recognized that he was martyred too early (A.D. 44) to have written the epistle (Acts 12:1–2).

Since at least the third century, the most prominent view has been that James, the Lord's brother (Mark 6:3), wrote the book. This was the belief of Origen (c. A.D. 185–253), Eusebius (c. 265–340), and Jerome (c. 340–420). In more recent times other views have been advanced, such as that the designation "James" (1:1) is a pseudonym, that the epistle was originally anonymous, that it was written by an unknown James, or that it was the product of a disciple of the Lord's brother and thus represented the teaching of James.

However, the evidence of the epistle itself favors the traditional identification of the Lord's brother as author. The characteristics of James the brother of the Lord as seen in Acts 21:17–25, in Galatians 2:12, and in the description of "James the Just" by Hegesippus (Eusebius *Ecclesiastical History* 2.23) all are in harmony with the heavy emphasis on genuine religious practice and ethical conduct apparent in the epistle. The vocabulary of James's speech and letter in Acts 15:13–29 reveals significant similarity to that of the epistle (Mayor, pp. iii–iv). The authoritative tone of the epistle (forty-six imperatives) agrees well with the authority exercised by James in Acts 15:13ff.; 21:18.

2. Date

Some writers, not accepting the view that James the Lord's brother wrote the epistle, have dated it either late in the first century or some time between A.D. 100

and 150. But if the Lord's brother is identified as author, the book must have originated prior to A.D. 62, when, according to Josephus, James was martyred.

Among those who hold the traditional view of authorship, there are two general opinions. Some argue for a date near the end of James's life, perhaps in the early sixties; others insist that the epistle was written before A.D. 50. If the latter date is correct, James may have been the first NT book written.

Several considerations make it probable that James wrote between A.D. 45 and 50.
1. The Jewish orientation of the epistle fits the earlier period much more naturally than the later. That the author does not refer to Gentiles or related subjects may well point to the time in the history of the early church when Gentiles were only beginning to be reached with the gospel.
2. The absence of any reference to the controversy concerning the Judaizers and their insistence on Gentile circumcision is best explained by the earlier date.
3. The close affinity of the teaching of James to that of the OT and Christ is significant. If the epistle were later, one might expect to find a greater similarity to the writings of Paul, such as is apparent in 1 Peter, for example.
4. Furthermore, the evidence of a simple church order favors the early date. The leaders are "teachers" (3:1) and "elders" (5:14).
5. Finally, the use of the Greek term *synagōgē* (synagogue; NIV, "meeting") to describe the church assembly or meeting place (2:2) points to the early period when Christianity was largely confined to Jewish circles.

3. Destination

The epistle is addressed to "the twelve tribes scattered among the nations" (1:1). Although this is quite indefinite, it does reveal something about the recipients. The expression "twelve tribes" is clearly Jewish and no doubt was intended to identify the readers as Jews. The description of their congregation or meeting place as a *synagōgē* (2:2) also supports this interpretation. Another indication that the recipients were Jews is the use in 5:4 of the Hebrew title *kyriou sabaōth* ("Lord Almighty"; lit., "Lord of hosts").

The author further limits his intended readership by statements that assume the recipients are Christians. The most explicit statement of this kind is the pointed imperative of 2:1: "My brothers, as believers in our glorious Lord Jesus Christ, don't show favoritism." Here James clearly assumes that the Jews he is addressing are followers of Christ. The same fact is less explicitly indicated in the insistence of 5:7, that the brothers should be patient until the Lord comes, and in the further instruction that they "stand firm, because the Lord's coming is near" (5:8). It would seem, then, that the epistle was addressed to Jewish believers in Jesus as Messiah.

The geographical location of these Jewish Christians is not specifically identified. They are merely described as "scattered among the nations" (1:1), which means they were not centered in one locality. Beyond this the biblical text does not take us. It is possible, however, to theorize about the identity of the addressees. Some have suggested that they were the believers who were forced to leave Jerusalem during the persecution that followed Stephen's death. These Jewish Christians spread out over Judea and Samaria (Acts 8:1) and even as far as Phoenicia, Cyprus, and Syrian Antioch (Acts 11:19).

It is most reasonable to assume that James, the leading elder of the Jerusalem church, would feel responsible for these former "parishioners" and attempt to instruct them somewhat as he would have done had they still been under his care in Jerusalem. The epistle reveals his intimate knowledge of their circumstances and characteristics. And he writes with the note of authority expected of one who had been recognized as a spiritual leader in the Jerusalem church.

4. Occasion and Purpose

If it is correctly assumed that James, the leader of the Jerusalem church, wrote this epistle to believers who had been dispersed from Jerusalem in the persecution following Stephen's death, the occasion for writing is fairly clear. These Jewish Christians, scattered throughout the area east of the Mediterranean Sea, no longer had contact with the apostles; nor was James among them to instruct and exhort them.

Difficulties—perhaps persecutions—were confronting them (1:2–4); the ungodly rich were oppressing them (5:1–6); the religion of some was becoming a superficial formality (1:22–27; 2:14–26); discriminatory practices revealed a lack of love (2:1–13); and bitterness in speech (3:1–12) and attitude (3:13–4:3) marred their fellowship. Apparently reports of such problems among the scattered brothers had reached James in Jerusalem. In response, he wrote as pastor *in absentia* to urge his people to make the needed changes in their lives and in their corporate relationships.

5. Canonicity

The epistle was not readily received into the collection of writings that were viewed as being on a par with the OT Scriptures. It was rejected by some as late as the time of Eusebius (c. 265–340). Few early Christian writers refer to it. The Muratorian Canon (c. 170) omits it, as does the OL version.

Such negative evidence could be taken as ground for doubting the authority of the book if it were not that, after a period of questioning, the churches finally granted unanimous recognition to it as canonical. It had successfully passed the test. Furthermore, there are reasonable explanations for the late acceptance of the epistle. Eusebius himself explained that some denied the book because few ancient writers had quoted from it (*Ecclesiastical History* 2.23). It was not questioned because any fault was found with its teaching, but merely because it had not been widely used. There are reasons why this condition existed. Among these are its untheological nature, its brevity, the question of James's identity, the fact that it was not written by one of the twelve apostles, and its general address (sent to no specific person or church).

In due time, such authorities as Eusebius and Jerome (c. 340–420) placed their stamp of approval on the book, and the Council of Carthage (397) recognized its canonicity. Ultimately, churches everywhere were reading it as authoritative Scripture.

6. Relation to Other Writings

Many attempts have been made to trace a connection between the Epistle of James and numerous biblical and extrabiblical writings (e.g., Prov, the synoptic Gospels,

Rom, 1 Cor, Gal, 1 Peter, Ecclus, Philo). In a number of cases it is uncertain who influenced whom. In other instances, the similarities prove no literary reliance of any kind.

There are, however, two areas where the literary relationships seem relatively well defined and significant. The similarity between the Epistle of James and the teachings of Jesus in the Sermon on the Mount has often been noted. A clear example of this connection is seen in James 5:12: "Above all, my brothers, do not swear—not by heaven or by earth or by anything else. Let your 'Yes' be yes, and your 'No,' no, or you will be condemned." This teaching was obviously derived from the words of Jesus recorded in Matthew 5:34–37. Jesus said, "But I tell you, Do not swear at all: either by heaven, for it is God's throne; or by the earth, for it is his footstool; or by Jerusalem, for it is the city of the Great King. . . . Simply let your 'Yes' be 'Yes,' and your 'No,' 'No'; anything beyond this comes from the evil one." Other related statements include James 2:5 (Luke 6:20), James 3:10–12 (Matt 7:16–20), and James 3:18 (Matt 5:9). From such parallels we may conclude that James reflects the thoughts and often the very words of Christ.

Another possible literary relationship is that between James and the wisdom writings. Some, in fact, have described James as NT wisdom literature. Ropes, on the other hand, writes, "In the Wisdom-literature, as a literary type, it is impossible to place James" (p. 17).

It is true that James was not written in the same style as Proverbs, where one finds long series of proverbial statements structured in the parallel form characteristic of Hebrew poetry. Nevertheless, the two have noteworthy affinities. For example, the pithy, proverbial style of James should be noted (1:8, 22; 4:17), as well as the juxtaposition of good and evil (3:13–18). Also James's use of the word "wisdom" is significant (1:5; 3:13–17). In James 1:5 wisdom is the understanding that enables a person to face trials, and in 3:13–17 it is an attitude that determines how one lives. The Book of Proverbs abounds with references to wisdom, always viewing it as the kind of understanding that produces a sensible and an upright life. And in Proverbs as in James wisdom has its source in God.

Another evidence of affinity between James and Proverbs appears in the area of quotation and allusion. James 4:6 is a direct citation of Proverbs 3:34. In addition, there are numerous concepts or expressions in James that may be traced back to Proverbs (cf. James 1:5 with Prov 2:6; 1:19 with Prov 29:20; 3:18 with Prov 11:30; 4:13–16 with Prov 27:1; and 5:20 with Prov 10:12). Parallels to other wisdom literature could also be cited.

7. Theological Values

The Epistle of James is without doubt the least theological of all NT books, with the exception of Philemon. In fact, one of the reasons for the delay in canonical recognition of the epistle was its lack of theological content.

Having recognized this, however, one must hasten to insist that the book is not without theological value. The practical emphases of James rest on a solid theological foundation, which is often explicitly revealed and perhaps more often assumed or implied.

Three doctrines come to the surface more often than any others, and of these the most prominent is the doctrine of God. In keeping with the ethical nature of the epistle is the repeated stress on the doctrine of sin. And, surprisingly, the third most prominent theological theme is eschatology.

God is seen as being generous (1:5) and holy (1:13), the unchanging source of good (1:17). He is the one and only God (2:19), the Father of his people and the prototype in whose likeness men were created (3:9). Furthermore he is sovereign (4:15) and just (5:4), filled with pity and tender mercy (5:11).

James views sin as universal (3:2), indwelling all persons (1:14–15) and resulting in death (1:15). It expresses itself in anger (1:20), moral filth (1:21), blasphemy (2:7), discrimination (2:9–11), bitterness and lust (4:1–3), intimate ties with the evil world (4:4), pride (4:6), and theft and oppression (5:4).

In the third area of theological emphasis, James sees the end time as the day of rewards (1:12), the day when God's kingdom will be introduced (2:5), the day of judgment (2:12; 3:1), and the day when the Lord will return (5:7–8).

Several other doctrines receive limited mention. Christ is described as Lord (1:1; 2:1), but the Holy Spirit is not referred to unless it be in 4:5. In the area of soteriology, James speaks of regeneration (1:18), salvation of the soul (1:21), and justification (2:21–25). He promises the believer forgiveness of sins (5:15). He discusses the relation of saving faith and resultant good deeds (2:14–26). And he makes incidental reference to church order when he speaks of elders (5:14).

8. Bibliography

Adamson, James. *The Epistle of James,* NIC. Grand Rapids: Eerdmans, 1976.

Barclay, William. *The Letters of James and Peter. The Daily Study Bible.* Philadelphia: Westminster, 1960.

Blackman, E.C. *The Epistle of James. Torch Bible Commentaries.* London: SCM, 1957.

Carr, A. *Epistle of St. James.* CGT. Cambridge: Cambridge University Press, 1895.

Easton, B.S. *The Epistle of James.* IB. Vol. 12. New York: Abingdon, 1957.

Hort, F.J.A. *The Epistle of James.* London: Macmillan, 1909.

Lenski, R.C.H. *The Interpretation of the Epistle to the Hebrews and of the Epistle of James.* Columbus, Ohio: Wartburg, 1946.

Mayor, J.B. *The Epistle of St. James.* 3rd. ed. Grand Rapids: Zondervan, 1954.

Metzger, Bruce M. *A Textual Commentary on the Greek New Testament,* A Companion Volume to the United Bible Societies' *Greek New Testament.* 3rd ed. New York: UBS, 1971.

Mitton, C. Leslie. *The Epistle of James.* Grand Rapids: Eerdmans, 1966.

Moffatt, James. *The General Epistles of James, Peter, and Judas.* MNT. Garden City, N.Y.: Doubleday, 1928.

Plummer, Alfred. *The General Epistles of St. James and St. Jude.* ExB. London: Hodder & Stoughton, 1897.

Ropes, James H. *A Critical and Exegetical Commentary on the Epistle of St. James.* ICC. New York: Charles Scribner's Sons, 1916.

Ross, Alexander. *The Epistles of James and John.* NIC. Grand Rapids: Eerdmans, 1954.

Tasker, R.V.G. *The General Epistle of James.* TNTC. Grand Rapids: Eerdmans, 1956.

9. Outline

Text and Exposition

I. Salutation

1:1

> [1]James, a servant of God and of the Lord Jesus Christ, To the twelve tribes scattered among the nations: Greetings.

1 In the discussion of the authorship of the epistle (cf. Introduction), James was identified as the brother of Jesus. More specifically, since Jesus was virgin born, James was his half brother. In the Book of Acts this same James appears as the leader of the Jerusalem church (Acts 15:13ff.; 21:18).

The author describes himself as "a servant [*doulos*] of God and of the Lord Jesus Christ." The *doulos* was neither a free man nor a hired servant; he was a slave, the rightful property of his master. The term "slave," however, did not necessarily carry the degrading connotation attached to the word today. James was a servant who was proud to belong—body and soul—to God and to Jesus Christ.

The letter is addressed to "the twelve tribes," a designation intended to identify the readers as Jews. They were not residents of Palestine but were "scattered among the nations" as part of the Jewish Dispersion (*diaspora*). James's designation of his readers as "believers in our glorious Lord Jesus Christ" (2:1) makes it clear that not all dispersed Jews are included. It is probable that the recipients were the members of the Jerusalem church who had been driven out of Jerusalem at the time of Stephen's martyrdom (Acts 8:1, 4; 11:19–20). If this identification is correct, James had formerly been their spiritual leader. As such, he wrote to them with rightful spiritual authority and with full knowledge of their needs.

II. Trials and Temptations (1:2–18)

1. *The Testing of Faith*

1:2–12

> [2]Consider it pure joy, my brothers, whenever you face trials of many kinds, [3]because you know that the testing of your faith develops perseverance. [4]Perseverance must finish its work so that you may be mature and complete, not lacking anything. [5]If any of you lacks wisdom, he should ask God, who gives generously to all without finding fault, and it will be given to him. [6]But when he asks, he must believe and not doubt, because he who doubts is like a wave of the sea, blown and tossed by the wind. [7]That man should not think he will receive anything from the Lord; [8]he is a double-minded man, unstable in all he does.
> [9]The brother in humble circumstances ought to take pride in his high position. [10]But the one who is rich should take pride in his low position, because he will pass away like a wild flower. [11]For the sun rises with scorching heat and withers the plant; its blossom falls and its beauty is destroyed. In the same way, the rich man will fade away even while he goes about his business.
> [12]Blessed is the man who perseveres under trial, because when he has stood the test, he will receive the crown of life that God has promised to those who love him.

2 In vv.2-4 James explains that trials are reason for rejoicing because of the wholesome effects they produce. The word "trials" (*peirasmois*) describes things that put a person to the test. They may be difficulties that come from without, such as persecution, or they may be inner moral tests, such as temptations to sin. James uses the word in the former sense in vv.2-4 and in the latter sense in vv.13-18. The outward trial, rather than being a reason for unhappiness, can be a ground for "pure joy." The expression is *pasan charan*, which speaks of full and complete joy. And it is not merely the coming of a single trial that is described; James speaks of the experience of "trials of many kinds." The verb *peripesēte*, translated "face," speaks of falling into the midst of people, objects, or circumstances, such as trials (as here) or robbers (as in Luke 10:30). The picture is that of being surrounded with "trials of many kinds." The primary meaning of *poikilois* is "many-colored," and thus, "variegated," "of many kinds." Being surrounded by all kinds of trials should be viewed as reason for genuine rejoicing.

3 The reason that trials are to be considered grounds for joy is that they are capable of developing "perseverance." They put the believer's faith to the test, and this experience produces the desired result. The question answered by the testing of faith is whether or not faith will persevere. If it is genuine faith, testing serves to develop its persistence. *Hypomonēn* is translated "patience" in KJV, but it is a much more active and forceful word. It speaks of tenacity and stick-to-it-iveness. Barclay explains that it is not the patience that passively endures; instead, it is the quality that enables a man to stand on his feet facing the storm (William Barclay, *New Testament Words* [London: SCM, 1964], pp. 144-45). It is in struggling against difficulty and opposition that spiritual stamina is developed.

4 "Perseverance" has a work to do, and this can be accomplished only by persistence in trials. If perseverance is to "finish its work," faith must not falter or give up. The goal in view is that believers "may be mature and complete" (*teleioi kai holoklēroi*). *Teleioi* can mean "perfect" (KJV), "complete," or "mature." There are three reasons, however, for understanding the word as referring here to maturity.
1. Scripture does not indicate that believers reach perfection in this life.
2. Since *holoklēroi* describes that which has all its parts, it is most natural when it occurs with *teleioi* to reserve the meaning of completeness for *holoklēroi*.
3. The statement that "perseverance must finish its work" indicates progress and development, the result of which may well be described as maturity. Thus, perseverance in facing trials develops maturity of character and a balance of all the graces and strengths needed for the Christian life.

5 Verses 5-8 contain God's offer of help for those who are facing trials. The repetition of the word "lack" shows that James is still discussing the subject of trials. In v.4 he assures his readers that when perseverance has finished its work, the believer will lack none of the needed virtues and strengths. In v.5, however, James speaks of the period of testing before perseverance has completed its work. During such testing, if anyone "lacks wisdom," he may have it by asking. The type of Greek conditional sentence found here assumes that people facing trials do lack wisdom. What they need is not the speculative or theoretical wisdom of a philosophical system. It is the kind of wisdom that plays such a large part in the Book of Proverbs (1:2-4; 2:10-15; 4:5-9). It is the God-given understanding that enables a person to avoid the paths of wickedness and to live a life of righteousness. In this context wisdom is understanding the nature and purpose of trials and knowing how to meet them victoriously. Such wisdom is available to the one who will "ask God" for it, not once only, but repeatedly (Gr., present tense). The promise is that "it will be given to him." There is nothing in God that keeps him from giving. It is his practice to give "generously" and "without finding fault." He does not scold his children for asking nor berate them for their deficiency.

6 Although there is nothing in God that prevents him from giving wisdom to his people, a barrier may exist in them. When they ask, they "must believe and not doubt." Their faith must be more than mere acceptance of a creed. To believe is to be confident that God will give what is requested; it is to expect him to do so. The extent of faith that God looks for is emphasized by the words "not doubt" (*mēden diakrinomenos*). The true force of this expression is "and not doubt at all" (BAG, p. 520). *Diakrinomenos* describes one who is divided in his mind and who wavers between two opinions. One moment he voices the yes of faith; the next moment it is the no of disbelief. Such an attitude is graphically illustrated by "a wave of the sea." Completely lacking in stability, it is "blown and tossed by the wind." First there is the crest, then the trough. Instead, prayer that moves God to respond must be marked by the constancy of unwavering faith.

The reference to the sea is the first of James's illustrations from nature. See also 1:10–11, 17–18, 26; 3:3–5, 7, 11–12; 5:7, 17–18. As Jesus drew numerous illustrations from life around him, so James revealed his love for nature by his repeated use of it for illustrative purposes.

7–8 "That man" is a somewhat derogatory reference to the doubter, whom James has just compared to the tossing wave. Here he is further characterized as "double-minded" and "unstable." The Greek *dipsychos* in strictest literalness means "double-souled." It is as though one soul declares, "I believe," and the other in turn shouts, "I don't!" This sort of instability is not only apparent when the man prays, it marks "all he does." In his personal life, his business life, his social life, as well as in his spiritual life, indecisiveness negates his effectiveness. A person like this will not "receive anything from the Lord." But one may wonder how this man is different from the anguished father who cried, "I do believe; help me overcome my unbelief!" (Mark 9:24). Such an exclamation seems to suggest that the father was "a double-minded man." But there is a difference. The father was not oscillating between belief and unbelief. He desired to believe—and even asserted his belief—but because he felt keenly the inadequacy of his faith, he asked for help in believing. He was not facing in both directions at the same time like the "double-minded man" of James 1:8. In spite of his conscious weakness, the father had set his heart to believe. And Christ responded to his faith and healed his son (Mark 9:25–27). In response to this kind of faith, God will give wisdom to those who ask for it, and will enable them to persevere in times of trial.

9 Verses 9–11 are thought by some to introduce an entirely new subject (EGT, 4:424). However, since v.12 explicitly deals with persevering "under trial," it is best to understand vv.9–11 to be related to the same general subject. James seems to be indicating that trials erase any superficial distinctions that may be thought to separate the rich brother from the poor one.

"Brother" shows that James is referring to a believer. To describe the "circumstances" of this brother, the author uses the word *tapeinos*, which has the basic meaning of "lowly," "mean," "insignificant," "weak," "poor" (TDNT, 8:1). In view of the constrast with the rich (*plousios*) man in v.10, it is best to understand that the man in v.9 is one who is financially poor, and thus "in humble circumstances." The "high position" in which this brother is to take pride has reference first of all to his position in Christ. In saving him, God lifts him up and gives him new dignity and worth. In this context, however, it seems most likely that James also has in mind the privilege of "suffering disgrace for the Name [Jesus]" (Acts 5:41). To endure persecution for Christ's sake lifts the believer to a position of honor that more than offsets his poverty.

10 The text does not explicitly state that "the one who is rich" is a believer, and for that reason some have insisted that he is unsaved. It would seem most natural, however, for James to omit the word "brother" in v.10 and assume that it would be carried over from v.9. The wealthy believer, then, is exhorted to glory "in his low position." Since the context deals with trials, the low position may be a description of the humbling experience of suffering persecution for Christ's sake. The very same treatment that exalts the poor man and gives him a new sense of worth also humbles the rich man. Suffering shows him that, instead of having a lasting lease on life, his life on this earth is no more permanent than "a wild flower" (cf. Isa 40:6–8.) Some interpreters understand James to say that it is the rich man's wealth that passes away, not the man himself (Ropes, p. 148). But it should be noted that the subject of the verb "pass away," is not riches but "the *one* who is rich." Again, in v.11b it is the rich man who will "fade away." Suffering and persecution reveal how tentative and short life really is.

11 The phenomenon James speaks of was a familiar one. Green grass and plants do not last long under the "scorching heat" of the Palestinian summer sun. More specifically, the reference may be to the sudden coming of a hot, searing wind known as the sirocco, which quickly withers and burns the vegetation. The withering of the plant and falling of its blossom are taken almost verbatim from Isaiah 40:7 (LXX). It may be that the "beauty" of the blossom is suggestive of the fine clothes that the rich wear. As impressive and attractive as the garments may be, they soon fade and wear out. And, what is even more important, "the rich man" himself "will fade away." Here again Ropes refers the wasting away to the loss of wealth (p. 149), but it should be noted that it is the man who fades away. Nothing is said about his wealth. This fading takes place "even while he goes about his business." Unexpectedly, in the midst of a busy life, the end comes. These are sobering thoughts that tend to reduce the rich to the level of men in general, just as the privilege of suffering for Christ lifts the poor man to a new plane of dignity and worth.

12 James concludes his discussion of the testing of faith with a promise of the reward to be given to the one who successfully stands the test. This verse is seen to be related to the preceding verses, rather than those that follow, by the repetition of terminology ("trials," v.2; "testing," "perseverance," v.3) and also from the fact that testings are to be endured ("perseveres"), whereas temptations are to be resisted (Ropes, p. 150). The expression "Blessed is the man" reveals the author's familiarity with the language of the OT (cf. Pss 1:1; 32:2; 34:8; 84:12; Prov 8:34; Isa 56:2; Jer 17:7) and the beatitudes (Matt 5:3–11). It is not sufficient to translate the word *makarios* as "happy." Even in secular Greek the word described "the transcendent happiness of a life beyond care, labour and death" (TDNT, 4:362). In biblical usage it speaks of "the distinctive religious joy" which is one of the benefits of salvation (ibid., p. 367). James uses the term to describe the enviable state of the man who does not give up when confronted with trying circumstances but remains strong in faith and devotion to God. The word *dokimos*, which indicates that the man "has stood the test," was used to describe the successful testing of precious metals and coins. It referred to the process of testing and also to the consequent approval of the tested object as genuine. Perseverance under trial results in approval, and approval results in "the crown [*stephanon*] of life." Although this term may designate a kingly crown, it more often refers to the crown given to a victorious athlete—a wreath of laurel, oak, or even celery. For James, the word refers to the reward to be given the believer who is victorious in his struggle against trials. It is evident that this "life that God has promised" is more than the eternal life given to every believer at the time of his salvation (John 5:24). Since it is a reward for an accomplishment subsequent to initial faith, it must refer to a still higher quality of life.

Notes:

3 The classical Gr. meaning of δοκίμιον (*dokimion*) is "a means of testing," but the papyri reveal that the word came to refer to that which is tested and approved. Adolf Deissmann has shown that the word is in reality the neuter of the adjective δοκίμιος (*dokimios*, "proved," "tried") and is here used substantively (*Bible Studies* [Edinburgh: T. & T. Clark, 1909], pp. 259ff.). Thus it is not the mere fact of testing that "develops perseverance;" it is faith that has been put to the test and approved.

10 KJV reads "flower of the grass," which is the literal rendering of ἄνθος χόρτου (*anthos chortou*). But James apparently borrowed this expression from the LXX of Isa 40:6, where it translates the Heb. ציץ השדה (*ṣîṣ haśśāḏeh*), "flower of the field," and thus "a wild flower."

2. *The Source of Temptation*

1:13–18

> [13]When tempted, no one should say, "God is tempting me." For God cannot be tempted by evil, nor does he tempt anyone; [14]but each one is tempted when, by his own evil desire, he is dragged away and enticed. [15]Then, after desire has conceived, it gives birth to sin; and sin, when it is full-grown, gives birth to death.
> [16]Don't be deceived, my dear brothers. [17]Every good and perfect gift is from above, coming down from the Father of the heavenly lights, who does not change like shifting shadows. [18]He chose to give us birth through the word of truth, that we might be a kind of firstfruits of all he created.

In these verses James declares that no one should assume that enticement to sin comes from God (v.13a); he then proceeds to give a series of reasons for his assertion (vv.13b–18).

13 The Greek noun *peirasmos* can refer either to an outward circumstance of trial or to a temptation to sin. The same is true of the verb form as well. Whereas the noun is used in vv.2–3 of "trials" and "testing," in vv.13–15, where the verb occurs, the obvious reference is to temptation. That this is the meaning is indicated by the words "evil" (v.13), "evil desire" (v.14), and "sin" (v.15).

The first reason why temptation does not come from God is that God "cannot be tempted by evil." That is, he cannot be successfully tempted. His omnipotent, holy will fully resists any invitation to sin. Furthermore, in him there is not the slightest moral depravity to which temptation may appeal. Therefore, it is inconsistent to think that God could be the author of temptation.

14 Instead, the source of temptation lies within man himself. He is tempted "by his own evil desire." James personifies man's sinful desire and identifies it as the efficient cause of temptation (RHG, p. 635). He does not blame any external person or object. It is by man's own sinful nature that "he is dragged away and enticed." These two verbs are taken from the sphere of fishing and hunting. Although "dragged away" is a possible translation of *exelkomenos* (BAG, p. 273), when it is coupled with *deleazomenos* ("enticed"), it may better be rendered by "drawn out." Mayor lists a number of examples where the word describes the "drawing of the fish out of its original retreat" (p. 51). James pictures man's "evil desire," first, as attracting his attention and persuading him to approach the forbidden thing and, second, as luring him by means of bait to yield to the temptation. Robertson entitles this verse "*Snared by One's Own Bait*" (A.T. Robertson, *Practical and Social Aspects of Christianity* [New York: Hodder & Stoughton, 1915], p. 76).

15 James changes his figure from a snare to conception and birth. The genealogy of evil desire is traced for three generations, as it were. A chronological order is suggested by the words "then" and "after." First, temptation comes (v.14); then desire, like a human mother, conceives and "gives birth to sin." In this graphic manner the author portrays the experience of yielding to temptation. Then sin, the child of evil desire, develops till it "is full-grown" and ready to produce offspring. When it conceives, it "gives birth to death." James is not suggesting that only when sin has reached its full development does it result in death. The penalty of sin of any kind or extent is spiritual death. The details of the illustration must not be pressed too far. The author's intention is simply to trace the results of temptation when one yields to it. The order is evil desire, sin, death.

16 "Don't be deceived" is an expression employed as a pointed introduction for a significant statement (cf. 1 Cor 6:9; 15:33; Gal 6:7; and a similar construction in 1 John 3:7). The warning in this passage is against being deceived into thinking that God is the author of temptation. In fact, the Greek construction used here (*mē* with the present tense imperative) often implies that the addressees have been engaging in the practice being prohibited. In that case James would be saying, "Stop being deceived."

17 Here follows the significant statement that the prohibition of the previous verse was intended to introduce. Instead of sending temptation, God is the giver of "every good and perfect gift." The concept of goodness rules out the possibility that God would send an influence as destructive as temptation. God's gifts are marked by kindness and helpfulness, not destructiveness. They are "perfect," which in this context excludes any possibility of moral evil, such as tempting his people to commit sin. The point of James's statement is that nothing but good comes from God. The second half of the verse shows that this is invariably true.

Here God is designated as "the Father of the heavenly lights." NIV has inserted the word "heavenly," even though it is not found in the Greek text. The context seems to indicate that the lights referred to are the stars and planets. "Father" probably has a twofold significance, pointing on the one hand to the creation of the lights and on the other to God's continuing sovereignty over them.

Unlike the "shifting shadows" that are caused by the sun, moon, and stars, God "does not change." With him there is no variation at all (ouk eni parallagē). The shadows cast by the sun are minimal at noon, but just before sunset they stretch out for yards across the landscape. God is not like that. He does not change. He is always the giver of good gifts, never a sadistic being who would entice his creatures to destroy themselves in sin.

18 James advances his final reason for denying that God is the author of temptation. Rather than acting destructively, God acts constructively. "He chose to give us birth." Inasmuch as this birth is "through the word of truth," that is, through the gospel, the birth referred to here must be spiritual rather than natural. God accomplishes this action by his own deliberate choice (boulētheis). His purpose in regeneration is "that we might be a kind of firstfruits." The figure the author has in mind is drawn from such OT passages as Exodus 34:22 and Leviticus 23:10. The term "firstfruits" referred to the first portion of the harvest given to God, a foretaste of that which was to come. So it was that the early Christians were a preliminary indication of the great host of people (tōn autou ktismatōn, "his creatures") who through subsequent centuries would be born again.

Notes

17 UBS has adopted the reading παραλλαγὴ ἢ τροπῆς ἀποσκίασμα (parallagē ē tropēs aposkiasma) following ℵ^c A C, numerous miniscules, and several versions. A straightforward translation would be "variation or shadow of [from] turning," referring to a shadow caused by the turning of an object such as a heavenly body. If this was the original text of James, he might well have been speaking of an eclipse.

However, a second reading has significant textual support. Three sources have παραλλαγὴ ἢ τροπῆς ἀποσκιάσματος (parallagē ē tropēs aposkiasmatos): ℵ* B P²³, all representatives of the Alexandrian text. Inasmuch as ancient Gr. MSS had few accents or breathing marks, η (ē) may originally have been the article ἡ (hē). In that case the translation would be "variation which is [consists in] the turning of a shadow." This reading is adopted by Ropes (pp. 162–64), Tasker (pp. 48–49), Edgar J. Goodspeed (Problems of New Testament Translation [Chicago: University of Chicago, 1945], pp. 189–90), RSV mg., NEB, and NIV.

Whereas the first-listed reading is more specifically astronomical, the second reading is more general. It may refer to any changing shadow. Although most translations are based on the former reading, the more general reading has much in its favor and is the one represented in the commentary above.

III. The Practice of the Word

1:19–27

> ¹⁹My dear brothers, take note of this: Everyone should be quick to listen, slow to speak and slow to become angry, ²⁰for man's anger does not bring about the righteous life that God desires. ²¹Therefore, get rid of all moral filth and the evil that is so prevalent, and humbly accept the word planted in you, which can save you.
> ²²Do not merely listen to the word, and so deceive yourselves. Do what it says. ²³Anyone who listens to the word but does not do what it says is like a man who looks at his face in a mirror ²⁴and, after looking at himself, goes away and immediately forgets what he looks like. ²⁵But the man who looks intently into the perfect law that gives freedom, and continues to do this, not forgetting what he has heard, but doing it—he will be blessed in what he does.
> ²⁶If anyone considers himself religious and yet does not keep a tight rein on his tongue, he deceives himself and his religion is worthless. ²⁷Religion that God our Father accepts as pure and faultless is this: to look after orphans and widows in their distress and to keep oneself from being polluted by the world.

Verses 19–21 may seem at first glance to be an isolated section of miscellaneous exhortations. Further examination, however, reveals significant links to the preceding and following contexts. The term "word" is found in vv. 18, 21–25 and refers to the Scriptures, the Word of God. Verse 18 indicates that regeneration comes through the instrumentality of the Word; v. 21 contains a call to receive the Word; and vv. 22–25 discuss the doing of the Word. It would seem, then, that vv. 19–21 emphasize listening to and receiving the Word, while vv. 22–25 stress the doing of the Word.

19 In vv. 19–21a, James is attempting to clear the way for the reception of God's truth (v. 21b). He begins by calling for the readers' attention: "Take note of this." (KJV's "Wherefore" is based on an inferior Gr. text.) The reception of the Word demands a readiness "to listen." Reluctance at this point will block the acceptance of truth. It also demands restrained speech. A continual talker cannot hear what anyone else says and by the same token will not hear when God speaks to him. Finally, the restraint of anger is demanded. Anger will close the mind to God's truth. Ross explains, "Ceaseless talkers may easily degenerate into fierce controversialists" (p. 38). And a fiercely argumentative attitude is not conducive to the humble reception of truth.

20 The connective "for" indicates that this verse gives the reasoning that lies behind the last exhortation. Anger does not produce "the righteous life that God desires." An angry attitude is not the atmosphere in which righteousness flourishes. James stresses this from the positive side when he says, "Peacemakers who sow in peace raise a harvest of righteousness" (3:18).

21 In further preparation for the reception of the Word, one must "get rid of all moral filth." The Greek word translated "get rid of" (*apothemenoi*) was primarily used of taking off garments. Hebrews 12:1 speaks of throwing off any excessive weight, such as unnecessary clothing, to make ready for the race of faith. The "moral filth" and the evil that is so abundant are to be stripped off like dirty clothes in preparation for "accept[ing] the word." The reception of truth must of necessity be marked by humility or meekness (Gr., *praytēti*). This is not to be construed as spineless weakness. Instead, it is the quality of a strong man that makes him docile and submissive rather than haughty and rebellious. Only in such a spirit can one fully receive God's truth. That the Word is described as "planted in you" suggests the readers were believers who already possessed the truth. The phrase "which can save you" simply describes the truth as saving truth. James is not calling for an initial acceptance of that message, but for a full and intelligent appropriation of the truth as the Christian grows in spiritual understanding.

22 The author next discusses putting the Word into practice. It is not enough merely to "listen to the word" or, by the same token, merely to read it. Those who congratulate themselves on being hearers of the truth are deceiving themselves. If they assume that this is all that is needed, they are sadly mistaken. If they think that merely listening to the message earns them a position of special favor with God, they are duped by their own faulty reasoning. In reality, the responsibility of those who hear is far greater than that of those who have never heard. If they do not combine doing with hearing, they put themselves in a most vulnerable position.

The call to "do what it says" lies at the center of all that James teaches. It sums up the message of the whole book: Put into practice what you profess to believe. Indeed, 1:22 may well be the key verse of James's epistle.

23 After urging the practice of the Word in v. 22, the author proceeds to explain why people should do more than merely listen to the truth. Here he uses the illustration (vv. 23–24) of a man who "looks at his face in a mirror." The Greek verb *katanoeō* does not describe a hasty glance as some have suggested. Instead, it refers to careful observation. It is "attentive scrutiny of an object" (TDNT, 4:975). So the man carefully studies his face and becomes thoroughly familiar with its features. This illustrative act is paralleled by the person who listens to the Word, apparently not momentarily but attentively, and at length, so that he understands what he hears. He knows what God expects him to do. Any failure to respond cannot be blamed on lack of understanding.

24 James further explains that upon going away the man "immediately forgets what he looks like." For him it is "out of sight, out of mind." In spite of thoroughly scrutinizing his face, he forgets what it was like. This is, of course, ludicrous, but no less ludicrous is the believer who listens carefully to God's truth and does not remember to put into practice what he has heard. Listening to truth is not an end in itself any more than gazing at one's face in a mirror is an end in itself. The purpose of listening to truth is to act upon it. Theoretical knowledge of spiritual truth is never commended in Scripture. In fact, it is discouraged and condemned. In the Judeo-Christian context, knowledge is inseparably tied to experience. The believer gains knowledge through experience, and his knowledge is intended to affect subsequent experience.

25 In contrast to the person who listens to the Word but does not do what it says, this verse describes one who both listens and puts what he hears into practice. "He will be blessed in what he does." The reason is fourfold. First, he "looks intently" into God's truth. This Greek verb (*parakyptō*) "denotes penetrating absorption" (TDNT, 5:815). It is the word used to describe John's act of stooping and peering into the tomb of Jesus (John 20:5). Here in James 1:25 it is as though a person stoops over the Scripture, zealously searching for its message. The second reason why this man is blessed is that "he continues to do this." He is the blessed man of Psalm 1 who meditates in God's law day and night. The third reason for his blessedness is that he does not forget "what he has heard." And the fourth and most important reason is that he puts the truth into practice.

James's use of the term "law" deserves special attention. He calls it "the perfect law of freedom" (Gr.). The use of the word "law" reveals his Jewish orientation and that of his readers. But James qualifies the word to make sure his readers do not misunderstand. He describes this law as "perfect" and as characterized by "freedom." It is not merely the OT law, nor is it the Mosaic law perverted to become a legalistic system for earning salvation by good works. When James calls it the "perfect law," he has in mind the sum total of God's revealed truth—not merely the preliminary portion found in the OT, but also the final revelation made through Christ and his apostles that was soon to be inscripturated in the NT. Thus it is complete, in contrast to that which is preliminary and preparatory. Furthermore, it is the "law of liberty" (Gr.), by which James means that it does not enslave. It is not enforced by external compulsion. Instead, it is freely accepted and fulfilled with glad devotion under the enablement of the Spirit of God (Gal 5:22–23). For similar uses of the term "law" in James, see 2:8, 12.

26 Verses 26–27 point out three specific areas where truth should be put into practice. The first is speech. James introduces a hypothetical case. The person involved "considers himself religious." The word *thrēskos* ("religious") occurs only here in the NT; and the corresponding noun *thrēskeia* ("religion") appears but four times in the NT, two of which are in James 1:26–27. The adjective *thrēskos* describes a person who performs the external acts of religion, such as public worship, fasting, or giving to the needy. The person James is referring to is the one who "does not keep tight rein on his tongue." Lenski says that he lets "his tongue go like an unbridled horse" (in loc.). He exerts no controlling restraint on his speech. Exactly how his speech offends is not indicated, whether it be by the cutting criticism of others, by unclean- ness, by dishonesty, or by other ways. His uncontrolled tongue reveals that "his religion is worthless," being merely external sham. Such a person has been playing the part of one who is religious and has convinced himself that he really is religious, but in so doing "he deceives himself." This is the second instance of self-deception in this chapter. In v.22 the person who hears the truth but does not put it into practice is self-deceived. In v.26 the self-deceived person is the one whose religious acts do not make a difference in the way he lives.

27 The kind of "religion that God our Father accepts" is the kind that exerts a positive influence on one's life. Notice that this verse does not give us a definition of religion. Instead, it presents a concrete way of insisting that genuine religion is a life-changing force. One's religion, then, should be more than external; it must spring from an inner spiritual reality that expresses itself in love to others and holiness before God. James next describes a specific example of love—the care of "orphans and widows." The verb *episkeptesthai* also appears in Matthew 25:36, 43 with reference to visiting the sick, not merely to make a social call, but in order to care for their needs. This is "faith expressing itself through love" (Gal 5:6). One whose religion is genuine will also avoid "being polluted by the world." "World" describes the total system of evil that per- vades every sphere of human existence and is set in opposition to God and to righteousness.

To summarize, vv.22–27 insist that a person's religion must consist of more than superficial acts. It is not enough to listen to the statement of spiritual truth (vv. 22–25), nor is it sufficient to engage in formal religious activity (v.26). The person whose religious experience is genuine will put spiritual truth into practice, and his life will be marked by love for others and holiness before God.

IV. The Condemnation of Partiality

2:1–13

[1]My brothers, as believers in our glorious Lord Jesus Christ, don't show favoritism. [2]Suppose a man comes into your meeting wearing a gold ring and fine clothes, and a poor man in shabby clothes also comes in. [3]If you show special attention to the man wearing fine clothes and say, "Here's a good seat for you," but say to the poor man, "You stand there" or "Sit on the floor by my feet," [4]have you not discriminated among yourselves and become judges with evil thoughts?

[5]Listen, my dear brothers: Has not God chosen those who are poor in the eyes of the world to be rich in faith and to inherit the kingdom he promised those who love him? [6]But you have insulted the poor. Is it not the rich who are exploiting you? Are they not the ones who are dragging you into court? [7]Are they not the ones who are slandering the noble name of him to whom you belong?

[8]If you really keep the royal law found in Scripture, "Love your neighbor as yourself," you are doing right. [9]But if you show favoritism, you sin and are convicted by the law as lawbreakers. [10]For whoever keeps the whole law and yet stumbles at just one point is guilty of breaking all of it. [11]For he who said, "Do not commit adultery," also said, "Do not murder." If you do not commit adultery but do commit murder, you have become a lawbreaker.

[12]Speak and act as those who are going to be judged by the law that gives freedom, [13]because judgment without mercy will be shown to anyone who has not been merciful. Mercy triumphs over judgment!

In 1:19–27 James has shown the importance of putting spiritual truth into practice. It is not too much to say that these verses comprise the bedrock on which the whole epistle rests. In each of the following sections James discusses at some length the application of the Word of truth to a specific aspect of life. In 2:1–13 he shows how partiality or discrimination violates the standard of God's truth.

1 James begins his discussion of partiality by a prohibition: "Don't show favoritism." The Greek construction here (*mē* with the present tense imperative) is used of forbidding a practice already in progress. That the recipients of this epistle were guilty of practicing discrimination is apparent from the context (v.6, "But you have insulted the poor"). Thus the prohibition means "Stop showing favoritism." The point James is making is that partiality is inconsistent with faith "in our glorious Lord Jesus Christ." To say that practicing favoritism contradicts one's profession of faith is another way of saying that one's action does not measure up to the truth he professes to believe. The stress on Christ as "glorious" heightens the gross inconsistency of allowing favoritism and discrimination to be associated with faith in such an exalted person as Christ.

2 A hypothetical illustration follows: "Suppose a man comes into your meeting." The word translated "meeting" is the Greek *synagōgē*, which had primary reference to the Jewish synagogue. The term need not be taken literally, however, as an indication that the Jewish Christians were still meeting in synagogue buildings. Even after leaving the synagogue, Jewish Christians no doubt continued to refer to their church meeting as a *synagōgē*.

James pictures two men entering this early assembly. The first one is "wearing a gold ring and fine clothes." The Greek word *lampra* ("fine") was a term used to describe the clothing of a rich person or a dignitary. In the Roman world it was the proper description for the toga of a candidate for public office. In sharp contrast are the "shabby clothes" of the "poor man." The word *rhypara* ("shabby") normally means "dirty" or "filthy." It is the adjective form of the noun in 1:21 that NIV translates as "moral filth." Inasmuch as this "poor man" is in reality a beggar (*ptōchos*), it seems most natural that his clothes should be described as filthy.

3 The rich man is shown "special attention." The Greek *epiblepsēte* means "to look with favor on" someone. This was the plea of the father of the demon-possessed boy: "I beg you to look at my son" (Luke 9:38). The verb refers not only to the favorable look but also to the consequent assistance. The rich man of James 2 is the object of solicitous attention as he is shown to "a good seat." It is possible, however, that the word *kalōs* does not refer to the proffered seat but should be translated "please" ("Sit here, please"). In contrast, "the poor man" is abruptly told to "stand there," perhaps in the back of the assembly or in some other out-of-the-way place. His other alternative is to "sit on the floor." The Greek text actually says, "Sit under my footstool," which probably means "by my footstool." The contrast between the speaker who has a stool for his feet and the beggar who must sit on the floor heightens the discrimination.

4 The expressed condemnation of this practice is put in question form. However, the Greek construction leaves no doubt as to James's opinion. The negative particle *ou* ("not") shows that he expects his readers to agree with his conclusion: "Have you not discriminated?" The practice illustrated in vv.2–3 rests on an unjustified distinction. The basis for showing favor is terribly wrong. Those acting in this way "become judges with evil thoughts." Here the play on words in the Greek is not apparent in the English translation. The word translated "discriminated" (*diekrithēte*) is built on the same root as the word for "judges" (*kritai*). In so judging between men, the readers had become unjust judges.

5 Verses 5–11 advance two arguments against the practice of favoritism. The first may be called the social argument (vv.5–7). The importance the author attaches to these arguments is seen in the imperative "Listen, my dear brothers." The early church was not drawn from the wealthy or ruling classes. It was largely made up of poorer people, those who are "poor in the eyes of the world." This is apparent in the gospels (e.g., Matt 11:5); Paul implies it (1 Cor 1:26–29); and James declares it (2:5). By saying that the believers' poverty is poverty "in the eyes of the world," James is suggesting that they are not really poor. They are "rich in faith" and heirs of the kingdom. The aspect of the kingdom James has in mind is yet future. It is the eternal kingdom that Christ equated with eternal life (Matt 25:34, 46). So James has shown us that the social snobbery of the world is short-sighted and superficial. And the favoritism James's readers practiced was based on this same shallow kind of evaluation.

James's concept of the blessed poor may be misunderstood. He does not say that all poor people are "rich in faith," nor does he exclude the rich from the ranks of the saved. Furthermore, God's choice of the poor must not be taken as based on any merit inherent in poverty. One reason God "has chosen those who are poor" may be seen in the account of the rich young ruler (Mark 10:17–27). There Jesus indicated that those who have riches find it exceedingly difficult to enter God's kingdom (vv.23–25), apparently because their wealth stands in the way. God blesses those who willingly recognize their spiritual bankruptcy (Matt 5:3). A second reason why God chooses the poor is explicitly stated in 1 Cor 1:26–29. God selects those who have nothing or are nothing in themselves "so that no one may boast before him" (v.29).

6 In sharp contrast to God's choice of the poor (v.5) is the way James's readers had treated them. God had chosen them, but they had "insulted" them! The incongruity of such treatment is dramatized by three pointed questions. Question number one: The rich are the ones "who are exploiting you," are they not? The word *katadynasteuō* ("exploit") is a strong term describing the brutal and tyrranical deprivation of one's rights. It occurs in a number of pasages in the LXX that speak of oppression of the poor, the widow, and the stranger (Ezek 22:29; Zech 7:10).

Question number two: Is it not the rich "who are dragging you into court?" Although *helkō* ("drag") may sometimes mean nothing more than "to draw or attract" (John 6:44; 12:32), in other situations it describes the act of forcibly dragging a person (Acts 16:19; 21:30), as seems to be the case here. The presence of the third personal pronoun *autoi* ("they") suggests that the rich men themselves ("with their own hands"—Mayor) dragged the poor into the courts.

7 Question number three: The rich "are slandering the noble name" of Christ, aren't they? Where God or his name are being spoken against, it is better to translate the Greek *blasphēmeō* by the English word "blaspheme," which has come to refer to speaking irreverently and disrespectfully of Deity. Christ's name is described as *kalon,* that is, "noble," "excellent," "honorable," rather than as *agathon,* which refers to that which is kind or morally good. NIV explains that this "noble name" is the name of "him to whom you belong." The word-for-word translation of James's Greek would read "the noble name that was called upon you." This expression clearly reveals its OT background (Deut 28:10; 2 Chron 7:14; Amos 9:12). A man was dedicated to God by calling God's name over him. The act indicated that he belonged to God. So Christians bear the worthy name of Christ as indication that they are his people. To show favoritism to those who blaspheme that wonderful name is the greatest incongruity of all.

8 James now proceeds to his moral argument in refutation of the practice of showing favoritism (vv.8–11). Here it is not a question of mere incongruity but of the rightness or wrongness of showing partiality. The commandment to love one's neighbor as oneself (Lev 19:18) is not described as "the royal law" simply because of its lofty character. Numerous commentators (Ropes, Mayor, Tasker, Ross, Lenski) agree that it is called "royal" because it is the supreme law to which all other laws governing human relationships are subordinate. It is the summation of all such laws (Matt 22:36–40). The one who keeps this supreme law is "doing right." NIV has translated *kalōs* ("well") as "right," since it seems to be contrasted with committing sin in v.9. The right course of action is to show favor to everyone, whether he is rich or poor. Love overlooks such superficial distinctions as wealth and quality of clothing. It shows kindness to a person in spite of any distasteful qualities he may have.

9 Whereas v.8 depicts the positive example of one who fully keeps the law, v.9 sets forth the negative example of one who breaks it. To "show favoritism" is not merely to be guilty of an insignificant fault or social impropriety; it is sin. Such a conclusion is based on solid legal ground rather than general human opinion. Those engaging in partiality "are convicted by the law as lawbreakers." Some understand this as a reference to the law in general; others assert that the law referred to is stated in Leviticus 19:15 or Deuteronomy 16:19. James, however, has already cited the law he is referring to. It is the "royal law" quoted in v.8. Anyone who shows favoritism breaks the supreme law of love for his neighbor, the law that comprehends all laws governing one's relationships to one's fellowmen.

10 By beginning this verse with the word "for" (*gar*), James indicates that he is going to explain how an act of favoritism makes a person a lawbreaker (v.9). It is obvious that he has set up a special case when he speaks of someone who "keeps the whole law" except for "one point," for in 3:2 he insists that "we all stumble in many ways." However, for the sake of his argument he imagines a person who "stumbles at just one point." Although *ptaisē*, ("stumbles") may describe an insignificant offense or error, it was also used as a synonym for the verb "to sin," but with no indication of the degree of seriousness. So James's reasoning is that to commit one act of sin, which breaks one commandment of the law, makes a person "guilty of breaking" the whole law.

11 Like v.10, this verse also opens with the explanatory "for," showing that the author is continuing his explanation. He does so with a simple illustration based on the unity of law. Although God's law has many facets, it is essentially one, being the expression of the character and will of God himself. To violate the law at any one point is not to violate one commandment only; it is to violate the will of God and to contradict the character of God. The same God who said, "Do not commit adultery," also said, "Do not murder." It is also the same God who gave the royal law of love for one's neighbor. The person who breaks just one of these laws has "become a lawbreaker." Although but one commandment is broken, the entire law of God has been flouted. When viewed like this, an act of favoritism is far from insignificant.

12 The section (2:1–13) is concluded with an urgent exhortation and warning (vv.12–13). The commands "Speak and act" are stronger in the Greek text than in the English. James says, "So speak and so act." His repetition of "so" (*houtōs*) is emphatic and also serves to distribute the emphasis equally between the two verbs. The present tense in both verbs calls for continuing action. James would have his readers continue to speak and act in light of the fact that they "are going to be judged." Since he is speaking to believers, the judgment to which he refers must be the judgment of believers at the judgment seat of Christ (2 Cor 5:10). The standard of judgment will be "the law that gives freedom," rather than the enslaving legalistic system developed by the scribes and Pharisees. It is the royal law of love (v.8), which the believer is enabled to keep by the Holy Spirit (Gal 5:22–23).

13 The reason for responding to the exhortation of v.12 is that "judgment without mercy" will be the lot of the unmerciful. No doubt mercy is singled out because James has the poor man of v.2 in mind. Instead of the mercy the man needed, he received cruel discrimination, and that at the hands of professing Christians. The basic principle that underlies v.12a was stated by Christ himself (Matt 18:33). The recipient of mercy should likewise be merciful. In fact, mercy should be the mark of the regenerated person. If it is present in the believer's life, he will have nothing to fear at the judgment. It is in this sense that "mercy triumphs over judgment." The believer will be able to smile triumphantly in the time of judgment. In the same vein John declares, "Love is made complete among us so that we will have confidence on the day of judgment, because in this world we are like him" (1 John 4:17). The presence of love (or mercy) shows that God has performed a work of grace in the believer's heart, making him like Christ. As a result, he can have confidence when he is judged.

Notes

4 A decided difference of opinion exists concerning the correct translation of διεκρίθητε (*diekrithēte*, NIV, "discriminated"). Most commentators point out that the common NT meaning of this verb in the passive voice is "to waver," "to doubt." It is to be divided within oneself as in James 1:6 (cf. Alford, Lenski, Mayor, Ropes, and Tasker). This view is also supported by TDNT (3:947–49) and is expressed in NEB and the translations of Goodspeed and Beck. The reasoning of James is usually explained as follows: The persons showing favoritism are wavering between worldly standards and true spiritual values. They take their place in the congregation as believers, but they judge men as the world views them.

On the other hand, a number of translations view the verb as meaning "to make a distinction." This is to treat the passive form as though it were active, a practice justified with certain verbs (RHG, p. 817). For example, NASB translates v.4a, "Have you not made distinctions among yourselves?" Similar renderings are found in ASV, RSV, Wms, Mof, *Centenary Translation*, Ph, TEV, and NIV. Several commentators agree (A.T. Robertson, *Practical and Social Aspects of Christianity* [New York: Hodder & Stoughton, 1915], p. 114; Ross). Although there is no parallel usage of this particular verb to support this interpretation, it is the most natural one in the light of the immediate context. The fault James was aiming at was discrimination against one person and favoritism toward another. To engage in such practices is clearly "to make distinctions." The view that the verb means "to waver" between worldly and spiritual standards is more contrived and thus less obvious to the average reader than the view just presented. The obvious sense of the passage argues that in this case there is a variance from the normal usage of the passive voice.

V. The Relation of Faith and Action

2:14–26

¹⁴What good is it, my brothers, if a man claims to have faith but has no deeds? Can such faith save him? ¹⁵Suppose a brother or sister is without clothes and daily food. ¹⁶If one of you says to him, "Go, I wish you well; keep warm and well fed," but does nothing about his physical needs, what good is it? ¹⁷In the same way, faith by itself, if it is not accompanied by action, is dead.

¹⁸But someone will say, "You have faith; I have deeds."

Show me your faith without deeds, and I will show you my faith by what I do. ¹⁹You believe that there is one God. Good! Even the demons believe that—and shudder.

²⁰You foolish man, do you want evidence that faith without deeds is useless? ²¹Was not our ancestor Abraham considered righteous for what he did when he offered his son Isaac on the altar? ²²You see that his faith and his actions were working together, and his faith was made complete by what he did. ²³And the

scripture was fulfilled that says, "Abraham believed God, and it was credited to him as righteousness," and he was called God's friend. [24]You see that a person is justified by what he does and not by faith alone.

[25]In the same way, was not even Rahab the prostitute considered righteous for what she did when she gave lodging to the spies and sent them off in a different direction? [26]As the body without the spirit is dead, so faith without deeds is dead.

This section has sometimes been misunderstood as conflicting with Paul's doctrine of justification by faith alone. No less a scholar than Martin Luther thought he saw an inconsistency between the teachings of James and Paul. However, careful study reveals that there is no disagreement between a Pauline statement like that in Ephesians 2:8–10 and the declaration of James 2:24.

The passage at hand (2:14–26) divides itself into three sections: the proposition (vv.14–17); the argument (vv.18–25); and the concluding statement (v.26). Here the author makes another application of the bedrock principle set forth in 1:19–27. As in that passage hearing must be accompanied by doing, so in 2:14–26 faith must be attended by action. This epistle leaves no place for a religion that is mere mental acceptance of truth.

14 James first states his proposition interrogatively. The two questions posed in this verse actually declare that faith not accompanied by good deeds is of no saving value whatsoever. The questions set up the hypothetical case of a person who "claims to have" genuine saving faith. Notice that James does not say that the person actually has faith. The question "Can such faith save him?" is so structured in the Greek text (using the negative particle *mē* interrogatively) that it expects a negative answer. The word "such" is the translation for the Greek article that appears before *pistis*, "faith." James is asking, "This faith can't save him, can it?" The article refers to the faith described in the preceding question—faith not accompanied by deeds. Faith without works cannot save; it takes faith that proves itself in the deeds it produces. James is not speaking of deeds performed to earn merit before God (as Paul uses the term in Rom 3:20). Genuine faith is a concomitant of regeneration and therefore affects the believer's behavior. Faith that does not issue in regenerate actions is superficial and spurious.

15 In vv.15–16 the proposition is illustrated by a supposition bordering on the ludicrous. It is the case of a believer ("brother or sister") who is in dire need ("without clothes and daily food"). The Greek *gymnoi* actually means "naked" and is probably to be understood as hyperbole. The purpose of the overstatement is to emphasize the drastic need of this believer. His is no mild case of need. He is desperate.

16 The statement "Go, I wish you well" is a modern idiom used to represent James's Greek *Hypagete en eirēnē* ("Go in peace"). This was a standard Hebrew farewell. The translation "keep warm and well fed" may be somewhat misleading in suggesting that the person is already warm and fed, which is not the case, as v.15 indicates. The two verbs are identified as passives by numerous commentators, with the understanding that they are commands to someone else to clothe and feed the unfortunate person. A.T. Robertson's suggestion that they are to be taken reflexively (as Greek middle voices) is more natural (*Word Pictures in the New Testament* [New York: Harper, 1933], 6:34–35). The meaning would be "get some warm clothes and eat your fill."

The preposterousness of such a command is no doubt intentional. "What good is it?" James asks. Its seeming concern for the welfare of the poor person is a worthless façade.

17 Here James states the proposition he intends to demonstrate in the following verses: "Faith . . . not accompanied by action is dead." Action is the proper fruit of living faith. Because life is dynamic and productive, faith that lives will surely produce the fruit of good deeds. Therefore, if no deeds are forthcoming, it is proof that the professed faith is dead. Notice that James does not deny that it is faith. He simply indicates that it is not the right kind of faith. It is not living faith, nor can it save.

18 James next proceeds to develop the argument in support of his proposition. His first point is that works are necessary to prove that a person has faith. There is some question as to the end of the quotation introduced by the words "But someone will say." Some translations, such as NASB and Wms, include all of v. 18 in the quotation. It seems preferable, however, to limit the statement to the words "You have faith; I have deeds," as do RSV, TEV, NIV, and Beck. The problem of identifying the persons referred to by the pronouns "you" and "I" is not easily resolved. Perhaps it is best to paraphrase the quotation as follows: "One person has faith; another has deeds." The statement then becomes an assertion that faith and works are not necessarily related to each other and that it is possible to have either one without the other (Tasker, pp. 64–66). To this assertion James responds with a challenge: "Show me your faith without deeds." The implication is that faith cannot be demonstrated apart from action. Faith is an attitude of the inner man, and it can only be seen as it influences the actions of the one who possesses it. Mere profession of faith proves nothing as to its reality; only action can demonstrate faith's genuineness. Hence James declares, "I will show you my faith by what I do."

19 The second argument offered in support of the proposition stated in v. 17 concerns the nature of saving faith. All faithful Jews believed the creed known as the Shema found in Deuteronomy 6:4: "Hear, O Israel: The LORD our God, the LORD is one." James commends his Jewish Christian readers for believing "that there is one God." This is "good!" That God is one was a basic truth of Jewish orthodoxy, but such acceptance of a creed is not enough to save a person. To prove his point, James declares that "even demons believe" the Shema. They know that there is but one God, and as a result they "shudder." The Greek term *phrissō* describes a shudder that results from fear. That the demons so respond to the fact of God is evidence that their belief is a thorough conviction. However, their response is also evidence that their faith is not saving faith, for they are terrified at the thought of God. Belief has not brought them peace with God. Saving faith, then, is not mere intellectual acceptance of a theological proposition. It goes much deeper, involving the whole inner man and expressing itself outwardly in a changed life.

20 James introduces the next argument in support of his proposition (v. 17) with the question "Do you want evidence?" His manner of addressing his imagined opponent is blunt, to say the least. The Greek adjective translated "foolish" means "empty." It refers to a deficiency that is intellectual, but in the theological and moral context of the NT the term also has a moral and spiritual flavor. So James addresses his opponent as one who has no comprehension of spiritual truth. He does not see "that faith without deeds is useless." In v.17 such faith is called "dead." Here it is described as something that does not work (*argē*); it accomplishes nothing. The evidence James offers his opponent is found in vv.21–25 and consists of two OT examples—Abraham and Rahab.

21 The designation of Abraham as "our ancestor" (*patēr*, "father") agrees with evidence found elsewhere in the epistle (e.g., 1:1) that James wrote for a Jewish readership. The Greek word *edikaiōthē* ("considered righteous") is the term the older versions translate as "justified." Its standard meaning is "to declare righteous." It is a forensic term, never referring to making a person subjectively righteous, but always describing the act of declaring a person righteous. So James states that Abraham was declared righteous "for what he did." It was a pronouncement that found its source (*ek*, "out of") in Abraham's obedient offering of his son (Gen 22:1–14). The explanation of this statement is given in the following verses.

22 Here James makes it clear that he is not talking about works as the sole source of Abraham's justification, as v.21 taken out of its context might lead one to believe. Instead, Abraham's "faith and his actions were working together." Faith and works are inseparable. It is not possible for one person to have valid faith without works and for another to have genuine works without faith, as James's opponent argued in v.18. But this may sound as if Abraham's justification resulted from a mixture of faith and works, each being equally efficacious. If this is what James meant, he is in conflict with Paul, who insists that faith is the only means of justification. However, it is not necessary to take James's statement in this way. Other NT passages show plainly that a person is justified by faith alone. James, assuming this fact, declares that this justifying faith has a certain quality, a vitality that makes it the producer of good deeds. It is an action-producing faith. Mayor wrote, "Abraham's faith was not mere profession but an extremely active principle" (p. 95). Paul described this quality of faith when he spoke of "faith expressing itself through love" (Gal 5:6). Faith, then, is the means of obtaining justification, but by its very nature it is faith that produces deeds. In this sense Abraham's faith was validated by his deeds. If there had been no good deeds following, faith would have been incomplete (v.22), dead (v.17), and useless (v.20). In this sense also Abraham was "considered righteous for what he did." If there had been no good deeds forthcoming, his faith would not have been genuine; and therefore it could not have been counted to him for righteousness.

23 "The scripture" to which James refers as "fulfilled" is Genesis 15:6. The account of the offering of Isaac on the altar appears in Genesis 22:1–14. Thirty years may have intervened between the events of these two chapters. In the former passage Abraham's faith is said to have been "credited to him as righteousness." The obedient offering of Isaac in the latter passage "fulfilled" the statement of the former passage. This is not to be understood as the fulfillment of a prophecy. Rather, it is fulfillment in the sense of completion (cf. v.22). What Abraham did in Genesis 22 was the outworking of the faith described in chapter 15. That it was the kind of faith that justifies is shown in chapter 22. God's act of crediting Abraham with righteousness because of his faith was vindicated by Abraham's act of obedience in offering his son. In this way Genesis 22:1–14 fulfilled Genesis 15:6. James adds, as a parallel description of Abraham's standing with God, that "he was called God's friend" (see 2 Chron 20:7; Isa 41:8). This is another way of saying that he was right with God. It was not that Abraham earned the favor of God by obeying him; instead, he acted as a friend of God should act and thus showed that he was in reality God's friend.

24 In this summary statement James assumes that a person is justified by faith but "not by faith alone." It is by faith *and* "by what he does." Taken by itself, this declaration may seem blatantly contradictory to such Pauline statements as that of Ephesians 2:8–9. If both passages are studied in context, however, the seeming contradiction disappears. James has indicated that deeds complete faith (v.22). They are the outworking of genuine faith. Thus deeds are the evidence that saving faith is present in a person's life (v.18). James was combating a superficial faith that had no wholesome effect in the life of the professed believer. Paul, on the other hand, was combating legalism—the belief that one may earn saving merit before God by his good deeds. Consequently Paul insisted that salvation is not by works but by faith alone. However, the following context of the Ephesians passage (2:10) reveals that Paul did not depreciate good works. He declared, "We are God's workmanship, created in Christ Jesus to do good works." In Paul, therefore, as well as in James, good deeds are the product of genuine faith. In both writers faith that produces no good deeds is incapable of saving a person.

25 The second OT person cited as an example of genuine faith is "Rahab the prostitute." She too was "considered righteous for what she did." Although her faith was like that of Abraham, she was unlike the patriarch in almost every other way. She had been a pagan; she was a woman; and she was a prostitute. Nevertheless, she chose to become identified with the people of Israel, a decision based on faith (cf. Josh 2:8–13; Heb 11:31). Far from being dead or worthless, her faith moved her to risk her life to protect the spies. As a result, "even" (*kai*) the prostitute was declared righteous. James does not give approval to Rahab's former life; it is her living faith, seen against the background of her previous immorality, he commends.

26 The argument of vv. 18–25 concludes with a statement that cites the human body as an illustration. "The body without the spirit" is nothing but a corpse. "Faith without deeds" is as dead as a corpse, and equally useless. James does not imply that deeds are the actual life principle that gives life to faith, but only that faith and deeds are inseparable. If there are no acts springing from faith, that faith is no more alive than "the body without the spirit."

Notes

19 The variant readings of the reference to Deut 6:4 can be divided into two categories: those that have the article before θεός (*theos*, "God") and those that do not. The articular reading adopted by UBS is tr. "there is one God" by NIV. But more literally it is "God is one," since the article identifies θεός (*theos*, "God") as the subject of the copulative sentence. The anarthrous reading εἷς θεός ἐστιν (*heis theos estin*, "there is one God") has good MS support (B), but it is the least conventional (Ropes, p. 215).

20 KJV translates the latter part of this verse "faith without works is dead," basing its rendering on the external evidence of the majority of MSS. However, since the word ἀργή (*argē*, "barren"; NIV, "useless") is supported by B and C, and since νεκρά (*nekra*, "dead") may well be a harmonization with vv.17, 26, ἀργή (argē) seems to be the best reading. A possible play on words (ἔργων–ἀργή, ergōn–argē, "works–useless") is pointed out by Metzger (p. 681).

VI. The Control of the Tongue

3:1–12

> [1]Not many of you should presume to be teachers, my brothers, because you know that we who teach will be judged more strictly. [2]We all stumble in many ways. If anyone is never at fault in what he says, he is a perfect man, able to keep his whole body in check.
> [3]When we put bits into the mouths of horses to make them obey us, we can turn the whole animal. [4]Or take ships as an example. Although they are so large and are driven by strong winds, they are steered by a very small rudder wherever the pilot wants to go. [5]Likewise the tongue is a small part of the body, but it makes great boasts. Consider what a great forest is set on fire by a small spark. [6]The tongue also is a fire, a world of evil among the parts of the body. It corrupts the whole person, sets the whole course of his life on fire, and is itself set on fire by hell.
> [7]All kinds of animals, birds, reptiles and creatures of the sea are being tamed and have been tamed by man, [8]but no man can tame the tongue. It is a restless evil, full of deadly poison.
> [9]With the tongue we praise our Lord and Father, and with it we curse men, who have been made in God's likeness. [10]Out of the same mouth come praise and cursing. My brothers, this should not be. [11]Can both fresh water and salt water flow from the same spring? [12]My brothers, can a fig tree bear olives, or a grapevine bear figs? Neither can a salt spring produce fresh water.

In this section the author picks up a subject first mentioned in 1:19 and reiterated in 1:26. Genuine religion should exert a controlling influence over a person's tongue. James's treatment of the topic may be broken into three subdivisions: the weighty responsibility of teachers (vv.1–2); the powerful influence of the tongue (vv.3–6); and the perversity of the tongue (vv.7–12).

1 James's first concern in this passage has to do with those who desired to be "teachers" in the scattered Jewish Christian congregations. A somewhat similar situation is reflected in 1 Timothy 1:7. The KJV "masters" is an Old English term for teachers (e.g., schoolmaster). The Greek construction (mē with the present imperative ginesthe) probably suggests that it had been a common practice for many of the readers to seek to become teachers. So James warns that they should stop becoming teachers in such large numbers. No doubt many who were not qualified by natural ability or spiritual gift were coveting the prestige of teaching. They are warned that teachers "will be judged more strictly." It is apparent from the words "we who teach" that James includes himself as a teacher. The KJV translation "we shall receive the greater condemnation" is unfortunate. The Greek word krima refers to the decision of a judge, whether it be favorable or unfavorable. In this context the term is neutral. James merely says that the judgment of teachers will be especially strict because greater responsibility rests on teachers. The reason for this is that the teacher's essential instrument—the tongue—which is so easily misused, has great influence.

2 In the Greek text this verse begins with gar ("for"), indicating an explanation for the previous statement. The teacher's responsibility is weighty because the tongue

is the most difficult member of the body to control. To say that "we all stumble" is not merely to declare that everyone makes mistakes (RSV). The literal meaning of *ptaiō* is "to stumble," but in both biblical and extrabiblical writings it was also used figuratively to refer to acts of sin (cf. 2:10). Thus the author declares the universality of sin, even among believers. The person who "is never at fault" in his speech (i.e., never commits sins of speech) "is a perfect man." If anyone could be found who never sins with his tongue, he would never sin in any other way, either. Since sins of the tongue are hardest to avoid, anyone who could control his tongue would surely be able to "keep his whole body in check"—i.e., keep it from being used as an instrument of sin.

3 James illustrates the powerful influence of the tongue by the practice of putting "bits into the mouths of horses to make them obey us." A very small bit "can turn the whole animal." So a man who controls his tongue can control his whole being.

4 The next illustration of the influence of the tongue is the rudder of a ship. James vividly introduces the illustration: "Take ships as an example." Three factors made ships of that day difficult to control: they were "so large"; they were "driven by strong winds"; and they were "steered by a very small rudder." The rudder was a small blade on the end of a tiller, extending through a form of oarlock from the rear of the ship. Compared to the size of the vessel and the power of the gale, the rudder was but a minute part; yet it guided the ship "wherever the pilot [wanted] to go."

5 With the words "likewise the tongue," the application of the two preceding verses is introduced. Like bits (v.3) and rudders (v.4), the tongue also is a small item. Yet, also like them, it exerts a powerful influence. "It makes great boasts," and these are not empty claims. The tongue is able to sway multitudes. It can alter the destinies of nations. Since *megala auchei* ("makes great boasts") is usually employed in a derogatory sense, it may be that the author uses the expression to apply the first two illustrations of the tongue's influence (vv.3–4) and also to introduce the third one (vv.5b–6). The destructive potential of the tongue is graphically pictured by a forest fire. Thousands of acres of valuable timber may be devastated by a "small spark." In the two former illustrations, animals and ships are controlled by small objects; in this last illustration, a huge forest is destroyed by a tiny spark. The tongue likewise can either control or destroy.

6 So, James says, "The tongue also is a fire." The inflammatory tongue has turned brother against brother, neighbor against neighbor, nation against nation. The tongue is also "a world of evil." It is as though all the wickedness in the whole world were wrapped up in that little piece of flesh. There are few sins people commit in which the tongue is not involved.

James describes the tongue's influence as both destructive and as corrupting "the whole person." The Greek word translated "person" by NIV is *sōma* ("body"). Since the person resides in the body and uses the body as his instrument, James seems to use "body" to refer to the whole man. In reality, he is not referring to the tongue of flesh but to the intelligent, communicating mind that uses the tongue as its instrument. So the mind corrupts the whole person. But the corrupting influence of the tongue reaches out in widening circles, for it "sets the whole course of his life on fire." The pronoun "his" in the NIV is not in the Greek text and therefore might better be omitted. It limits the sphere of influence to the speaker, whereas James seems to refer to the whole of human existence. Finally, James traces the inflaming nature of the tongue back to its source. It is, he says, "set on fire by hell," a way of saying that it comes from the devil. The term *geennēs* or *gehenna* comes from the Greek form of the Hebrew name of the valley of Hinnom (*gê-hinnōm*), a spot just south of Jerusalem where the rubbish of the city was deposited and burned. This continual burning of rubbish became a figure for eternal punishment.

7 James shifts almost unnoticeably from discussing the power of the tongue (vv.3–6) to a discussion of its perversity (vv.7–12). Actually v.6, in depicting the tongue's influence, is already describing its perversity. According to vv.7–8, man's inability to tame his tongue shows the perversity of the tongue. At creation God gave man the dominion over the animals that he has exercised ever since (Gen 1:28). "All kinds" of creatures of land, sea, and air have been subdued by mankind. To emphasize the continuing aspect of man's dominance over the animals, James uses both the present and the perfect tenses—"are being tamed and have been tamed."

8 But even though man has retained his dominion over all kinds of animals, Tasker says, "Because of the fall man has lost dominion over himself" (p. 77). When he says, "No man can tame the tongue," James is stating that no man by himself can subdue the tongue. This is not to say that God cannot bring it under control. While the tongue cannot be controlled by man, the tongue of the regenerate person can be controlled by the indwelling Holy Spirit. In its natural state the tongue "is a restless evil," like a ferocious beast that will not be subdued. It is "full of deadly poison," like a serpent ready to inject venom into its victim.

9 James goes on to speak of inconsistency as an aspect of the tongue's perversity (vv.9–12). We use the same instrument to "praise our Lord and Father" and to "curse men." But praising God and cursing men is tantamount to praising and cursing the same person, for in v.9 James describes man as "made in God's likeness" (cf. man's having been created in the image of God [Gen 1:26–27]). Although marred by sin, that image is still very much a reality; and man's intellect, emotion, and will show that he bears God's likeness. Obviously, James is not referring to such words as those of Paul when he invoked a curse on anyone who perverts the gospel (Gal 1:6–9). Instead, it is the cursing that grows out of bitterness and hatred that he speaks of.

10 Again, James stresses the inconsistency of the tongue in that it is the source of such direct opposites as "praise and cursing." He does not have only the unsaved in mind because he introduces his rebuke with the words "my brothers," the term used throughout the epistle to address believers (1:2, 16, 19; 2:1, 5, 14; 3:1; et al.). Although the believer has in the indwelling Holy Spirit the potential for controlling the tongue, he may not be appropriating this potential. Hence, James insists that "this should not be." The mouth should be used consistently to praise God and to express love and kindness to men.

11 James again turns to nature for his illustrations. He asks, "Can both fresh water and salt water flow from the same spring?" The word *bryei* ("flow") is a poetic term describing water that pours out, almost as being under pressure. The water is sweet (*glyky;* NIV, "fresh") and bitter (*pikron;* NIV, "salt"). "Sweet" describes fresh water that is good for drinking; "bitter" refers to water so brackish or even salty as to be unfit for drinking. James may have had the Dead Sea in mind.

12 James concludes his discussion of the tongue by going behind the physical organ to the real source of speech. He asks, "Can a fig tree bear olives?" A plant produces according to its nature, whether figs, grapes, or any other fruit. So with "a salt spring." It cannot "produce fresh water" because it is not a fresh water spring. Therefore, out of the mouth of a good man come good words, and out of the mouth of a sinful man come sinful words.

Notes

6 The question of punctuation in this verse is a difficult one. It is clear from the repetition of ἡ γλῶσσα (hē glōssa, "the tongue") that καὶ ἡ γλῶσσα πῦρ (kai hē glōssa pyr, "the tongue also is a fire") is a complete clause, with the verb ἐστίν (estin, "is") being assumed. It is possible that this clause should be followed by a comma and that ὁ κόσμος τῆς ἀδικίας (ho kosmos tēs adikias, "a world of evil") is a second predicate nominative after the assumed ἐστίν (estin, "is"). This, however, makes the following clause to be a rather pointless statement: ἡ γλῶσσα καθίσταται ἐν τοῖς μέλεσιν ἡμῶν (hē glōssa kathistatai en tois melesin hēmōn, "the tongue is placed among our members"). It seems best, therefore, to assume a period after πῦρ (pyr, "fire") and to take ὁ κόσμος τῆς ἀδικίας (ho kosmos tēs adikias, "a world of evil") as the predicate nominative after καθίσταται (kathistatai, "is placed"). The verse would then read, "The tongue also is a fire. The tongue is constituted a world of evil among the parts of the body, which corrupts. . . ." For a parallel use of καθίσταται (kathistatai, "is placed") followed by a predicate nominative, see Rom 5:19.

The expression τὸν τροχὸν τῆς γενέσεως (ton trochon tēs geneseōs, "the course of nature") is both difficult and interesting. Τροχός (trochos), when accented on the ultima, means "wheel," or when accented on the penult, τρόχος (trochos), means "course" (from τρέχειν [trechein, "to run"]). Γενέσεως (geneseōs) may mean "birth" or "origin." BAG (s.v.) also gives "existence" as a meaning in certain extrabiblical passages. In Judith 12:18 (LXX) it is used in the expression πάσας τὰς ἡμέρας τῆς γενέσεώς μου (pasas tas hēmeras tēs geneseōs mou, "all the days of my existence"). Since extensive research has yielded no exact parallel for the phrase employed by James, it seems best to assume that he did not borrow it from any pagan philosophical or religious source, but rather coined the expression himself. Whether we understand τροχόν (troch'on) to mean "wheel" or "course" makes little difference. James refers to the whole of existence, which is set on fire by the tongue.

VII. Two Kinds of Wisdom

3:13–18

[13]Who is wise and understanding among you? Let him show it by his good life, by deeds done in the humility that comes from wisdom. [14]But if you harbor bitter envy and selfish ambition in your hearts, do not boast about it or deny the truth. [15]Such "wisdom" does not come down from heaven but is earthly, unspiritual, of the devil. [16]For where you have envy and selfish ambition, there you find disorder and every evil practice.

[17]But the wisdom that comes from heaven is first of all pure; then peace loving, considerate, submissive, full of mercy and good fruit, impartial and sincere. [18]Peacemakers who sow in peace raise a harvest of righteousness.

This passage is a natural outgrowth of the discussion of the tongue. The six verses divide into three sections: an exhortation (v. 13); earthly wisdom (vv. 14-16); and wisdom from heaven (vv. 17-18).

13 James addresses the person who is "wise and understanding." The word *sophos* ("wise") was the technical term among the Jews for the teacher, the scribe, the rabbi (TDNT, 7:505). It appears that the author is still speaking to those who would be teachers (cf. 3:1); here it is not what they say that he is concerned with, but rather how they live. The term *epistēmōn* describes one who is expert, who has special knowledge or training. Thus anyone who would be a teacher, who claims to be an expert with special understanding, is under obligation to "show it by his good life." He should possess "knowhow" and be skilled in applying God's truth to practical, everyday living. The KJV term "conversation" is not to be restricted to speech. In 1611 it possessed the much broader meaning of "conduct," "manner of life," and was at that time a good translation of *anastrophēs* (NIV, "life").

The particular characteristic stressed in this verse is "humility that comes from wisdom." The word translated "humility" in NIV is *prautēti*, more commonly rendered "meekness." "Humility" may not be the best translation, since it confuses *prautēs* with the word *tapeinophrosynē*, more normally translated "humility." A better translation might be "gentleness," but even this does not adequately render the Greek word (see remarks on 1:21). *Prautēs* is gentleness, but not a passive gentleness growing out of weakness or resignation. It is an active attitude of deliberate acceptance (TDNT, 6:645). The word was used to describe a horse that had been broken and trained to submit to the bridle (William Barclay, *New Testament Words* [London: SCM, 1971], pp. 241-42). So this gentleness is strength under control, the control of the Spirit of God (Gal 5:22-23). It is a gentleness "that comes from wisdom" or is characteristic of wisdom (see remarks on 1:5). James does not have in mind the Greek concept of speculative or theoretical wisdom but the Hebrew idea of practical wisdom that enables one to live a life of godliness.

14 Apparently some of James's readers were harboring "bitter envy and selfish ambition" in their hearts. The Greek simple conditional sentence assumes the existence of the situation described. The determinative word is *eritheian* ("selfish ambition"), which speaks of a self-seeking attitude bent on gaining advantage and prestige for oneself or one's group. This forceful term colors the word *zēlon* ("envy"), so that *zēlon* here means "selfish zeal." The word is often used to describe fanatical zeal for a cause (1 Kings 19:10 [3 Kings 19:10 LXX]; Ps 69:9 [68:10 LXX]; Isa 9:7), either in a good or a bad sense. James makes it clear by the adjective "bitter" that he is referring to a sinful zeal. Because this condition existed among his readers, he insists that they must "not boast about it or deny the truth." The phrase "about it," which has been added by the translators, could be taken to mean "Do not boast about your bitter zeal and selfish ambition." James's readers may have been priding themselves in their partisan defense of the truth—a defense that was to their own advantage and advancement. Through such bitter and partisan defense, they were in reality denying the very truth they were attempting to defend.

15 Though James refers to the attitude described in v. 14 as "wisdom," he obviously does not mean that it is genuine wisdom. On the contrary, it is the wisdom claimed by the would-be teachers of v.14 whose lives contradict their claims. Such "wisdom" evaluates everything by worldly standards and makes personal gain life's highest goal. Yet even this spurious use of the term reflects the Hebrew concept of wisdom as practical rather than theoretical. God is the source of genuine wisdom (Prov 2:6), but this pseudo-wisdom is not from him, because, as James declares, "such 'wisdom' does not come down from heaven." Instead of being from above (*anōthen*), it is "earthly" in source as well as kind. It views life from the limited viewpoint of this world rather than from heaven's vantage point. Its mind is set on earthly things (Phil 3:19).

James also calls wisdom *psychikē* ("unspiritual"). In 1 Corinthians 2:14–15 *psychikos* ("unspiritual") is contrasted to *pneumatikos* ("spiritual"). The *pneumatikos* ("spiritual") man has received the Spirit of God (1 Cor 2:12), but the *psychikos* ("unspiritual") man does not have the Spirit (Jude 19). Thus "wisdom" that is *psychikē* ("unspiritual") characterizes unregenerate human nature. James also says that it is "of the devil" (more lit., "demonic" [*daimoniōdēs*]).

16 The conjunction "for" (*gar*) indicates that bitter zeal and selfish ambition always result in "disorder and every evil practice." *Akatastasia* ("disorder") is a common word for anarchy and political turmoil. Luke uses it to refer to political uprisings (Luke 21:9). James is no doubt speaking of disturbance and turmoil in the church. The "evil practice" refers specifically to worthless activity, to deeds that are bad because they are good for nothing and cannot produce any real benefit (Trench, pp. 305–6). Selfish zeal and ambition, then, always tend to destroy spiritual life and work.

17 In contrast to the denial of v.15—"Such 'wisdom' does not come down from heaven"—James next turns to a description of "the wisdom that comes from heaven." It is "first of all pure." This is its basic characteristic. The reference is not to sexual purity but to the absence of any sinful attitude or motive. It is the opposite of the self-seeking attitude of vv.14–16. From this inner quality flow the outward manifestations given in the rest of the verse. James describes this wisdom as "peace loving" in contrast to the bitter spirit of competitiveness and selfish ambition described in v.14.

Next, this godly wisdom is "considerate" (*epieikēs*). This is one of the great words of character description in the NT. In the LXX it is used mostly of God's disposition as King. He is gentle and kind, although in reality he has every reason to be stern and punitive toward men in their sin. God's people also are to be marked by this godlike quality, not insisting on their rights according to the letter of the law, but exercising love's leniency instead.

Likewise, "the wisdom that comes from heaven is . . . submissive." This quality is the opposite of obstinacy and self-seeking; it is a readiness to yield. The attitude that comes from God is "full of mercy and good fruit." Altogether compassionate, heavenly wisdom is always ready to help those who are in need. Furthermore, it is "impartial," showing no favoritism, and discriminating against no one. Finally, this wisdom is "sincere" (*anhypokritos*, "without hypocrisy"). Far from being theoretical and speculative, James's concept of wisdom is thoroughly practical. It is the understanding and attitude that result in true piety and godliness.

18 James concludes his discussion of "the wisdom that comes from heaven" by reiterating the second quality listed in v.17. To "raise a harvest of righteousness" demands a certain kind of climate. A crop of righteousness cannot be produced in the climate of bitterness and self-seeking. Righteousness will grow only in a climate of peace. And it must be sown and cultivated by the "peacemakers." Such persons not only love peace and live in peace but also strive to create conditions of peace.

VIII. The Worldly Attitude

4:1–10

¹What causes fights and quarrels among you? Don't they come from your desires that battle within you? ²You want something but don't get it. You kill and covet, but you cannot have what you want. You quarrel and fight. You do not have, because you do not ask God. ³When you ask, you do not receive, because you ask with wrong motives, that you may spend what you get on your pleasures.

⁴You adulterous people, don't you know that friendship with the world is hatred toward God? Anyone who chooses to be a friend of the world becomes an enemy of God. ⁵Or do you think Scripture says without reason that the spirit he caused to live in us tends toward envy, ⁶but he gives us more grace? That is why Scripture says:

> "God opposes the proud
>   but gives grace to the humble."

⁷Submit yourselves, then, to God. Resist the devil, and he will flee from you. ⁸Come near to God and he will come near to you. Wash your hands, you sinners, and purify your hearts, you double-minded. ⁹Grieve, mourn and wail. Change your laughter to mourning and your joy to gloom. ¹⁰Humble yourselves before the Lord, and he will lift you up.

In 3:14–16 James has discussed a philosophy of life that is characteristic of the unregenerate mind and is a major ingredient of worldliness. In 4:1–10 he examines this worldly attitude in greater detail. First he identifies the source of worldly antagonisms (4:1–3); next, he reproves spiritual unfaithfulness (4:4–6); and, finally, he pleads for submission to God (4:7–10).

1 Instead of the climate of peace necessary for the production of righteousness (3:18), James's readers were living in an atmosphere of constant "fights and quarrels." These two nouns (*polemoi* and *machai*) were normally used of national warfare, but they had also become common, forceful expressions for any kind of open antagonism. James asks, "What causes fights and quarrels among you?" His answer, with which he expects his reader to agree, is "Don't they come from your desires?" The term *hēdonōn* (NIV, "desires") means "pleasures." It is the source of the English word "hedonism," the designation of the philosophy that views pleasure as the chief goal of life. James pictures these pleasures as residing within his readers, there carrying on a bitter campaign to gain satisfaction. Pleasure is the overriding desire of their lives. Nothing will be allowed to stand in the way of its realization.

2 The NIV translation "You want something" is not quite forceful enough to fit the context or to represent the Greek verb. *Epithymeite* expresses longing and eager desire. Buchsel says, "*Epithymia* is anxious self-seeking" (TDNT, 3:171). And in Exodus 20:17 (LXX) and Romans 7:7 *ouk epithymēseis* is the Greek translation of the tenth commandment, "Do not covet." So James says, "You eagerly desire something, but you don't get it." So strong is the desire that "you kill and covet."

This last statement has aroused much discussion. First, it is difficult to believe that James's readers, whom he elsewhere addresses as Christians (2:1), were actually guilty of murder. Some, insisting that the word must be taken literally, say that James is not referring to any specific occurrences but is indicating what happens when men desire pleasure rather than God (Ropes, p. 255). This interpretation, however, does not do justice to the pointed accusation "You kill." In the context of forceful words such as *polemoi* ("wars") and *machai* ("battles"), it seems better to take *phoneuete* ("you kill") as hyperbole for hatred. This also resolves the problem of seeming anticlimactic word order. To say "You hate and covet" is a much more natural order than to say "You murder and covet." Furthermore, Matthew 5:21–22 and 1 John 3:15 show that hatred is equal to murder. James repeats his assertion that, with all their consuming desire and bitter antagonism, his readers were not able to obtain what they wanted. The reason was that they were going after it in the wrong way. They did "not ask God" for it. They were lusting and fighting rather than praying.

3 And even when James's readers did ask God for things, they did "not receive" what they requested. Why? They asked "with wrong motives." Their purpose was to "spend" (*dapanēsēte*) what they got for pleasure. The prodigal son exemplifies one who spent (same Gr. verb) his money in this way (Luke 15:14). "Pleasures" (*hēdonais*) is the same word translated "desires" in v.1. It was the desire of James's readers for pleasures that was battling within them for satisfaction (v.1) and even leading them to try to use prayer as a means of gratification (v.3). They were not actually asking for gratification but for things, such as money, that they intended to use for pleasure. They wanted to gratify themselves rather than help others and please God.

4 Having identified the source of the bitter fighting as being the desire for pleasure (4:1–3), James next rebukes his readers for spiritual unfaithfulness (4:4–6). The noun translated "adulterous people" is feminine, meaning "adulteresses." The people of God in the OT are considered the wife of the Lord (Jer 31:32), and in the NT, the bride of Christ (Eph 5:23–32). It is reasonable, therefore, to understand "adulteress" as a figure of speech for spiritual unfaithfulness. It is a blunt and shocking word, intended to jar the reader and awaken him to his true spiritual condition. The concept of spiritual adultery was no doubt taken from the OT (cf. Hos 2:2–5; 3:1–5, 9:1).

For the believer, however, there are two objects for affection: the world and God, and these two are direct opposites. James uses the word *kosmos* ("world"), as do Paul and John, to refer to the system of evil controlled by Satan. It includes all that is wicked and opposed to God on this earth. James is thinking especially of pleasures that lure men's hearts from God. By its very nature, then, "friendship with the world is hatred toward God." To have a warm, familiar attitude toward this evil world is to be on good terms with God's enemy. It is to adopt the world's set of values and want what the world wants instead of choosing according to divine standards. The person who deliberately "chooses [*boulēthē*] to be a friend of the world" by that choice "becomes an enemy of God."

5 This verse is one of the most difficult in the epistle. Various translations have been suggested, but there is good reason to believe that the translation given in the NIV footnote for the last part of the verse is correct, "that God jealously longs for the spirit that he made to live in us." This rendering fits the immediate context better than the

NIV text, "that the spirit he caused to live in us tends toward envy." Verse 4, which is closely tied to v.5 by the conjunction "or," indicates that the believer who is a friend of the world is guilty of spiritual adultery. Although his love and devotion belong to God, he has fallen in love with the world. It is natural, therefore, to expect v.5 to speak of God's jealous longing for his people's love, rather than of their envious spirit. And there are OT passages that refer to God as jealously desiring the devotion of his people. Since there is no passage of which James 4:5 is a verbatim quotation, it is best to understand it as giving the gist of such passages as Exodus 20:5 and 34:14.

A second reason for preferring the NIV footnote rendering is that it more accurately represents the Greek text. It is true that the words *pros phthonon* can literally mean "to envy," but BAG indicates that this phrase was a Greek adverbial idiom meaning "jealously" (p. 718; cf. Ropes, p. 262). Furthermore, the Greek verb *epipothei* is not adequately represented by "tends." *Epipothei* means "to long for," "to yearn for" something or someone. It is much better, therefore, to translate *pros phthonon epipothei* as "longs jealously for." Thus, in v.4 James has accused his readers of spiritual unfaithfulness. If they are not willing to accept this indictment, he asks in v.5 what they think about the OT passages dealing with God's jealous longing for his people. This is the significance of the introductory conjunction "or." Do they think Scripture speaks "without reason" or emptily? Of course they don't think this. Consequently, it is necessary to believe that friendship with the world is enmity toward God, and thus it is spiritual unfaithfulness.

6 NIV makes the words "but he gives more grace" a part of the question of v.5. However, this arrangement is contrary to almost all other current translations of the verse. It should be noted that the words "he gives more grace" are not found in the OT in connection with any statement about the jealousy of God. Instead, they are taken from Proverbs 3:34, which is quoted in the latter part of James 4:6. It is better, therefore, to end v.5 with a question mark and to make the clause "but he gives more grace" a new sentence. The meaning of vv.4–6 would then be that God has set a high standard for wholehearted love and devotion on the part of his people, but he gives grace that is greater than the rigorous demand he has made. This assurance is documented with a quotation from the OT. The point of the quotation, as James uses it, is in the second clause. The reference to the gift of grace looks back to God's demand for loyalty (vv.4–5). God in grace gives his people the help they need to resist the appeal of the world and to remain loyal to him. The reference to "the humble" constitutes the theme for vv.7–10, where James pleads for submission to God. "The humble" are the people who willingly submit to God's desire for them rather than proudly insisting on satisfying their own desires for pleasure (cf. vv.1–3).

7 The command to submit to God is the logical response to the quotation from Proverbs 3:34. This is indicated by the word "then" (*oun*), which has the inferential meaning of "therefore." Since "God opposes the proud" but helps "the humble," believers should submit to him. Submission is not the same as obedience. Instead, it is the surrender of one's will, which leads to obedience.

James issues a series of ten commands in vv.7–10 ("submit," "resist" [v.7]; "come near," "wash," "purify" [v.8]; "grieve," "mourn," "wail," "change" [v.9]; "humble" [v.10]). In each instance the Greek aorist imperative calls for immediate response. It is a pointed and forceful way to demand action. Rather than resisting God's will for us, we should "resist the devil." James seems to suggest that the spiritual unfaithfulness of v.4 was the result of the devil's influence. The promise "he will flee from you" gives assurance that, as powerful as he may be, Satan can be resisted.

8 The series of imperatives continues with the command "Come near to God." In setting their hearts on pleasure, James's readers had drifted away from God. Though still his people, they had become estranged from him. But the assurance that God will welcome them back accompanies the command to return. God jealously yearns for their devotion (v.5). The call to "wash your hands" is a command to make one's conduct pure. Similarly, the call to "purify your hearts" insists on purity of thoughts and motives. The eager quest for pleasure (vv.1–5) had resulted in sins of heart and hand. So James bluntly addresses them as "you sinners," a strong term, showing the extent of their involvement in worldly attitudes and actions. The designation "double-minded" is used somewhat differently than in 1:8. Here it describes the attempt of the readers to love God and the pleasures of the world at the same time.

9 Four of the ten imperatives of vv.7–10 occur in this verse, and all four are calls to repentance. *Talaipōrēsate* ("grieve") is a strong word meaning "to be miserable," "to be wretched." In contrast to the worldly pleasures they had sought so eagerly, James's readers are to repent in misery. They also are commanded to "mourn." This verb (*pentheō*) usually depicts passionate grief that cannot be hidden. Similar outward grief is called for in the verb *klausate* ("wail"). In the past, when the readers had pursued pleasure, their lives had been marked by "laughter" and "joy"; but now they are to change their "laughter to mourning" and their "joy to gloom." Some have imagined that the attitude expressed in this verse is to be the constant characteristic of the Christian. Such an interpretation, however, overlooks the situation that gave rise to these commands. It was the burning desire for pleasures that led James to issue this powerful call to all-out repentance.

10 With the words "humble yourselves," James returns to the text quoted from the OT (cf. v.6). God graciously gives aid to the humble; therefore "humble yourselves." Here the specific form of humbling is that of repentance for the sin of transferring affections from God to pleasures of the world. However, the principle stated in this verse is much more comprehensive in its application. That God exalts those who humble themselves is a consistent biblical principle (cf. Matt 23:12; Luke 14:11; 18:14; Phil 2:5–11; 1 Peter 5:6.)

Notes

2 This verse has been punctuated in several ways. Many have a semicolon, a comma, or no punctuation after ἔχετε (*echete*, "you have"; NIV, "get") and a period or a semicolon after φονεύετε (*phoneuete*, "you kill") (RSV, NASB, NEB, TEV, Wms, Beck, AmT). This seems to necessitate a translation similar to the following: "You desire and do not have; so you kill. And you covet and cannot obtain; so you fight and wage war" (RSV). A number of others place a period or a semicolon after ἔχετε (*echete*, "you have") and a comma or no punctuation after φονεύετε (*phoneuete*, "you kill") (TR, WH, UBS, KJV, ASV, Mof, NIV). Three factors argue in favor of the latter punctuation. First, the necessity to supply the word "so" makes the former punctuation questionable. Second, the καί (*kai*, "and") before ζηλοῦτε (*zēloute*, "you covet") would no doubt have been omitted if the former punctuation had been intended. Third, the identification of φονεύετε (phoneuete, "you kill") as hyperbole for hatred removes the seeming anticlimax that gave rise to former punctuation in the first place.

4 The KJV reads, "Ye adulterers and adulteresses," following the TR. The MS support for this reading comes from the eighth and ninth centuries, with a host of minuscules from the ninth century on. The reading adopted by the NIV and most modern versions is μοιχαλίδες (moichalides, "adulteresses"), omitting the masculine μοιχοί (moichoi, "adulterers"). The textual evidence strongly favors the latter reading. In addition, Metzger explains the probable origin of the reading that includes μοιχοί (moichoi, "adulterers"). It apparently was inserted at a time when the words were understood literally. Being puzzled by the omission of reference to men, the copyists inserted μοιχοί (Metzger, p. 683).

IX. Faultfinding

4:11-12

[11]Brothers, do not slander one another. Anyone who speaks against his brother or judges him speaks against the law and judges it. When you judge the law, you are not keeping it, but sitting in judgment on it. [12]There is only one Lawgiver and Judge, the one who is able to save and destroy. But you—who are you to judge your neighbor?

11 The prohibition introducing this verse would more accurately be translated "Do not speak against one another" rather than "Do not slander." Although the verb *katalaleite* may be used of "slander," it is a broader term than that. To slander is to make false charges or misrepresentations that damage a person's reputation. *Katalaleite* refers to any form of speaking against a person. What is said may be true in its content but harsh and unkind in the manner of its presentation. The grammatical construction used here (*mē* with the present imperative) usually forbids the continuation of a practice already in progress. James's readers had fallen into the habit of criticizing one another, and so he says, "Stop speaking against one another." The reason he gives is that the one who criticizes or judges his brother "speaks against the law and judges it." The law referred to is probably the command of Leviticus 19:18: "Love your neighbor as yourself." To speak against your neighbor is to violate this law. The person who does so places himself above the law and, by his action, declares that law to be a bad or unnecessary statute. Rather than submitting to it and "keeping it," he passes judgment on its validity and sets it aside.

12 In passing judgment, this critic of his brother has usurped a position of authority that is reserved for God alone. God is the "one Lawgiver and Judge." Since he gave the law, he is qualified to judge those who are responsible to keep it. That he is "able to save and destroy" is proof that he is in a position to enforce the law, rewarding those who keep it, and punishing those who violate it. God stands supreme as giver of the law and as its judge. The NIV's "But you—who are you?" catches the full force of the Greek construction. With shattering bluntness, James crushes any right his readers may have claimed to sit in judgment over their neighbors. This is not to rule out civil courts and judges. Instead, it is to root out the harsh, unkind, critical spirit that continually finds fault with others.

X. Arrogant Self-Sufficiency

4:13-17

> [13]Now listen, you who say, "Today or tomorrow we will go to this or that city, spend a year there, carry on business and make money." [14]Why, you do not even know what will happen tomorrow. What is your life? You are a mist that appears for a little while and then vanishes. [15]Instead, you ought to say, "If it is the Lord's will, we will live and do this or that." [16]As it is, you boast and brag. All such boasting is evil. [17]Anyone, then, who knows the good he ought to do and doesn't do it, sins.

13 This section gives another example of the "wisdom" that characterizes the world (cf. 4:15). James addresses businessmen, probably Christians, since v. 17 seems to suggest that the readers know that their practice is wrong. "Now listen" (*age nyn*) is a pointed call for attention that indicates the seriousness of what follows. The present tense *legontes* ("say") seems to indicate that the situation under consideration was not an isolated instance. It was something that occurred frequently. Business travel in the first century was very common, and Jews, especially, traveled widely for business purposes; NT examples are Aquila and Priscilla (Acts 18:2, 18; Rom 16:3) and Lydia (Acts 16:14). Notice the well-laid plan: (1) "go to this or that city," (2) "spend a year there," (3) "carry on business," and (4) "make money." The starting time is arranged—"today or tomorrow." The city has been selected—the Greek text simply says "this city" (*tēnde tēn polin*). But God has no place in the plans.

14 No allowance is made for unforeseen circumstances. These businessmen are confident that they will be able to carry their plans through to completion. And so James points out their fallacy. They "do not even know what will happen tomorrow," to say nothing about a year from now. They have been planning as if they know exactly what the future holds or even as if they have control of the future. Not only is their knowledge limited, but their very lives are uncertain. They may not be here next year. To point up the transitory nature of life, James employs another illustration from nature—"You are a mist." In the morning it covers the countryside; before noon it is gone. But some of James's readers had been planning as if they were going to be here forever!

15 Instead of saying, "Today or tomorrow we will go to this or that city . . . and make money" (v. 13), the Christian businessman "ought to say, 'If it is the Lord's will.'" No Christian can safely assume that he can live independently of God. For a believer to leave God out of his plans is an arrogant assumption of self-sufficiency, a tacit declaration of independence from God. It is to overlook reality. Whether men recognize it or not, they "will live and do this or that" only "if it is the Lord's will." A study of the use of this conditional clause in the NT makes it clear that we are not to repeat it mechanically in connection with every statement of future plans. Paul, for example, employs it in Acts 18:21 and 1 Corinthians 4:19, but he does not use it in Acts 19:21; Romans 15:28; or 1 Corinthians 16:5, 8. Yet it is obvious that whether Paul explicitly stated it or not, he always conditioned his plans on the will of God.

16 Some of James's readers, however, rather than subjecting their plans to God's will, made it their practice to "boast and brag." To make plans without considering God's plan is the same thing as arrogantly claiming to be in full command of the future. The Greek text literally means "You are boasting in your arrogant pretentions" (*kauchasthe en tais alazoneiais hymōn*). *Alazoneia* refers to proud confidence in one's own knowledge or cleverness, hence, arrogance. It implies that these qualities are not really possessed (so Mayor, in loc.). The businessmen addressed by James were proud of their arrogant assumption that they could foresee and control the future. Some interpreters, however, have taken *en tais alazoneiais hymōn* to be adverbial, describing the manner of the boasting. But the verb *kauchaomai* ("to boast") followed by the preposition *en* ("in") occurs in sixteen other NT passages, and in every instance the prepositional phrase expresses the ground of the boasting (cf. Rom 2:17, "brag about your relationship to God"; 2:23, "you brag about the law"). Thus it is best to understand that it was about their arrogant pretentions concerning the future that James's readers were boasting. "Such boasting," says James, "is evil." It not only lacks the quality of being good, it is aggressively and viciously wicked.

17 Although this statement may apply to any number of situations, James intended it to refer to the immediately preceding context. He says, "Anyone, then, who knows." The word "then" (*oun*) introduces a concluding summary statement. Ropes suggests that it is a maxim that means something like "You have been fully warned" (p. 281). It is like saying, "Now that I have pointed the matter out to you, you have no excuse." Knowing what should be done obligates a person to do it.

Notes

14 Whether the text reads τῆς αὔριον ποία ἡ ζωὴ ὑμῶν (*tēs aurion poia hē zōē hymōn,* "what your life will be tomorrow") or τὸ τῆς αὔριον. Ποία ἡ ζωὴ ὑμῶν (*to tēs aurion. Poia hē zōē hymōn,* "what will be tomorrow. What is your life?") affects the meaning of the verse. NIV follows the latter as the best reading, which Metzger says is supported by "a wide diversity of witnesses" (p. 684). It should also be noted that a third variant has τὰ τῆς αὔριον (*ta tēs aurion,* "the things of tomorrow"), which may argue for the presence of an article, whether singular or plural. If τῆς αὔριον (*tēs aurion*) is adopted, the tr. of the verse must be somewhat as follows: "You do not know what your life will be like tomorrow. You are just a vapor" (NASB). This reading, however, has a built-in inconsistency, as Ropes points out (p. 278). It is not a question of what the conditions of life will be tomorrow, but of whether you will still be alive tomorrow. This is indicated by the statement "You are a mist that appears for a little while and then vanishes." The best reading, therefore, seems to be τὸ τῆς αὔριον (*to tēs aurion,* "what will be tomorrow").

XI. Denunciation of the Wicked Rich

5:1–6

¹Now listen, you rich people, weep and wail because of the misery that is coming upon you. ²Your wealth has rotted, and moths have eaten your clothes. ³Your gold and silver are corroded. Their corrosion will testify against you and eat your flesh like fire. You have hoarded wealth in the last days. ⁴Look! The wages you failed

to pay the workmen who mowed your fields are crying out against you. The cries of the harvesters have reached the ears of the Lord Almighty. ⁵You have lived on earth in luxury and self-indulgence. You have fattened yourselves in the day of slaughter. ⁶You have condemned and murdered innocent men, who were not opposing you.

In these six verses James first declares the fact of coming judgment (v. 1) and then lists the crimes against which this judgment will be meted out (vv. 2–6). Those crimes are four in number: hoarded wealth (vv. 2–3); unpaid wages (v. 4); luxury and self-indulgence (v. 5); and the murder of innocent men (v. 6).

There is good reason to believe that the persons referred to in this section are not believers. It might be argued that they are personally addressed in the same way other groups are addressed in previous sections (3:1; 4:13). Since the epistle in general is written to Christians, it might be assumed that the rich of 5:1–6 are Christians just as the rich of 1:9–11 are. However, there are significant differences between 5:1–6 and the rest of the epistle. These individuals are not addressed as "brothers" (cf. 1:2, 16, 19; 2:1, 5, 14; 3:1, 10, 12; 4:11; 5:7, 9, 10, 12). Furthermore, they are not called on to repent and change their ways but only to "weep and wail" because of the judgment they are going to undergo. It is, therefore, more reasonable to understand the section as similar to OT prophetic declarations of coming judgment against pagan nations. It will be noted that the latter also are interspersed among sections addressed to God's people (e.g., Isa 13–21, 23; Ezek 25–32).

1 That this verse begins a new section is indicated by the repeated call for attention: "Now listen" (cf. 4:13). The rich are to "weep and wail." While the first word, *klausate,* may describe audible weeping, the second term, *ololyzontes,* most certainly does. It is an onomatopoeic word that sounds like howling. In 4:9 James's readers are commanded to make themselves miserable (*talaipōrēsate,* "grieve") in all-out repentance. But here in 5:1 the rich are told that God will send the miseries (*tais talaipōriais*) of judgment upon them.

2 The first crime charged against the wicked rich is that of hoarding various forms of wealth. They have so much wealth stored up that it "has rotted"; their clothes also are moth eaten. Wealth in those days consisted of both money and such commodities as grain, oil, and costly garments. Evidence that costly garments were stored as wealth and used as payment for services rendered occurs in such passages as 2 Kings 5:5, 22; 1 Maccabees 11:24; and Matthew 6:19. Thus it was the commodities that had rotted and the stored garments that had been invaded by moths. There is no reason to take these happenings as figurative or as predictive of the future. The tragic fact was that the rich had hoarded so much food and clothing that it was going to waste. Their crime was uncontrolled greed that resulted in oppression of the poor (v. 4).

3 An obvious form of wealth was "gold and silver," and this is said to have become "corroded." The Greek word *katiōtai* may refer to rust, tarnish, or corrosion. Since gold and silver do not rust or even corrode, James must refer to tarnished metal. The tarnish was indication of how long the hoarded wealth had lain idle. He warns the rich, "Their corrosion will testify against you." It witnessed to the greed and selfishness of these wicked men, who had far more than they could ever use, while their

workers were deprived of their wages. The idea that the corrosion will eat the flesh of the rich "like fire" is a graphic way of declaring that their greed will result in their own destruction, as if the corrosion that ate their riches actually will eat their very flesh.

James's statement that the rich had "hoarded wealth in the last days" shows that he had the future judgment in mind. The NT regards the whole period between Christ's first and second comings as the last time or last days (Heb 1:1–2; 1 John 2:18). In comparison with the preparatory days of the OT, this is the last period before Christ comes to set up his kingdom and to judge all men. It was even in the last hour, as it were, before Christ comes to judge, that the rich "hoarded wealth."

4 The second crime the rich are charged with is that they "failed to pay the workmen" who harvested their crops. Here James vividly pictures the unpaid wages, still in the possession of the unscrupulous rich farmers, as continually accusing them of their dishonesty. It was as though the very coins cried out the guilt. The harvesters complained about their treatment, and their complaints "reached the ears of the Lord Almighty." God heard their cries as he always hears the voice of his suffering people (cf. Exod 3:7). The designation "the Lord Almighty" represents a Hebrew expression that literally means "Lord of hosts" or "Lord of the armies." In 1 Samuel 17:45 it refers to the armies of Israel. The word "host" is also used to refer to God's angels (2 Chron 18:18) and to all the stars (Deut 4:19). God is Lord of the armies of earth, of the angelic armies, and of all the starry host. This is a graphic way of declaring that God is almighty. The God who hears the cries of his suffering people is "the Lord Almighty," and he will vindicate them in due time.

5 The third charge against the rich is that they have lived "in luxury and self-indulgence." These two words (*etryphēsate* and *espatalēsate*) are synonyms, but there is a shade of difference between them. The first refers to a soft, enervating luxury that tends to demoralize. The second word describes extravagant and wasteful self-indulgence. Ropes says that in its secular use it seems to have had certain immoral associations (p. 290). In their unrestrained indulgence, the rich had "fattened" themselves. The Greek text says that they had fattened their hearts (*kardias*). The heart is viewed as desiring luxury and pleasure, and the rich are pictured as giving their hearts everything they desired. The "day of slaughter" is a designation of the day of judgment (Jer 12:3). James uses graphic imagery to indicate that the rich are on the brink of judgment. On the very day when judgment was due to come, they were fattening themselves, like cattle completely unaware of their impending destruction.

6 The final crime of the wicked rich was that they had "murdered innocent men." In 2:6 the rich are accused of dragging believers into court; here they are charged with murder. This is not to be taken figuratively but literally. Examples were Christ, Stephen, James the son of Zebedee, and, later, the author himself. The word *dikaion*, here translated "innocent men," literally means "righteous." It is that class of people who were known as the righteous that James had in mind. More than being "innocent," they were believers. And they came largely from the ranks of the poor. (cf. 2:5–7). The NIV translation "who were not opposing you" misses the bluntness of James's indictment. The Greek text abruptly declares, *ouk antitassetai hymin* ("He does not oppose you"). The rich were guilty of attacking not merely a righteous man but a man who was defenseless or who refused to fight back.

Notes

---

3 WH, RSV^mg, and Ropes place a period after τὰς σάρκας ὑμῶν (*tas sarkas hymōn,* "your flesh") and no punctuation after πῦρ (*pyr,* "fire"). Both RSV^mg and Ropes then tr. as follows: "And will eat your flesh, since you have stored up fire." Ropes argues that ἐθησαυρίσατε (*ethēsaurisate,* "you have hoarded") without an object is impossible (p. 287). However, the verb does occur without any possible object in Luke 12:21 and 2 Cor 12:14. Furthermore, "since" is not a normal meaning of ὡς (*hōs*); and the phrase ὡς πῦρ (*hōs pyr,* "like fire") goes with the preceding clause more naturally than with the one that follows. Consequently, the UBS punctuation is preferable.

XII. Miscellaneous Exhortations (5:7–20)

1. *Concerning Patience*

5:7–11

> [7]Be patient, then, brothers, until the Lord's coming. See how the farmer waits for the land to yield its valuable crop and how patient he is for the autumn and spring rains. [8]You too, be patient and stand firm, because the Lord's coming is near. [9]Don't grumble against each other, brothers, or you will be judged. The judge is standing at the door!
> [10]Brothers, as an example of patience in the face of suffering, take the prophets who spoke in the name of the Lord. [11]As you know, we consider blessed those who have persevered. You have heard of Job's perseverance and have seen what the Lord finally brought about. The Lord is full of compassion and mercy.

This exhortation concerning patience is built around three illustrations: the farmer (vv. 7–9); the prophets (v. 10); and Job (v. 11).

7 The exhortation is addressed to the "brothers," indicating that James is turning his attention from the unbelieving rich back to the believing Jews to whom the epistle was sent. The word "then" (*oun*) suggests that the oppression of the righteous poor described in vv. 1–6 is what gives rise to the call for patience in vv. 7–11. In the former section James warns the oppressing rich of coming judgment; in the latter section he encourages the oppressed poor to "be patient." The verb *makrothymēsate* ("be patient") describes the attitude of self-restraint that does not try to get even for a wrong that has been done (so J. B. Lightfoot, *St. Paul's Epistles to the Colossians and to Philemon* [London: Macmillan, 1890], p. 138). It usually represents long-suffering patience toward persons rather than things (so Trench). So James calls for a patience toward the rich oppressors that will last "until the Lord's coming." The word *parousias* ("coming") was a common term used to describe the visit of a king to a city or province of his kingdom and thus depicts Christ as a royal personage.

The first illustration of patience is that of the farmer who waits patiently "for the fall and spring rains" (KJV, "the early and latter rain"). In Palestine the early rains came in October and November soon after the grain was sown, and the latter rains came in April and May as the grain was maturing. Both rainy seasons were necessary for a successful crop. Knowing this, the farmer was willing to wait patiently until both rains came and provided the needed moisture.

8 With the words "You too, be patient," James applies the illustration of the patient farmer. In addition, he urges his readers to "stand firm." The clause *stērixate tas kardias hymōn* literally means "strengthen your hearts," that is, be strong in the inner man. The verb has the idea of providing solid support, of establishing a person, and thus enabling him to stand unmoved by trouble. The reason given for standing firm is that "the Lord's coming is near." The day when things will be set right is imminent. This confident expectation will undergird the faint heart and make it strong.

9 The believers are to be patient toward both outsiders who oppress them and insiders who irritate them. Christians are not to "grumble against each other." *Stenazete,* translated "grumble," commonly means "to sigh," "to groan." It speaks of inner distress more than open complaint. What is forbidden is not the loud and bitter denunciation of others but the unexpressed feeling of bitterness or the smothered resentment that may express itself in a groan or a sigh. James uses the Greek *mē* with the present imperative to prohibit the continuation of this hateful practice. To continue it would result in judgment. And the Judge is represented as "standing at the door," as if his hand is on the latch, ready to enter at any time.

10 The second illustration of patience is that of "the prophets who spoke in the name of the Lord." In their position as his representatives, they experienced affliction (*kakopatheias*) and responded to it with long-suffering patience (*makrothymias*). Although James refers to "the prophets" as a group, Jeremiah certainly stands out as one who endured mistreatment with patience. He was put in the stocks (Jer 20:2), thrown into prison (32:2), and lowered into a miry dungeon (38:6); yet he persisted in his ministry without bitterness or recrimination. Such men constitute a model (*hypodeigma*) for believers who are oppressed and mistreated.

11 The third illustration is Job. "Those who have persevered" are considered blessed. No doubt James has in mind his words in 1:12, where he points out the enviable joy of the person who does not cave in under trial. In 5:7–10 the plea is for patience (*makrothymia*), the self-restraint that does not retaliate; but here in 5:11 it is *hypomonē*, perseverance in difficult circumstances. (For a brief discussion of this word, see the comments on 1:3.) It is significant that James does not speak of Job's patience, for despite the popular phrase "the patience of Job," he hardly exemplified that quality (cf. Job 12:2; 13:3–4; 16:2). He was, however, an outstanding example of perseverance in the most trying situations (cf. Job 1:21–22; 2:10; 13:15; 19:25–27). His experience also was proof that "the Lord is full of compassion and mercy," as we see in "what the Lord finally brought about" for him. Because Job persevered, God gave him "twice as much as he had before" (Job 42:10–17). To sum up, in James 5:7–11 the author is urging his readers not to fight back but to exercise long-suffering patience toward the rich who oppress them; and he is calling for stout-hearted perseverance in the trying circumstances that confront them.

2. Concerning Oaths

5:12

> ¹²Above all, my brothers, do not swear—not by heaven or by earth or by anything else. Let your "Yes" be yes, and your "No," no, or you will be condemned.

12 In addition to the preceding exhortations to patience and perseverance, James next places special emphasis on the prohibition of oaths: "Above all, . . . do not swear." As in v.9, the grammatical construction shows that the use of oaths was an existing practice that ought to be discontinued. James is echoing the words of Jesus in Matthew 5:34-37, which forbid swearing altogether. It should be obvious that what is referred to in Matthew and James is the light, casual use of oaths in informal conversation—not formal oaths in such places as courts of law. God himself is said to have taken an oath (Ps 110:4), and Paul sometimes called God to witness (2 Cor 1:21; Gal 1:20). Rather than employing an oath to convince people that a statement is true, the Christian should let his " 'Yes' be yes," and his " 'No,' no." That is, he should be honest in all his speech so that when he makes an affirmation or denial people will know it is unquestionably the truth. In the careless use of oaths a person is in danger of taking God's name in vain, for which he will come under judgment (cf. Exod 20:7).

3. *Concerning Prayer*

5:13-18

> ¹³Is any one of you in trouble? He should pray. Is anyone happy? Let him sing songs of praise. ¹⁴Is any one of you sick? He should call the elders of the church to pray over him and anoint him with oil in the name of the Lord. ¹⁵And the prayer offered in faith will make the sick person well; the Lord will raise him up. If he has sinned, he will be forgiven. ¹⁶Therefore confess your sins to each other and pray for each other so that you may be healed. The prayer of a righteous man is powerful and effective.
>
> ¹⁷Elijah was a man just like us. He prayed earnestly that it would not rain, and it did not rain on the land for three and a half years. ¹⁸Again he prayed, and the heavens gave rain, and the earth produced its crops.

This passage on prayer falls into two sections. Verses 13-16 constitute a call for prayer in every circumstance of life; vv.17-18 illustrate the effectiveness of sincere prayer.

13 One circumstance that calls for prayer is the experience of being "in trouble." Here James has used the verb form (*kakopathei*) of the noun *kakopatheias,* which he employed in v.10 to describe the trouble experienced by the prophets. When such an experience comes, the Christian needs patience. He is not to grumble in bitter disgust (v.9), nor is he to express himself in oaths (v.12). Instead, "he should pray." Patience comes from God, and prayer is an effective way to obtain it. James also urges anyone who is in good spirits to "sing songs of praise." This too is prayer.

14 Sickness is another circumstance where prayer is needed, and concerning such prayer James gives detailed instructions. The sick person "should call for the elders of the church." In Titus 1:5, 7 and Acts 20:17, 28 elders and bishops (or overseers) are equated. In Acts 20:28 the elders are instructed to shepherd (*poimainein*) the church of God; that is, to do the work of an overseer or pastor. That "elder," "bishop," "pastor" refer to the same office is also suggested in 1 Peter 5:1-4. Thus, the sick person is to call the pastors of the church "to pray over him and anoint him with oil." Prayer is the more significant of the two ministries performed by the elders. "Pray" is the main verb, while "anoint" is a participle. Moreover, the overall emphasis of the

203

paragraph is on prayer. So the anointing is a secondary action. There are a number of reasons for understanding this application of oil as medicinal rather than sacramental. The word *aleipsantes* ("anoint") is not the usual word for sacramental or ritualistic anointing. James could have used the verb *chriō* if that had been what he had in mind. The distinction is still observed in modern Greek, with *aleiphō* meaning "to daub," "to smear," and *chriō* meaning "to anoint." Furthermore, it is a well-documented fact that oil was one of the most common medicines of biblical times. See Isaiah 1:6 and Luke 10:34. Josephus (Antiq. XVII, 172 [vi. 5]) reports that during his last illness Herod the Great was given a bath in oil in hopes of effecting a cure. The papyri, Philo, Pliny, and the physician Galen all refer to the medicinal use of oil. Galen described it as "the best of all remedies for paralysis" (*De Simplicium Medicamentorum Temperamentis* 2.10ff). It is evident, then, that James is prescribing prayer and medicine.

15 The assurance is given that prayer "will make the sick person well." In the final analysis this is what effects the healing. In answer to "the prayer offered in faith," God uses the medicine to cure the malady. The statement "the Lord will raise him up" means that the sick man will be enabled to get up from his sick bed. If it was sin that occasioned his sickness, "he will be forgiven." This suggests the possibility that, because of persistence in sin, God sent sickness as a disciplinary agent (cf. 1 Cor 11:30). The conditional clause "if he has sinned" makes it clear that not all sickness is the result of sin.

16 From the promise of v. 15 an inference is drawn ("therefore"). Since confession of sin and the prayer of faith bring healing, Christians should confess their "sins to each other and pray for each other." It is not merely the elders who are told to pray, but Christians in general. If a person has sinned against a brother, he should confess the sin to him. This will no doubt result in mutual confession—"to each other." Then the two believers should "pray for each other." If the sin has caused sickness, healing will follow confession and prayer. James proceeds to add the assurance that prayer "is powerful and effective." The "righteous man" here referred to is the man whose sins have been confessed and forgiven. His prayer is fully able to secure results, such as healing of the sick.

17–18 Verses 17 and 18 offer illustrative proof that a righteous man's prayer is "powerful and effective." "Elijah," James says, "was a man just like us." He had no superhuman powers; he was by nature a human being and nothing more. However, when he prayed "that it would not rain, . . . it did not rain" (cf. 1 Kings 17:1; 18:42–45). The explanation of his power in prayer is twofold: he was a righteous man, and "he prayed earnestly." So James assures his readers that such answers to prayer are within the reach of any believer. It is true that 1 Kings 17–18 does not explicitly say that Elijah prayed, but this may be assumed from 17:1 and especially from 18:42. The three and one-half years is a round number based on 18:1.

4. Concerning the Wanderer

5:19–20

> [19] My brothers, if one of you should wander from the truth and someone should bring him back, [20] remember this: Whoever turns a sinner from the error of his way will save him from death and cover over a multitude of sins.

19-20 It is clear from the words "my brothers" that James addresses this last exhortation to believers. It is also apparent that he speaks of the possibility that one of them may "wander from the truth." Verse 20 gives reason to believe that the truth from which the wanderer turns is the saving truth of the gospel. James's purpose in these closing verses is to encourage Christians to make an effort to bring the wanderer back. Two worthy results of such an accomplishment are cited. First, it will "save him from death." That this cannot be physical death may be inferred from the literal translation of the Greek text: it "shall save his soul from death." So it would seem that spiritual death is in view. Since Scripture teaches that once a person is regenerated he can never be lost, it may be assumed that his hypothetical wanderer is not a genuine believer. He would be one who had been among the believers and had made a profession of faith, but his profession had been superficial. To bring him to genuine faith in the truth is to save his soul from eternal death. The result of bringing the wanderer back is that "many sins" will be covered. Genuine faith brings full forgiveness of the wanderer's sins; and they are covered, never to be held against him again. As difficult as it may be to win such a person to saving faith, the eternal results make it infinitely worthwhile. For a similar situation see Hebrews 6:4-8.